MORE THAN MONEY

MORE THAN

MONEY

FIVE FORMS OF CAPITAL TO CREATE
WEALTH AND ELIMINATE POVERTY

Paul C. Godfrey

STANFORD BUSINESS BOOKS
An Imprint of Stanford University Press
Stanford, California

Stanford University Press
Stanford, California

Special discounts for bulk quantities of Stanford Business Books are available to corporations, professional associations, and other organizations. For details and discount information, contact the special sales department of Stanford University Press. Tel: (650) 736-1782, Fax: (650) 736-1784.

Printed in the United States of America on acid-free, archival-quality paper.

Library of Congress Cataloging-in-Publication Data

Godfrey, Paul C., author.
  More than money : five forms of capital to create wealth and eliminate poverty / Paul C. Godfrey.
      pages cm
  Includes bibliographical references and index.
  ISBN 978-0-8047-8279-1 (cloth : alk. paper) — ISBN 978-0-8047-8280-7 (pbk. : alk. paper)
  1. Poverty. 2. Social capital (Sociology). 3. Capital. 4. Self-reliance. 5. Organization.
  6. Economic development. I. Title.
  QH79.P6G68 2013
  658.15'2—dc23
                                2013021446

  ISBN 978-0-8047-8920-2 (electronic)

Typeset at Stanford University Press in 10.5/15 Adobe Garamond.

.

To the people on the streets of Accra,
thank you for helping me see more clearly.

CONTENTS

ACKNOWLEDGMENTS

Although the by-line for the book indicates that I'm the author, many others helped to co-create the project that led to this publication. Thanks first to my deans at the Marriott School: Ned Hill offered a timely invitation to immerse myself in the search for solutions to poverty, and Gary Cornia has not only provided enthusiastic support, he's also run interference with the university administration to free up needed time to complete the manuscript. Todd Manwaring's moral leadership, intellectual rigor, and emotional engagement to the cause of the poor has inspired and shaped my work in this area. The Melvin J. Ballard Center for Economic Self-Reliance at Brigham Young University, founded by Todd, has financially underwritten many of my travels as well as furnished a forum for discussion, debate, and collaboration on these important issues.

Margo Beth Fleming from the Stanford University Press improved the manuscript; more important, she taught me the difference between sharing ideas and writing a book, a difference for which I will ever be grateful. My friend and colleague at the University of Utah, Bill Schulze, taught me several lessons that have found their way into these pages.

I owe a debt of gratitude to many colleagues at BYU's Marriott School. Lee Perry and Gibb Dyer have been colleagues in the truest sense of the word; they've been mentors, friends, and wise counselors for the larger project of my academic life. John Bingham, Barclay Burns, Robb Jensen, and Christian Mealey (currently pursuing a Ph.D. at Rice University) gave me insightful feedback on earlier drafts of the book.

My student assistants have contributed in ways beyond their years and experience. Jon Mangum spent a summer with people in Ghana; his work helped me understand the roles of the different types of capital, especially the role of social capital. Justin Oldryod and Andrew Scheuermann uncovered insights about the James Watt story that illustrates the book's central concepts. Their enthusiasm kept me going and made me reflect on the potential of these ideas to inspire a new generation of officers in the war on poverty. Janelle Gordon dragged me, reluctantly, into the twenty-first century and helped me develop materials and media to support the book. I am better for the journey. Melissa Lundgren and Nathanael Read employed their substantial skills to make the figures and tables in the book concise and engaging.

And, finally, my family. Grant, Kate, and Charlie said that having a dad who wrote a book would be "way cool," even on the days I wasn't so sure I was either a writer or cool. Lilly read the entire manuscript to make sure my thoughts came through completely and coherently. Sam proved an excellent traveling companion on flights to and from Ghana; his ability to connect with the people there added a wonderful richness to our interactions and subsequent learning. Last, but far from least, I owe so much to my wife, Robin. Her frank critique and faultless companionship pushed me to hone and refine my ideas, prose, and presentation. As with every other aspect of my life, I'm far better with her than alone.

MORE THAN MONEY

INTRODUCTION

Eliminating, Not Alleviating Poverty

IS POVERTY PERMANENT? The Hebrew leader Moses offered a sanguine assessment in his final discourse to his people: "There will never cease to be needy ones in your land" (*Tanakh*, Deut. 15:11). His successor Jesus Christ would say, fourteen centuries later, "Ye have the poor always with you" (Matt. 26:11). Twenty one centuries later the world's political leaders joined arms to promise, "[We] will spare no effort to free our fellow men, women and children from the abject and dehumanizing conditions of extreme poverty."[1] The fine print clarifies that grand goal as cutting by half the number of people living on $1 per day. It seems that Jesus spoke truth; the poor will always be with us.

Moses and Jesus may have based their bleak forecasts on the reality that poverty, as a macrosocial problem, persists because its causes are deeply entrenched in social life. The four ancient horsemen—war, pestilence, famine, and death—ride alongside generational population dynamics, recent decades of failed efforts at education and literacy, and the ongoing evolution of global trade to subject billions to surviving at what scholars term the base of the pyramid.[2] We can think of this poverty as "Big P" poverty: large groups trapped in lives of destitution created and perpetuated by sweeping social forces beyond their control.

Moses instructed his followers to "open your hand to the poor and needy kinsman in your land" (*Tanakh*, Deut 15:11). Jesus enjoined his followers that "inasmuch as ye have done it unto the least of these"—the hungry, naked, estranged, or imprisoned—"ye have done it unto me" (Matt. 25:40). The Koran teaches a similar doctrine: "Whatever wealth you spend, it is for the parents and the near of kin and the orphans and the needy and the wayfarer, and whatever good you do, Allah surely knows it" (*Koran*, 2:215); and Tirukkural admonishes Hindus to "find and follow the good path and be ruled by compassion . . . compassion will prove the means to liberation" (Kural, 242). In the face of Big P poverty the world's spiritual traditions admonish us to provide relief and compassion to individuals and families, or work on "little p" poverty.

Jesus' injunction in particular raises a troubling implication for his followers: is it enough to merely succor the poor in their poverty or must they try to lift them out of it? Could one leave the Lord sated but in squalor, or does the injunction to do it "unto me" invite, perhaps require, an attempt to eliminate, as opposed to merely alleviate or palliate, little p poverty? For me, Jesus' insertion of "unto me" implies an obligation not to merely relieve suffering but to remove squalor.

The title of this book claims we can *eliminate*—not just *alleviate*—little p poverty. That bold claim builds on my experience, observations, and research over the past eight years. In 2004 my dean, Ned Hill, asked me to become involved with a new research center at Brigham Young University's Marriott School of Management that focused on fighting poverty through an emerging set of market-based approaches. The goals of what would become the Melvin J. Ballard Center for Economic Self-Reliance seemed like a natural extension of the work I was doing around philanthropy and corporate social responsibility; after all, business plays a huge role in society and leveraging its capabilities in the fight against poverty could potentially yield powerful results.

I dived in and began reading about development economics, the branch of economics focusing on Big P poverty; I attended conferences to understand current approaches and refine my own thinking. I climbed on airplanes to see poverty firsthand; traveling to Ghana, the Navajo Nation (an impoverished sovereign nation located within the continental United States), and to Paraguay on a regular basis to learn more about both Big P and little p poverty. Personal interviews, extended observations, and the stories of those mired in and moving out of deep poverty began to reveal a consistent pattern among those who escape little p poverty, even in societies mired in Big P poverty.

This book builds on three key lessons about the process and promise of eliminating poverty. First, *we* don't eliminate poverty; *individuals and families* work themselves out of poverty and into prosperity. Our efforts can be quite effective when they help people eradicate poverty in their own lives. Unfortunately our efforts can hurt as well; we can create conditions and incentives that perpetuate the poverty we loathe. The lesson is more nuanced than merely empowering people; we must create a context where people's natural tendencies toward self-reliance flourish. That's why the title claims that we eliminate poverty through self-reliance.

Second, eliminating poverty requires more than money, as the title of the book suggests. Money thrown toward the poor often ends up in alleviating the symptoms of poverty but usually fails to create lasting solutions. Poverty abates when people become self-reliant and leverage five different types of capital—institutional, social, human, organizational, and physical. This book considers each type of capital and how they interact with self-reliance to lift people out of poverty. A holistic and sophisticated focus on the five types of capital helps us end little p—and maybe Big P—poverty.

Third, our work, when it is most effective, involves organization. An effective organization has the capability to look past the thick branches of poverty and attack the roots. These organizations have a clear vision, a set of partners, and accountability systems that sustain their efforts over the decades it takes to move a generation from poverty to prosperity. This book outlines how to build enduring organizations that can bring the lessons of the five capital accounts to bear on the long-term fight against little p poverty.

In my travels and tutoring experiences, I've rubbed shoulders with a number of social entrepreneurs, NGO leaders, foundation directors, government officials, and business men and women. A common pattern emerges among those who seem to succeed. They begin their work full of passion and commitment and have some early successes in their efforts. After about three to five years, however, they look over what they've built and ask, "What have we really accomplished?" They've relieved some suffering among the poor but have a nagging feeling they've failed to find lasting solutions to poverty. They recognize the gap between alleviation and elimination.

If questions about the effectiveness of your, and your organization's, efforts nag you, or if you are just beginning to organize and work, *and you want to be more effective in your efforts*, then this book is for you. As you understand the five types of capital and their relationship to poverty and the poor you'll see mistakes you can avoid and design principles you can employ to improve your efforts. You'll also learn some simple, yet powerful, lessons to help you build an organization that can succeed. I'll offer strategic suggestions and lasting principles to create substantive and sustainable organizations rather than tactical steps or temporary patches; temporary tactics can't go the distance in the fight against poverty.

One final note. In the interest of readability and literary ease I'll sometimes refer to those living in poverty as "poor people." The adjective *poor* carries objective, but no normative, meaning. *Poor* represents a factual statement of deprivation—of the necessities of life or of opportunities for self-fulfillment. I do not intend, nor should you infer, any normative or evaluative, either condemning or extolling, assessment of those living in these conditions.

The fight to eliminate poverty, at least its little p version, is winnable, but to win we need to be deliberate in the design and doing of our work. This book hopes to help you do that. So, turn the page and begin to see why it takes more than money to eliminate poverty.

CHAPTER ONE

MORE THAN MONEY

There are a thousand hacking at the branches of evil to one who is striking at the root.

—*Henry David Thoreau*

IT'S NOT ABOUT THE MONEY! In the global wars on poverty money has served as both the primary weapon and chief foot soldier for both academics and practitioners. If we deploy the right amount to the right place at the right time, the right things would happen, poverty would abate, and misery give way to human happiness. Development economists, business scholars, social entrepreneurs, and thought leaders all trumpet the right amount and mix of investment and spending by government, businesses, and consumers, as critical to meaningful gains by the world's poor.[1]

I like Thoreau's observation. Most of the billions, or trillions, of dollars thrown at the poverty problem ends up in the branches—alleviating the symptoms of poverty—but little gets at the root and creates lasting prosperity for individuals. Money doesn't eliminate poverty. Money fails, primarily, because it does little to develop or encourage self-reliance; I'll make a case in these pages that self-reliance leads to a lasting solution to poverty. First, however, let's truly understand the fascination with money as the key to battling the curse of poverty.

The focus on money conforms to our *conventional* wisdom about what poverty is, and by implication how it can be overcome. The World Bank's operating definition of poverty tells us that

> Poverty is "pronounced deprivation in well-being." The conventional view links wellbeing primarily to command over commodities, so the poor

are those who do not have enough income or consumption to put them above some adequate minimum threshold. This view sees poverty largely in monetary terms.[2]

Specialists and lay people alike may intuitively realize that it takes more than just money to create meaningful change, but requests for aid—often urgent—in monetary terms often force other critical conversations to the background. The "conventional view"—deeply engrained into our mental maps of poverty—means that the conversations about strategic solutions quickly devolve into tactical talk about fund raising, potential donors, and expected receipts.

Money also provides a seductively *convenient* soldier to deploy. When we move past the simple symptoms of want we begin to see the complex causes of need, and those deeper causes constitute what planners refer to as wicked problems: ones that defy definition, have multiple causes and potential remedies, and no definite or optimal solution.[3] At one level, writing a check is easier than finding the causal roots in the quagmire of wicked complexity. At a deeper level, money-as-the-solution appeals to a deeper belief that money is the apparent solution to *our* own problems, so giving money to the poor should help them with *their* problems. Money acts as a quick palliative for the pain of the destitute.

For some, maybe many, money represents not only a convenient way to engage in a worthy cause; it also *consoles* the conscience. Living lives at or near the top of the economic pyramid, our drive for justice, or perhaps our sense of guilt over our abundance, encourages us to do something. But again, doing something requires getting our hands dirty and admitting our weakness in the face of an intractable problem. Giving money relieves our feelings of helplessness and hopelessness. Money becomes a palliative for the pain of the donor.

Money may conform to convention, provide a convenient and consoling way to get involved. What it hasn't shown, at least to date, is a *curative* effect on poverty. That's a bold claim, one I'll back up in a moment, but it will prove helpful to think more about poverty and the different levels where it exists. We can think of two overarching types of poverty, Big P and little p.

Big P poverty describes poverty driven by macrosocial forces and measured at very aggregate levels. Big P poverty isn't about people, at least not ones with names and faces; it's about people as statistics and the metalevel forces that drive them: famine, ignorance, marital and family institutions, political oppression, and war, to name a few. Percentages and aggregates matter in the fight against Big P poverty, the percent of people with clean drinking water, access to sanitation, or secondary education. It's not about whether the Agbetes of Accra or the Walkers of Window Rock have any of those things. The focus lies in *alleviating*—mitigating the effects of—poverty but tacitly frames its underlying causes as intractable.

Little p poverty focuses on individuals and families. It's about the Agbetes, the Walkers, and millions of other people with names, faces, lives, and real needs. Real people live in corrupt or fragile states; they often lack access to formal educational opportunities or participation in the formal economy. The causes of Big P poverty put real people in little p poverty, as do things like physical or mental handicaps, family dynamics, and personal choices. Fighting little p poverty means improving the lives and livelihoods of individuals, one at a time. Little p poverty can be *eliminated,* individuals and families can move from poverty to prosperity.

If Big P poverty focuses on statistics, then little p poverty concerns stories, the intimate arcs of individual lives. Slicing poverty into Big P and little p does more than provide a memorable metaphor; it highlights that those fighting it will be more effective when their efforts and organizations match the realities operating at each level. We'll talk more about that throughout the book. The division also illuminates the failure of money to make much of a dent in the global problem of poverty.

Money and Big P Poverty—the Failure of Foreign Aid

The most public debate about money and the fight against Big P poverty features cross-town dueling economists Jeffrey Sachs of Columbia and New York University's William Easterly. Both admit that foreign aid has proven less than stellar—more like an abject failure—in eradicating poverty and enabling sustained development. Much of the more than $620 billion that USAID has granted or loaned to foreign countries for economic aid from 1946 to 2010 in the form of foreign aid has not delivered anything like an adequate return on investment.[4] Sachs and Easterly offer radically different explanations and proffer different solutions.

For Sachs the problem lies in the paucity of aid: the problems and shortcomings in developing countries are so extensive that foreign donations are too small to make a difference.[5] For example, aid to Kenya for health care came to about $100 million per year a decade ago; to build a health system capable of providing substantive care to all Kenyans would cost about $1.5 *billion* per year, fifteen times the amount earmarked.[6] Not surprisingly, Sachs calls for a new a massive infusion of aid large enough to get developing countries over the hurdle; we should supersede the big push of the 1960s with an even bigger push in the twenty-first century. Big P poverty requires staggeringly big sums to eradicate.

Easterly proffers the exact opposite explanation: foreign aid has presented developing country leaders with a glut of resources that creates and reinforces dependency, institutionalizing and enshrining Big P poverty into the fabric of these societies in the form of graft and corruption.[7] Aid to improve the educational systems in Africa, for example, doesn't lead to economic growth (and may not do much for substantive learning either).[8] Easterly's remedy lies in cutting foreign aid and replacing free public money with the miracle of the market; development policies should create a proper set of incentives for investment and private business.[9] The abstract nature of Big P poverty requires an equally abstract institution, the Big M market, to fight it.

Given the failures of previous efforts, and the seeming inability of many developing markets to adopt Big M market mechanisms, it comes as no surprise that nations, businesses, and individuals express cynicism at worst, or suffer fatigue at best, toward well-intended efforts to attack Big P poverty. One response has been to abandon the focus on large-scale interventions and focus instead at the smallest scale of economic activity.

Money and Little p Poverty—The Unfilled Promise of Microcredit

The fight against little p poverty changed in the mid-1970s when future Nobel Laureate Muhammad Yunus discovered that many of the poor women in the villages of Bangladesh captured only subsistence wages, rather than the market price, for their work.[10] What shut the women out of the market? Their inability to purchase the small amounts of raw materials on their own; they lacked the financial capital and relied on a middleman. Yunus lent $27 to a group of forty-two women and initiated the microcredit movement.

Undoubtedly microcredit has helped millions improve their livelihoods and given them a measure of control; unfortunately, it has also become a panacea for solving the problems of the poor. I attended a lecture given by a high-profile management guru who asked: "[Do] you want to eliminate poverty? Well, just give every woman a small loan and she'll pull her family out of poverty." That's a bold claim.

Does the reality of microcredit match the hype? The best research on microcredit shows that the tool appears to increase income; however, the biggest gains in income come to those who are the best off among borrowers;[11] one study found that the poorest borrowers actually saw their incomes decrease.[12] Microcredit produces contradictory outcomes; many borrowers see incomes rise but measures of health, housing, and nutrition decline. A devil's bargain: borrowers appear forced to trade off economic or social gains.[13]

One challenge lies in the fact that microcredit is micro—small scale. Financing helps individual entrepreneurs purchase raw materials or other consumables but often leaves no slack to fund asset purchases or employees.[14] Microcredit may facilitate individual self-sufficiency, but the model doesn't lead to job creation or growth in business scale; the ripple effects of microcredit don't extend out very far into the broader community.[15]

Whether fighting Big P or little p poverty, a financial focus fails to eliminate poverty because at best it helps people *have* more; it can't help them *be* more. Having more relates to external things: what people own, possess, or can access. Being more happens inside; it captures capabilities, character, and desires that help people reach their full potential. Money may be the ticket that helps us have more, but being more requires more than money. Having more alleviates the suffering of poverty; being more eliminates the situation of poverty.

This book is about self-reliance, its role in eliminating little p poverty and helping people become more. Self-reliance interacts with five elements in our economic and social lives that I refer to as types of capital. The book presents and argues a simple thesis for those interested in eliminating little p poverty: real development—the kind that permanently lifts people out of poverty—requires harnessing and focusing five different types of capital in ways that enhance and leverage people's self-reliance.

SELF-RELIANCE AND THE FIVE TYPES OF CAPITAL

What is real development and how does it influence self-reliance? Jane Jacobs was not a professional economist but a writer and activist. In *The Nature of Economies* she offers a wonderfully concise way to understand real economic development as opposed to mere growth.[16] Growth consists of a *quantitative* change in the output of an economic system, while development captures a *qualitative* change in the types of outputs of that system. Growth is about having more, development about being more.

For some, talk of self-reliance evokes images of Jim Bridger, the early nineteenth-century trapper who scratched out a meager existence in the rugged and untamed American West. Living and working alone, Bridger, like most Mountain Men, relied solely on his own skill, strength, and cleverness. Self-reliance, as I'll discuss at length in Chapter 2, captures something vastly different; two distinct, yet related, elements of people's economic actions: the inputs they use and outputs they produce. Self-reliance represents both a *disposition*, a bundle of beliefs and attitudes that drive behaviors, and a *condition*, or configuration of assets and resources that result from those behaviors. We all have the potential to become self-reliant, and our natural tendencies to be so will either be nurtured or hindered by the social settings in which we live.

Those social worlds provide sets of resources that strongly influence both the disposition and configuration that defines self-reliance. Individuals and families employ and leverage these resources to produce economic income as well as social satisfaction. I describe them as types of capital because they are durable sources of wealth that produce wealth. The types of capital are:

Institutional: The large social structures that provide meaning and structure to social life.

Social: The resources available to us by virtue of our relationships with family members, friends, or associates.

Human: Knowledge, skills, and attitudes that produce tangible outcomes and create wealth.

Organizational: Collective social endeavors we engage in or interact with that harness the powers of cooperation between and competition among people.

Physical: The tangible, and financial, resources we employ to produce products or services or exchange with others to create value.

To illustrate the role of the five types of capital and self-reliance in creating real, sustainable development, let's look at what may be history's greatest episode of development: the Industrial Revolution. More specifically, let's consider a single actor who made a big difference: James Watt, developer of the steam engine, the machine that powered the industrial economy. We'll return to Watt's story throughout the book to illustrate in greater detail each type of capital, but for now I'll sketch out the basics of the fascinating story of Watt's steam engine.

James Watt's Steam Engine

There are at least two great myths about the Industrial Revolution: that it was a revolution and that it began with James Watt's invention of the steam engine in the 1760s. The term *Industrial Revolution* appeared well after the supposed "revolution" began and didn't become the description de jour until historian Arnold Toynbee popularized the term almost a century after the supposed revolution took place.[17]

Economic historians see industrialization beginning in the thirteenth century, with the Magna Carta and the gradual rise of the rule of law throughout Europe playing a starring role.[18] Religious historians argue that the spirit of inquiry in thirteenth-century Christian theology that re-emerged with Thomas Aquinas enabled scientific progress and discovery. Military historians point further back to the twelfth-century Crusades, which planted the seeds of large-scale organizations, sophisticated communication and logistics networks, and the development of a banking industry. All these scholars argue that industrialization resulted from social evolution, not revolution.

The invention of the steam engine has been relegated to the stuff of a children's bedtime story, and legend has it that James Watt, as a very young boy, watched steam lift the lid of a tea kettle at his grandmother's home and had the epiphany that steam would be a tremendous source of power.[19] James would then spend his life doggedly bringing that boyhood vision to life, first in the laboratory and then in industry. The reality of the steam engine includes trial and error, happenstance meeting, good fortune, and cleverness worthy of the best grown-up novel.

The power of steam had been known since Hero of Alexandria, who made steam-powered toys in the first century A.D., but that technology would lie fallow for more than a millennium and a half. By 1712 Englishman Thomas Newcomen had developed a commercially viable steam engine that became a familiar fixture in England's coal mining regions by the 1720s. Newcomen's engine, a huge, stationary steam-powered pumping arm, allowed English coal miners to pump water from their mines and thus pursue coal in deeper veins to fuel an already expanding industrial base.

While a marvel of technology and a quantum leap in industrial development, Newcomen's engine suffered from two major drawbacks. First, the machine couldn't be moved. The "engine" was really a large building; once constructed it became the embodiment of fixed capital. Second, the engine wasn't efficient, as it generated very little power for each ton of coal that fired its boiler. In consequence the expensive giant could be used only where coal was cheap and close—the rural coal regions of England and Scotland. Newcomen's marvel could fuel only the coal industry, but an engine that could fuel an entire economy would come within a generation at the hands of James Watt.

Scotsman James Watt (1736–1819), the reputed father of the Industrial Revolution, was born a frail and sickly child with a pessimistic and cautious disposition, hardly the traits of the prototypical entrepreneur. His poor health led to a home-schooled education at the hands of his bookish mother and extensive exposure to his father's business selling navigational instruments. Watt's father built him his own workshop and provided the tools for young James to develop his skills in metal work. James seemed to have a talent for instrument making, and he would enrich those skills through a much abbreviated apprenticeship in London in the late 1750s.

By 1763 Watt owned a successful scientific instrument manufacturing company and held the position of official instrument maker at the University of Glasgow. One of Watt's tasks consisted of repairing a small model of a Newcomen engine brought to the university for study. The model failed to work properly, and Watt was assigned to "repair" it; that repair job would change the course of scientific and economic history. He quickly realized just how inefficient Newcomen's engine was and began to search for improvements.

Watt was by no means an academic, but his fascination with the scientific discoveries of the Enlightenment and his willingness to master the theories of the day would prove vital to the development of his machine. Throughout his career, Watt supplemented his formidable skills as a craftsman and model builder with the best science of the day. He learned first about steam, heat transfer, and productive work—topics we know today as basic thermodynamics but that represented cutting-edge science in the eighteenth century.

In this endeavor Watt had the good fortune to work with Joseph Black, a professor at Glasgow University. Black later lent Watt £150 (about $5,500 in current dollars) based on the strength of his emerging designs and encouraged Watt to approach his friend John Roebuck as the potential of a new engine became clear. Mine owner Roebuck had the financial incentive and resources to push development of the engine forward. Roebuck became Watt's "angel investor"—to borrow a current phrase. Roebuck's capital, and his patience in the interminable delays in the process, allowed Watt to create a patentable design for the new engine by 1768.

Roebuck also introduced Watt to William Small, a local physician and scientist, who would in turn introduce Watt to Matthew Boulton. Boulton, a successful Birmingham entrepreneur and manufacturer, became Watt's business partner, financier, and advisor in 1769 after Roebuck suffered a financial reversal. While Watt would gain fame for his mechanical and technical prowess, Boulton would prove equally ingenious in the business side of their partnership. Today Boulton and Watt grace the British £50 note, a lasting symbol of their joint contribution.

Boulton and Small would prove invaluable in the patent process; their cleverness and political connections helped Watt secure a rather broad patent for a steam engine "concept" and several related off-shoots. Boulton saw the economic potential if Watt could turn the direction of force from his engine 90 degrees; indeed, Watt's rotary engine moved steam power from the mines to the mills and factories that constituted British industry. Boulton's Soho Works and organizing abilities facilitated a massive expansion of the scale of the enterprise.

James Watt's sickly childhood belied a self-reliant disposition. He conquered his pessimistic, cautious nature through a deep-seated sense of moral responsibility to provide for himself and his family. He exhibited a trait psychologists label self-efficacy, the belief that he could master new skills and knowledge. Watt's story shows us someone willing to invest and work from a long-term perspective. He acquired, husbanded, leveraged, and preserved each of the five types of capital introduced above.

Let's highlight three other key lessons for economic development from Watt's work before discussing those five types of capital. First, Watt's innovation took a long time. Work on the steam began in 1764, but the original patent wouldn't come for half a decade. It would take *three decades* for Watt's engines to finally outnumber Newcomen engines in service. Sustainable development and the innovations that fuel it take time; vision, persistence, strategy, and leadership play outsized roles in bringing projects to fruition.

Second, the title "Watt's steam engine" pays homage only to the innovator and relegates other critical players to the supporting cast. Watt, the workers in his instrument company, Black, Small, Boulton, and a host of others you'll meet in Chapters 4 and 9 all played important roles in the process. Take one away and history might look very different. The fight against poverty, and the changes it fosters, is a team sport; sustainable and long-term economic progress won't occur if individuals and their organizations can't work and play well with others—that is, if they can't form, maintain, and grow networks of like-minded individuals and organizations all working toward common goals.

Finally, the market—that marvel that William Easterly sees as the key to real advancement—had ways to judge the superiority of Watt's engine, and that market led industrialists and others to allocate resources to his designs. Watt developed the metric of horsepower so that customers could compare the work capacities of different engines. In the long-term fight to eliminate little p poverty, decision-makers, donors, and other partners clamor for, and find relief in, clear measures with which to judge which projects work.

With these lessons laid out, let's turn our attention back to the five types of capital and provide more of an introduction to these critical cognitive, social, and physical resources that create and reinforce the disposition and condition of self-reliance.

GOING DEEPER

The story of Watt's steam engine illustrates how each of the five types of capital helped breed lasting development; we'll now consider these types of capital more formally. As we dive into the five types of capital here, and much more deeply in Chapters 3–7, you should keep in mind one central idea: the importance of each type of capital comes as individuals, families, or maybe even communities use it to eliminate poverty in their own lives. Figure 1.1 illustrates this central point; indeed, a book could be written about how the five types of capital work with each other. My interest lies in how they work within individuals.

Before moving on I want to offer a bit more about the choice of the term

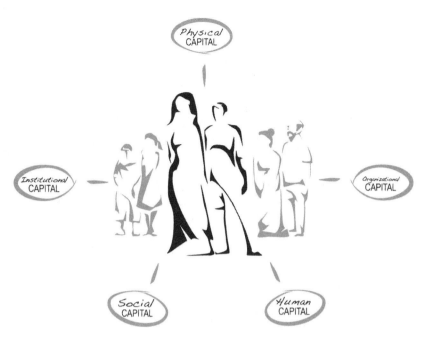

FIG. 1.1. The Five Types of Capital. (Source: Created by Nathanael Read.)

capital to describe these five elements. I previously portrayed capital as a durable resource that produces wealth; a more technical, yet equally simple, definition says that capital is the "accumulated wealth of an individual, company, or community, used as a fund for carrying on fresh production; *wealth in any form* used to help in producing more wealth."[20] Money is clearly capital, wealth that when properly invested produces more wealth. Each of the other types of capital similarly self-perpetuates and grows. Taken together, they embody the notion of "wealth in any form" in the definition above.

Capital, like energy, represents the capacity to do work—energy creates movement in the physical world, capital creates value, utility, or wealth, in the economic one. The analogy proves useful but imperfect because energy gets consumed as it becomes useful work. Capital, on the other hand, energizes useful work but also regenerates itself for use in the future; a more perfect analogy portrays capital as an engine. Capital represents a durable, but not perpetual, asset because even engines wear out over time and need continual maintenance to ensure productivity. Let's now introduce the five types of capital in more detail.

Institutional capital. Sociologist Dick Scott of Stanford University defines institutions as "regulative, normative, and cultural-cognitive elements that, together with associated activities and resources, provide stability and meaning to social life."[21] Institutions have two major components: tangible *regulatory* structures, the laws and regulations that become enacted and enforced by organizations, such as the legal and administrative structures that constituted the English Patent system in the eighteenth century, and intangible *cognitive/ normative* structures, the ways people frame the world and how they think about what is right and wrong, appropriate or inappropriate.

Institutions figure prominently in the fight against Big P poverty as that battle takes on the large and fundamental institutions of a country or region. Meta (high-level) institutions—for example, religious systems such as Christianity, Islam, Hinduism, or the dictatorial or democratic political systems we know as states—and their regulatory machinery loom large as they set the context for Big P poverty and often perpetuate it.[22] Cognitive/normative institutions influence both Big P and little p poverty because they establish the mental and moral maps that govern individual behaviors.

Institutional capital grounds the other types of capital because institutional strength underpins and facilitates their development. Beliefs about the role of families or community involvement shape the nature and strength of social capital available to individuals; the value people place on schooling and credentials figures prominently in the level of education individuals pursue. Regulatory institutions such as property rights and the courts that enforce them determine what types of physical and organizational capital can form. Chapter 3 considers institutional capital and introduces the metaphor of yarn-dyeing to illustrate its foundational role in eliminating poverty.

Social capital. Sociologist Alejandro Portes defines social capital as the sum total of resources available to individuals by virtue of the strength of relationships between them and other social units—or to put it briefly, whom an individual has relationships with.[23] Watt met his angel investor John Roebuck through his professional associate and friend Joseph Black. Social capital comes in two forms, *strong* or *weak* ties, and plays roles of *bonding* groups together or *bridging* different groups and resources.

The family or clan represents the prototypical strong tie relationship. Family life entails sustained, detailed, and deep interactions that transmit worldviews and norms of behavior from one generation to the next. Strong ties are thick, deeply embedded social relations.[24] Membership in a clan, tribe, or larger ethnic or geographic group locates and centers an individual's identity and underpins both attitudes and behaviors. Strong tie relationships bind us to that identity; bonding social capital articulates and reinforces how abstract cognitive and normative institutions play out in the concrete nature of daily life.

Relationships with school, work, or church associates usually exist as weak ties. The emotional bonds may be as strong, but the number, range, and intensity of those interactions are weaker than in strong tie relationships; they constitute the thin, temporary, and limited interactions we have with others. When we access our broader network of associates we often do so to gain access to resources we don't have; this is the role of bridging capital. Bonding capital typically has intrinsic value in our lives by providing meaning, but bridging capital has instrumental value as it helps us acquire and leverage resources for our gain. Chapter 4 explains that social capital can be a double-edged sword that enhances or hinders the escape from little p poverty.

Human capital. Economist Gary Becker formalized the concept of human capital in the 1960s as the "imbedding of resources in people."[25] Since Becker's initial foray into this area, economists think about human capital as primarily knowledge resources embedded in people, whether that knowledge comes from formal education or on-the-job training. Indeed, the two most prevalent measures of human capital are years of schooling and years of work experience. These measures capture the *head* (knowledge) and *hands* (skills) aspects of human capital.[26]

Human capital needs to capture the *heart* to complete the picture suggested by the head and hands. The heart captures a set of attitudes and the abilities they foster, or the psychic and emotional resources embedded within people that both facilitate their framing of challenges and provide the energy to respond. The attitudinal component of human capital includes things like the willingness of individuals to set goals and the ability to work to reach those goals, especially when they represent a real stretch for the individual.

Perseverance (the ability to keep working to accomplish tasks, even when the task is difficult), hopefulness and optimism, level of fear and anxiety, and a host of other emotions and character traits could be considered important to the heart, in fact too many to create an exhaustive list. You'll see in Chapter 5 that James Watt had a good head, skilled hands, and a strong heart, and that each played a role in his lifetime of invention.

Organizational capital. Organizations are, at the very core, vehicles for coordinating human action in order to accomplish things that individuals can't do alone. Matthew Boulton's Soho Works pioneered the factory system, a new way of organizing production. Organizational capital can be defined as the different recipes and methods for coordinating activity. Management scholars have considered organizations and their nuances for decades, but few have considered organization itself as a source of capital. That must change for the fight against poverty to move forward.

Two elements play an outsized role in the functioning of organizations: the distribution of ownership and offices. Ownership entails a set of obligations, usually backed up by contract law that defines who owes what to whom and who gets what from whom. It determines that the effort and energy people expend in their work and ownership arrangements play a critical role in determining the effectiveness of collective action. The concept of offices traces back to sociologist Max Weber's writings on bureaucracy.[27] Offices determine what people do in an organization. Decisions about what people do create opportunities for organizations to exploit the gains from the division of labor.

Ownership and offices come in two broad flavors: informal and formal. Organizations with informal offices take as their template the family, clan, or tribe; authority rests on tradition and social or kinship status. Formal organizations, on the other hand, rest on principles or rational choice and law. Explicit roles and job descriptions exist and tasks are parceled out based on expertise and authority from the legal ability of the organization to sanction behaviors. Chapter 6 shows the importance of organizational capital, but also its neglect in many efforts to eliminate poverty.

Physical capital. Physical capital may be a misnomer for the last type of capital because some of the elements of physical capital aren't physical (tangible) at all; physical capital can be divided into solid (substantive) and liquid (financial) components. Watt needed, and found, the eighteenth-century version of venture capital to bring his engine to market. He and Boulton also used credit and creative financing to introduce their machines to skeptical customers. Watt's engine also incorporated the latest technological advances in iron production.

Solid physical capital refers to tangible assets such as buildings, homes, autos, bicycles, or tools and other equipment. Liquid physical capital refers to money—the original subject of this chapter—and things closely related to money, such as insurance policies, investments, and credit. The value of physical capital depends on how well the solid and liquid components fit with the other types of capital. Complementarity with other resources, then, represents a crucial aspect of physical capital, including financial capital. Think of how little your computer matters if you don't have the right power adapter for the country you're in! Chapter 7 describes physical capital's importance as a piece of the puzzle in fighting poverty.

GOING FORWARD

The next chapter argues that if the five types of capital represent the energy people use to escape poverty, then self-reliance acts as a set of gears that focuses and directs that energy in the most productive ways. Part I of the book, Chapters 3–7, will give substance and content to the five types of capital described above. The other three lessons from Watt's engine—it's a long haul; working with others; and measuring success—matter because they shape the nature and structure of organized effort to eliminate little p poverty.

Chapter 8 discusses vision, strategy, and leadership as three tools to help manage the long-term nature of development efforts. In Chapter 9, I'll provide some guidance for selecting partners and creating and managing alliances, joint ventures, or other ways to work with others to implement programs and policies. Chapter 10 takes up measurement issues, both the fundamental need for measurement as well as a critique of some currently popular ways of measuring the success of development efforts.

The fight against poverty, little p or Big P, requires effective organizations and effort, for the war on poverty can only be won by organized militias, not by individual combatants. Part II explains how you can use the five types of capital, as well as lessons about mission, partnerships, and evaluation to mold an organization that becomes an effective weapon in the fight against poverty. My lessons will give you strategic guidance and principles, not tactical instructions or plans to help you succeed *in* time (today) and *over* time (many tomorrows). You won't find the "five steps you need to take today" in these pages. How you implement these principles depends on your particular *programs*, *places* you operate, *people* you serve, and *priorities* that drive your work. Principles allow you to tailor; plans provide off-the-rack, often ill-fitting advice.

Chapter 11 brings the book to a close, with a twist. The title captures the central premise of the book, that money alone can't eliminate poverty; it's not the *means* to lifting people into prosperity. But is money, or income or wealth, the *end* of eliminating poverty? What does it mean to prosper? I'll reach back as far as Aristotle for the answer to that question. For now, though, let's settle in to eighteenth-century Scotland to learn more about what it means to be self-reliant.

CHAPTER TWO

SELF-RELIANCE

The Mechanism That Eliminates Poverty

The dictionary is the only place that success comes before work.

—*Vince Lombardi*

NINETEEN-YEAR-OLD JAMES WATT left Glasgow for London on 7 June 1755.[1] After the death of his mother in 1754, Watt spent a year in Glasgow seeking an apprenticeship to master his father's profession, mathematical instrument making. He brought to his chosen profession the self-taught skill and natural dexterity of a young man raised in the trade, including his own tools and workshop; however, Watt needed formal training in the technically sophisticated work of navigation and measurement devices to master his craft. A local optician took the young Watt on, but the young man quickly outstripped the optician's skills. Further development could only take place from the experts in London.

Armed with 2 guineas (about $1,200 in 2011 currency),[2] James set out for London to pursue his trade. Watt ran headlong into two significant barriers when he arrived in London after a fortnight's journey. At nineteen he was too old to begin a traditional apprenticeship program in any trade, and having not worked under a certified master he could not work as a journeyman. The rules of the profession left him in an administrative no-man's-land that closed off the entry routes into his craft. Second, he was a Scotsman; although Watt was subject to the British Crown, eighteenth-century London considered him a "foreigner," a status that shut the doors of shops to him.

Crafts like instrument making operated under the vestiges of the medieval guild system: a system designed to create local monopolies that protected the livelihoods of those lucky enough to claim guild membership. Young James Watt felt the sting of those rules; those affecting his trade had been in force since 1631 in the charter of the Worshipful Company of Clockmakers.[3] Watt finally found John Morgan, a specialist in brass instruments with a willingness to overlook the guild's harsh rules. Morgan gave Watt a "bench," a position as an apprentice; Watt gave Morgan a commitment to hard labor for meager wages. He would survive on 8 shillings ($100) a week—a sum that covered both room and board.

Watt biographer H. W. Dickinson described the situation: "Watt was allotted the least eligible bench in the shop—that nearest the door and in the draughts—but full of determination he set to work. Although he was well grounded, he was attempting the well-nigh impossible feat of crowding into one year work that normally required three or four."[4]

Within two months Watt had completed a Hadley Quadrant, a type of sextant, more quickly and of higher quality than Morgan's apprentice two years his senior. He accomplished this feat by working from dawn until 8:00 or 9:00 at night, six days a week. No matter that he had little time or inclination for recreation: walking the streets of London ran the risk of encountering "press gangs." England's war with France had created a need for sailors, and that need was filled by forced impressment of young men through kidnap by marauding gangs.

Watt completed the work of the apprenticeship within his appointed year and, by June of 1756, told his father that he could "make a brass sector with a French joint, which is reckoned as nice a piece of framing as is in the trade."[5] He returned to Glasgow in July of 1756 with £20 ($5,000) worth of tools and materials and the knowledge and skill needed to set up his own shop. Eighteenth-century guild politics again plagued Watt: since he had not completed the seven-year internship required by the guilds in Glasgow, he could not open a shop in the city.

In October, while recovering his strength from the brutal regimen of his apprenticeship and with the help of friend and mentor Dr. Robert Dick, Watt began to restore a set of astronomical instruments for the University of Glasgow that had been damaged by exposure to the salty Atlantic air en route from Jamaica. The university gave Watt space to set up shop; Watt would leverage that space and the contract with the university to establish his business, and later would open another shop in the heart of Glasgow. By the early 1760s Watt was a prosperous instrument maker in Glasgow, carrying on a thriving trade in mathematical and even musical instruments.

Professor John Anderson walked into the university shop one day in late 1763 and asked James to work on a scale model of a Newcomen steam engine that the university had just acquired. The small scale model failed to work properly, and Anderson tasked Watt with its repair. Understanding the failure of that model would lead Watt to the insights and discoveries that would result in a patentable new engine five years later. After another twenty years, Watt's efforts would transform English—and global—manufacturing and usher in the Industrial Revolution.

Those fighting little p poverty can find many similarities between Watt and our clients. Many of them risk their personal safety to engage in trade, and they battle against institutional systems designed to exclude them from participation and progress. Watt worked hard, and Vince Lombardi would be proud of Watt's work ethic—twelve-hour days for a year. It took more than hard work, however. Watt possessed a self-reliant disposition that fostered a set of behaviors; those behaviors helped him create and sustain an ever-deepening capital pool to fuel his personal economic development.

In the last chapter I compared the five types of capital to an engine, with the capitals providing energy for useful work in a way that preserves and (much like a car's alternator) generates new energy. Self-reliance acts as a set of gears that focus and channel that energy toward its most productive uses. If the five capitals represent the engine that powers development, then self-reliance is the transmission that facilitates forward motion. This chapter defines self-reliance, explaining how it relates to the five types of capital and what we can do to encourage and develop self-reliance among those we serve.

SELF-RELIANCE

After I had related Watt's history to a group of philanthropists, one approached me and said that she appreciated my description of self-reliance, even though she was a big fan of Ralph Waldo Emerson. Emerson (1803–82), the pre-eminent American transcendentalist, portrayed the self-reliant individual as one who rejects society's norms and replaces those with the high virtues of nonconformance and individuality, much like Jim Bridger and the mountain men of the nineteenth century.[6] For me, self-reliance has more in common with a set of virtues—dependability, hard work, thrift, and the ability to play well with others—that eighteenth-century Enlightenment philosophers and theologians, including economic giant Adam Smith, saw as central to economic success and personal character.[7]

My colleague Eva Witesman studies the fight against poverty in the not-for-profit sector. When she and I started working together we often spoke past each other in terms of self-reliance; Eva used external terms such as level of income, savings, housing, living conditions, food, and the like to define self-reliance. She looked at the bundle of things that people *have* to define self-reliance. I described self-reliance in internal terms of values, outlooks, dispositions, and actions, or a collection of things people *think and do*.

We can define self-reliance in two ways: a person's possession of resources in excess of survival needs, and that person's ability to garner and hold those resources. Possession is an external outcome, one that causally depends on a person's internal abilities. The gear of self-reliance contains two sprockets that embody ability, one that captures how people think, the other how they act. The operation of that gear over repeated cycles then determines what people have. Self-reliance is a configuration of *assets* produced by ability, a consistent set of *behaviors* motivated by a stable framework of *cognitions*. I refer to this as the ABC model of self-reliance.

The causal arrow in the ABC model runs from cognitions through behaviors then to assets, or CBA. The model implies that the cognitive beliefs held by the poor create their poverty; however, that doesn't mean we blame the poor for their own poverty because many of those beliefs reside, but did not originate, in the person. As you'll see in Chapters 3 and 4, many of the beliefs that drive and sustain poverty originate in groups or the societies in which they live. What matters is not where those beliefs originated but that they cease to govern the lives of those we hope to help.

The Cognitive Beliefs of Self-Reliance

Psychologists define beliefs as propositions or tenets that we hold to be true or accurate descriptions of our existence.[8] Beliefs constitute the basic cognitive structures—mental organizing frameworks—that we use to describe the world in which we live and our place in it; they allow us to orient ourselves and determine what types of behavior will be appropriate. Beliefs guide and shape behavior; behavior enables the exit from poverty.

A fundamental insight in the management literature about behavior links effective performance—how well we execute behaviors—with effort, or motivation, and ability. The equation reads Performance (P) = Motivation (M) X Ability (A).[9] Individuals engage in the behaviors of self-reliance to the extent that they incorporate three critical beliefs that determine motivation and ability: responsibility, self-efficacy, and a long-term orientation. Responsibility provides strong motivation, as it gives us the *Why* behind our behaviors. Self-efficacy and a long-term orientation constitute abilities; self-efficacy supplies the *Can Do*, and a long-term view makes clear *What* things to do and *How* to do them.

Responsibility. We often think of responsibility in a negative sense of blame or fault. We learn early in life we don't want to be responsible when things go wrong; we figure out ways to deflect responsibility and place the blame on someone else. If we can't lay the fault at the feet of others, we can at least show that we have no control over the situation in order to absolve ourselves of responsibility. Placing blame and finding fault uses our energy to look outward to others and backward to what has happened; blame provides little impetus for self-introspection and forward progress.

Self-reliance builds on a positive notion of responsibility: that each of us has certain duties we are morally obligated to fulfill. There are things we must do. Philosophers since Plato and Aristotle have recognized and mused about positive responsibility in terms of our obligations or duties.[10] What *must* I do to be a good person? Positive responsibility turns our focus inward toward our own actions, and our time horizon forward; instead of justifying what we did last we concentrate on what we need to do next. The *must* in questions of responsibility deals with fundamental and ultimate notions of what is right and wrong, not merely efficient or practical, in terms of our actions and efforts. Responsibility is a moral concept.

Self-reliance entails the deeply rooted moral belief that individuals have a duty to provide for their own support and that active and hard work defines our humanity and enables our growth. The economic and physical work that responsibility invites provides us with the means to self-actualize and unlock the social and even spiritual graces within us. Auguste Comte, a French contemporary of James Watt, succinctly noted that "all human progress, political, moral, or intellectual, is inseparable from material progression."[11]

The virtue of responsibility arises from a combination of three sources: individual differences, familial teachings, and societal values. Our lived experience with others teaches us that, whatever the source, people vary in the intensity of their sense of responsibility. Parents, siblings, and extended families provided us with a number of role models who teach us (or not) its definition, and the imperative for and consequences of responsible behavior. The initial imprint about what constitute our duties and obligations may not be indelible, but it requires substantial effort to redraw those initial impressions. The home is where we learn to practice responsibility.[12]

The values and norms of the larger society come into play as well. Families often draw their normative templates from larger social institutions, such as legal standards or religious practices. Social institutions such as educational systems and the day-to-day culture of commerce and exchange establish and reinforce notions of responsible behavior among citizens; these abstract values provide either a complementary or jarring contrast to the day-to-day entrenched beliefs about responsibility coming from families.[13]

Self-efficacy. Stanford psychologist Albert Bandura defines self-efficacy as "people's beliefs about their capabilities to produce designated levels of performance that exercise influence over events that affect their lives."[14] If responsibility creates the moral obligation that we must provide for our own well-being, then self-efficacy gives us confidence in the endeavor: that we can do what responsibility says we must. People with self-efficacy face new challenges or unknown situations with the preloaded belief that they will succeed and thrive.

Four decades of research on self-efficacy show that self-efficacy explains a number of performance differences between individuals.[15] People who believe they can accomplish new or uncertain tasks are far more likely to make the attempt than those who are ambivalent about success; more important, however, higher levels of self-efficacy engender higher energy levels, over a longer time, with more focused effort and persistence in the face of adversity. Self-efficacy endows people with greater coping skills when hardships occur. Interestingly, people who view themselves as capable may enjoy greater mental health and higher levels of satisfaction and positive emotion.

In terms of economics, capable people see the business environment as malleable and believe their actions can mold and influence the nature of that environment and its outcomes. The beliefs opposite to self-efficacy are fatalism and powerlessness, the dual doctrines that the world can't be changed and our actions don't matter. Common sayings such as "It is what it is" or cultural beliefs such as "God willing" (for Christians) or *Insha'Allah* (for Muslims) allow people to avoid action that contributes to their own well-being. Fatalism allows us to play the victim, while self-efficacy invites us to become victors.

Bandura and his colleagues suggest two sources of self-efficacy. We gain self-efficacy best through our own *mastery experiences*; when we try, complete, and conquer unfamiliar tasks, we gain not only specific skills but also a general sense of confidence.[16] The trial and error process we all went through learning how to ride a bike exemplifies the role of individual mastery experiences in self-efficacy. Riding the bike by ourselves provides the most potent way to build our confidence; future success builds upon past mastery.

Self-efficacy also arises through *vicarious experiences*, watching others do well. As we observe others achieve, our beliefs about our own ability deepen. The experiences of others prove particularly valuable when we get to see the detailed steps they take to succeed, or when they describe how they did it. To paraphrase Isaac Newton, rubbing shoulders with giants increases the likelihood that we'll stand on their shoulders and accomplish our own great things. Many of us watched older siblings or friends master the bicycle before we made our first attempt.

Long-term view. Dutch social scientist Geert Hofstede made his mark by defining important dimensions of national cultures, his book *Culture's Consequences* provided the first serious foray into the difficult terrain of explaining national cultures.[17] The book drew from his survey work at IBM. He had six years of employee responses covering topics such as attitudes toward the company to views of the general business environment. Since the corporate culture of IBM was common to his respondents, Hofstede analyzed the data on the hypothesis that differences in attitude lay in national origin. His results confirmed his hypothesis.

In the 1980s Hofstede extended his work with data collected from the Chinese Value Survey (CVS). The CVS represented a major advance because its contributors, Chinese scholars, asked a different set of questions than the IBM survey. The CVS data confirmed the original findings with a twist: the CVS revealed a new cultural dimension that the IBM survey, with its Western orientation, had missed. Hofstede labeled the dimension Long Term Orientation because the dimension sorted people on how they treated the past and the future.

Short-term thinkers practice carpe diem; they live for the thin slice that is today because they see little connection between the past, present, and future. People with a long-term orientation value social orderings and respect traditions, they give gifts and attend to the reciprocal give and take that maintains relationships. They also value personal steadiness and stability, thrift, frugality, and persistence. Put simply, long-term thinkers see themselves as embedded in an ongoing stream of events and relationships where the future draws, and depends upon, the past.

Similar to our sense of responsibility, Long Term Orientation stems from our individual makeup, family imprinting, and larger societal values. We all emerge from the womb with a very short-term orientation: feed us, clean us, give us some love, and we're happy, at least until we're hungry, messy, or bored. Emerging neuroscience research teaches us that the part of the brain that controls long-term thinking, judgment, prudence, and the ability to calibrate risk develops at about age seventeen. Some part of a long-term orientation has genetic roots.

The family and larger culture play significant roles as well. Some families venerate the past, others vilify it. As parents and adults in the extended family make decisions about work, play, finances, and romances, children see whether the focus lies in immediate gratification, or if longer-term, potentially unforeseen consequences come into play. Paradoxically, the thick details of our daily lives provide the best setting to instill a view that looks far beyond today's concerns. As with the other virtues of self-reliance these early lessons strongly imprint our minds toward short- or long-term thinking.

Society plays an unusually large role in Long Term Orientation. Hofstede's work suggested that a long-term orientation arose from a Confucian philosophy that places heavy emphasis on intergenerational obligations and traditions. Religious doctrines that focus on an afterlife, such as John Calvin's concern for God's ultimate election by grace, inculcate and legitimate a concern for tomorrow among its adherents. Popular Western culture, with its heavy emphasis on instant gratification through material possessions, generates a strong headwind against this type of thinking, which may help explain why a long-term orientation didn't surface in the original, Western-oriented survey.

Responsibility answers *why*, self-efficacy the *can*, and long-term orientation the *what* and *how to* of self-reliance. These virtues reinforce and strengthen each other. The lack of one degrades the other two and stymies effective behavior. Responsibility without self-efficacy or a long-term view produces high-anxiety individuals. Self-efficacy alone leads to a cavalier arrogance and the often sporadic action of the talented, yet mercurial person. A long-term orientation without the other two leads to tepid and ineffective action: we know what to do but we don't know why and lack deep confidence in our abilities to do it well. Two Ghanaian entrepreneurs I met during my trips there illustrate the disposition of self-reliance.

Freddie and Warner

On my first trip to Ghana in 2005 I became acquainted with a group of successful entrepreneurs operating a group of handicraft shops at the Tetteh Quarshie Circle, a roundabout that connected roads linking downtown Accra and Ghana University in Legon to the north, Tema in the east, and Cape Coast to the west. The location of the shops along the roundabout provided easy access for visitors, particularly expatriate visitors, to Accra. The seller's trade association enforced rules among the members about selling tactics and business conduct; they aimed to provide easy shopping to accompany easy access on this thoroughfare.

Freddie and Warner both operated shops at Tetteh Quarshie. I've changed their names to protect their privacy. I met Freddie on my first and Warner on my second visit. Freddie's mom worked as a seamstress and his dad a woodcarver who taught him how to carve as a boy. Freddie feels that he was born with special gifts. On vacations all through his schooling he would go to the workshop with his father and learn the craft. His father taught him how to carve an antelope, but Freddie learned how to carve most everything else on his own.

Freddie started carving for money while still in school. He took a construction job for one month to save enough money to buy one log for his own carvings. The ensuing sales funded polytechnic school, but shortly after graduation he returned to carving. Freddie started with a small shed but now has three shops in the roundabout. Each shop cost 200,000 cedis ($200), to purchase a small shed and initial inventory. Pricing for profitability was a key to success, and continued sales depend on meeting customer expectations. He said, "[Y]ou have to study the market and find out what people like."

Freddie served as chairman of the trade association for many years. The quality of his carving work, and his attention to marketing, attracted the attention of foreign buyers. During one of my visits Freddie busily packed a moving box to ship his work to New York. The success of his shops, the international sales, and his leadership of the market allowed Freddie to prosper while many other vendors left the market. When we last met in 2012, Freddie described the challenges of paying for schooling for his nephew and his own children. His shops had been successful for a long time, and Freddie now looked to helping the next generation.

Freddie's long-term success is surprising given the changes I witnessed at the roundabout over several years of visits. I first went to Ghana in 2005, and the market bustled with activity and sales. By my second visit three years later a new, Western-style mall had just opened less than a half-mile away, and the roundabout had been replaced by a modern cloverleaf interchange. This one-two punch of development had devastating consequences on the number of visitors and the associated sales at the roundabout.

By my third visit, a year later, the best shops had seen business drop by 50 percent, while others saw 90 percent of their business evaporate. One of the entrepreneurs summarized the impact of the changes: in good times he cleared about $500 per month, but now, he noted, "[We] are just working for bread." My last visit, in 2012, revealed signs of a rebound as those who had successfully weathered the storm emerged with enough capital and acumen to continue their businesses.

That storm—Schumpeter described it as a "perennial gale of creative destruction"—significantly impacted Warner.[18] Warner sold crafts in the space his brother once occupied. His brother had been a talented wood carver like Freddie but sensed the impending implosion of the market and left to pursue work as a certified electrician in Accra; economic development both threatened small handicraft producers and beckoned qualified workers in the building trades. Warner had little aptitude for carving but was a natural salesman and could market what his brother or others produced. As the customer base eroded, Warner supported his family by turning his sales skills in a new direction—selling cigarettes.

Warner arrived at the cigarette wholesaler about 4:30 a.m. to buy cartons. He peddled cigarettes all day, working within a five-mile radius in and around Accra and traveling by bicycle for eight to nine hours in 90-degree, 90 percent humidity weather. Sales went well; Warner netted about $1.50 per carton and typically came home with $20 to $30 per day. Riding the bike drained

Warner, however, and he could sell only every other day, sometimes less. Warner's wife sold food in the local marketplace; together with their four-year-old daughter they lived as squatters in a nearby shed.

The couple had enough to eat and some rough shelter, no small feat among Accra's urban poor. Their immediate goal was to afford a small apartment, and Warner hoped to cobble together enough to purchase a motorcycle. A motorcycle would allow him greater reach in selling cigarettes; more important, however, he could sell every day. The motorcycle, while taking months to purchase, could easily double Warner's income.

Freddie and Warner both illustrate the disposition of self-reliance. A strong ethic of responsibility drives both men to support themselves and their immediate and extended families. Both have a sense of self-efficacy; Freddie developed his special gift into a worldwide client list, and Warner's confidence in his abilities motivated him to change industries and take the risk of purchasing inventory. Both men exhibit the long-term perspective to start with the most basic business and grow it over time. Freddie and Warner demonstrate the cognitive sprocket of the self-reliance gear; now let's consider the behavioral one.

The Behaviors of Self-Reliance

The cognitive beliefs of responsibility, self-efficacy, and a long-term orientation must engender behavior for self-reliance to become a true disposition. Behavior bridges the cognitive disposition and physical configuration of self-reliance. Four behaviors follow from the cognitive mindsets and values of self-reliance: acquiring, husbanding, leveraging, and preserving. These behaviors determine how we *get* stuff, how we *grow* it, and how we *hold* it.

Acquiring. First and foremost self-reliance engenders acquisition: self-reliance as a disposition encourages people to acquire useful capital, and one way we measure the *condition* of self-reliance is by what they have acquired. Warner employed his financial capital to purchase his inventory, his human capital in terms of physical effort and formidable sales skills; he relied on the institutional advantages of his urban location—a dense concentration of shops and buyers, and roads to connect them—to create a new opportunity for himself and his family. His action brought income today and created capital to use tomorrow. Many of Warner's colleagues at the Tetteh Quarshie market literally sat around and waited for customers that never seemed to come. When a person employs the capital she possesses she sows the seeds from which income, security, and forward progress sprout.

Husbanding. To husband is to cultivate and nurture, to make the most of a resource.[19] Freddie husbanded his human capital as he diligently learned from his father and the other carvers while he was a young man. He has continued to cultivate his skills by selling in the highest quality and caliber venues for traditional African art. Freddie also nurtured his financial capital by wise investing, smart work, and diligent saving; what began as one raw log that allowed him to wholesale rough carvings for "cut money" has transformed into finely finished goods, first sold in one shop, then three, and now in the global web-based art market and bazaar known as Novica (www.novica.com).

Leveraging. The self-reliant wisely combine their resources to leverage others' capital stocks to complement and enhance the value of their own. Freddie tells the story of his entry into the Novica global website. He had printed business cards as a way to market his shop locally and to the expatriates that frequented the Tetteh Quarshie market during its heyday. One day a buyer for global handicrafts showed up looking for Freddie; he had been given Freddie's card by one of his friends who bought at the shop. The buyer had been impressed by the quality of craftsmanship Freddie's carvings exhibited; the business card allowed him to find Freddie quickly amid the (literally) thousands of small art shops in and around Accra. A very traditional marketing tool provided the hook that allowed Freddie to tap into a very global marketplace.

Preservation. Self-reliant people acquire capital, husband its growth and development, bundle and leverage it with other types and sources of capital, and then preserve these assets. Prosperous environments provide ample formal infrastructure and cultural norms that encourage saving, investment, insurance, and other forms of capital preservation. Whether we heed those norms and preserve our assets is an individual matter; however, the institutional and organizational opportunities exist.

The culture of poverty generates and maintains a different set of norms around capital preservation, one of the most powerful being the unwritten rule that those who have share with those who don't. This norm acts as a form of insurance; I share with you now while I have so you'll share with me later when I don't. The poor face a seeming dilemma in that preserving the social capital of rich relationships implies dissipating physical and financial capital.

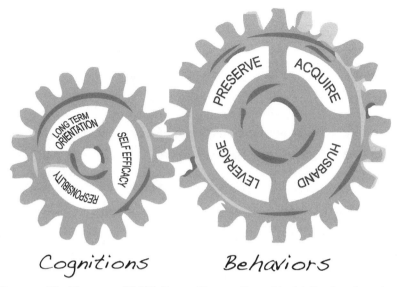

FIG. 2.1. The Elements of Self-Reliance. (Source: Created by Melissa Lundgren.)

Getting out of poverty means learning to say no when family and friends ask, or more often expect, a slice of the emerging pie. The tradeoff between preserving relationships or financial capital is false; profits and surpluses represent future capital to be deployed, not merely income to be consumed.[20]

Freddie, Warner, and many microentrepreneurs like them face another challenge in terms of financial capital preservation: they have money but rarely in chunks large enough to open a formal bank account. Microfinance institutions really help here, as they allow entrepreneurs to save in very small amounts, eventually yielding large enough savings to open formal accounts. Warner saves through another vehicle, Ghana's well-established Susu network. Susu's are individuals who operate informal savings banks targeting those who can save only pennies per day.[21] Whether saving under a mattress, with a Susu, or in a bank, preserving capital allows Freddie to purchase inventory and Warner to accumulate capital for a motorbike.

Figure 2.1 illustrates these two essential cogs in the disposition of self-reliance. The ABC model of self-reliance pictures movement beginning with the small, cognitive gear as energized by an individual's effort and capital stocks; however, as individuals employ those stocks through the behavioral sprocket the cognitive wheel turns as well. The thought and actions that create the disposition of self-reliance reinforce each other in a virtuous circle.

The cognitive disposition to be self-reliant means little without the essential behaviors. These four behaviors represent the crucial crucible that turns cognitive desires into tangible asset stocks. Those asset stocks endow the poor with capabilities that go beyond the mere financial value of their balance sheets; they create the *condition* of self-reliance that my colleague Eva rightfully concerns herself with. The condition of self-reliance empowers people to survive hard times and thrive during the easy ones. It is to the power of self-reliance that we know turn.

The Power of Self-Reliance

Self-reliance helps people to prosper and move their lives forward in meaningful ways; however, it is not a rule for riches. Warner may earn more and his earnings may be more stable, but he is unlikely to become wealthy by Ghanaian or U.S. standards; Freddie, on the other hand, is wealthy by Ghanaian standards, as he earns probably twice the going wage in Ghana. Why does being self-reliant matter? Self-reliance endows individuals with the ability to bounce back during bad times and to bound forward during good ones.

Bounce Back—Self-Reliance as Resilience. Bad things happen to everyone; few make it through life without experiencing some economic reversal of fortune. Businesses fail, or the broader economy turns down and people lose jobs. Inflation, illness, natural disasters, family emergencies, and other forces large and small eat away at our income and assets. Even the successes of others—in Freddie's and Warner's case the opening of a new mall and highway interchange—can wreak havoc on our economic well-being. Self-reliance bestows resilience in the face of negative shocks.

Resilience means that a system—individuals and families are systems—can withstand shocks either without damage or with the ability to recover quickly. The *condition* of self-reliance allows many shocks to occur without damage. Warner's brother held human capital in the form of training as a certified electrician. His human capital stock allowed him to approach the damaging opening of the mall as a simple job change, moving where his income would be greatest. Similarly, Warner's skills in sales made his economic transition easier than for many others, although the lack of financial capital to purchase a motorbike has made that transition far more uncertain and difficult.

The *disposition* of self-reliance plays an important role in helping people recover quickly when negative events occur. The fundamental beliefs of responsibility and self-efficacy point us in the right direction when the harsh winds of adversity blow. Unlike many others, Warner didn't wait for new customers to show up, or come to terms with a lowered standard of living. He believed that he was responsible for himself and his family, and he knew he was capable of finding some way to fulfill that obligation. He acted and found another viable opportunity, investing to acquire a cigarette inventory. He bounced back from the loss of one income source by creating another.

Bounding forward—self-reliance as robust growth. The self-reliant prosper during good times. Responsibility, self-efficacy, and a long-term orientation bestow two advantages: one provides the emotional and economic resources that allow us to survive, the other the things that allow us to thrive. The need to survive comes to us as a biological heritance. The need to thrive comes as a spiritual heritage; our innate tendency to flourish has been reinforced for centuries by philosophers, theologians, and now social scientists.[22]

Freddie's skills in carving and marketing continue to evolve. His capital accounts, particularly the social and organizational capital that allowed him to exploit the Novica opportunity, protected him against the drop in business from the new interchange. The condition of self-reliance made him resilient. Those same characteristics, responsibility, self-efficacy, and a long-term vision have facilitated his growth and development as an organization leader and role model of others. Freddie has served as the chairman of the market association at Tetteh Quarshie, a role that has provided ample opportunity for personal and professional growth.

Ghana hosted the Africa Cup soccer tournament in 2008. To prepare for the regional spotlight on Accra, city officials sought to clean up several areas by evicting squatters and merchants with no land title. The Tetteh Quarshie market was one target because no one has formal title to property; however, their association is formally registered as a trade union, which provided them with a claim on their shops and a way to preserve their livelihood.

Freddie hired an attorney to represent the group, and he personally met with the minister of trade to plead their cause. The group's legal status coupled with their formal protest and lobbying overturned the local initiative to drive them out. Membership in the association doubled after that episode as nearby merchants saw the power of organization and the effects of Freddie's leadership. The association now has more than one hundred member businesses.

During our last visit Freddie told me of his latest project. Sometime during 2010 a private group agreed to lease the land on which the shops sit from the government. The lease would run for fifty years and cost 107,000 cedis (just over $75,000). Some process during the negotiations violated public laws, and still other elements of the lease agreement were found fraudulent. The potential lease was declared invalid. Freddie has been negotiating with the government to grant a similar lease to the shop-owner's association. Having a long-term lease on the land would allow them to make capital improvements to the shops and more effectively compete with the mall and attract shoppers.

Bounding forward, like bouncing back, entails movement; the disposition of self-reliance encourages us, like Freddie and Warner, to move in ways that enhance the condition of self-reliance. Individuals deepen their accounts in each of the five types of capital. If self-reliance has the potential to help the poor lift themselves out of poverty, can social innovators create organizations, programs, and resources that help the poor acquire, husband, and leverage self-reliance? We'll answer that question in the next section.

BUILDING SELF-RELIANT ORGANIZATIONS

Self-reliance acts as a transmission that enables movement by individuals; it can also focus our organizational efforts to eliminate poverty. Self-reliance sharpens our ability to distinguish poignant from pointless actions we may take. Its overarching role lends to some philosophies and broad orientations to guide our work. Let me conclude this chapter by outlining how self-reliance can act as a design principle for interventions and the organizations that undertake them.

Let's think about how you can build self-reliance *in* your organization and *for* your clients, or how you can create a self-reliant organization that helps its clients become self-reliant. In both cases the elements are the same; self-reliance entails a strong foundation of moral responsibility, a healthy dose of self-efficacy and confidence, and a guiding commitment to long-term action.

Responsibility. Responsibility requires autonomy—the true exercise of independent choice in action—and autonomy engenders responsibility. Responsible people must have the space, either within the organization or its programs, to exercise their agency, making choices and following through with action. For associates inside the organization, this means having some degrees of freedom in what they do; they must be self-directed and self-initiating in their work.

Clients must be active participants, not merely recipients of programs and interventions. They have to do more than simply make room for the largesse of donors or programs; they must exert effort and make choices to bring program roles to fruition. The self-reliant organization develops responsibility by making its members responsible for something.

Autonomy and agency have a great ring to them as empowering words and concepts, but autonomy without accountability leads to unstructured action, risk taking, and cavalier behavior. In fact, unrestricted agency *dis*-empowers people, making them slaves to poor choices and actions. Give people positive responsibility for action, but hold them responsible for whatever actions they take, whether blameworthy or praiseworthy. Choice always carries a consequence in the natural and social world; the principle of accountability makes sure that individuals, not the organization, accept those consequences.

How to do this? The design feature lies in the "incomplete" organization. Well-intentioned social entrepreneurs often design "end-to-end" solutions to implement their innovative ideas. Associates have no real involvement other than to follow the checklist of tasks; they have no incentive to think or own what they do. Clients sit at the end of the pipeline and just receive whatever comes, with no transformative effort required. The principle of incompleteness leaves space for action; it means the program won't be complete without others taking responsibility. Incomplete organizations and interventions leave holes—holes filled by individual actions.

Self-efficacy. Self-efficacy comes first through vicarious experiences but best through mastery experiences, ones with ample time to learn, practice, and then master the skill. The sequence: train first through word or demonstration, then transition skill development to the individual. It simply takes time, and lots of repetitions, for someone to master a skill, whether associate or client. A good sequence requires proper pacing; social entrepreneurs tend to be a hurried lot; they want mastery, but they want it now! Competence takes time. Frustration, anger, and disengagement appear when people can't truly master what they've learned; they lose confidence in themselves and the organization that discourages them.

Mastery requires practice, but also proper feedback, a cousin to accountability.[23] Accountability is all about consequences, feedback about communication. Communication, to be effective, must be close enough in time to the behavior to make sense, clear enough to be heard and understood, and delivered in developmental, rather than critical ways. Good feedback encourages further trial and ennobles and energizes individuals; bad feedback enfeebles and enervates. Practice doesn't make perfect, but perfect practice does; perfect practice requires lots of feedback.

Long-term orientation. We all say that we operate from a truly long-term perspective and even believe we do. It's easy to say but hard to do. Relentless pressures seek to turn our gaze from long-term goals and broad visions toward today's exigencies. Pressure comes in the very worthy appeals, such as the demand for immediate, measurable results, annual planning cycles, or the cash flow demands of running any type of organization. These forces invite us to compromise the long-term gains for short-term results. Internally, training and skill mastery—the development of self-efficacy—face off against spending time on current problems and crises. Current pain usually trumps long-term gain.

The incomplete organizations I described above may be *effective* at developing responsibility, but typically they're not as *efficient* as their complete counterparts. Efficiency doesn't eliminate poverty, only effectiveness does. Given the pressure to focus on today, how do we embed a long-term orientation into the identity of the organization and the programs we run?

First, take the past seriously. One common misconception we have is that people show up at our door, either as employees or clients, with no history; they arrive with no past. In fact, everyone comes with a rich history, one that we ignore at our peril. History is an essential part of our identity; who we are depends on where we've been. In the rush to be innovative and entrepreneurial (which we all believe means something new), we denigrate—explicitly or implicitly—what went on before. In our rush to try something new we create fear and anxiety by removing people's connections to the past. Fear and anxiety stymie rather than encourage progress.

The second implication comes from the Bible. In the New Testament Jesus taught his followers about the challenges of taking the long-term view, and consequences of failing to do so. He said, "Suppose one of you wants to build a tower. Won't you first sit down and estimate the cost to see if you have enough money to complete it? For if you lay the foundation and are not able to finish it, everyone who sees it will ridicule you, saying, 'This person began to build and wasn't able to finish'" (Luke 14:28). Failure to complete our work may end up in ridicule or embarrassment, but it always ends with half-finished projects.

Jesus offers sensible advice, but given demands for immediate success, or the pressure of compelling needs, it becomes very easy for us, or for our clients, to forget to "count the cost." Counting costs effectively certainly means planning and budgeting systems. It also entails clear expectations about time lines, deep discussion about the details of projects and sequences, and developing a culture where people ask the simple, yet profound, hard question: and then what?[24] Not just once, but several times in order to truly open our view to the longer term.

Building self-reliant organizations allows us to develop and encourage self-reliance among those we work with: the individuals and families hoping to lift themselves out of little p poverty. Self-reliance represents the keystone and the types of capital the building blocks of the archway from poverty to prosperity.

CONCLUSION: SELF-RELIANCE AND THE FIVE TYPES OF CAPITAL

Self-reliance and the five types of capital move people forward, the capitals providing needed energy and self-reliance equally necessary focus and direction. The different capital accounts help us develop the dispositional virtues of responsibility, self-efficacy, and a long-term orientation. These virtues lead us to acquire, husband, leverage, and preserve these capitals in a fashion that makes us self-reliant. That specific configuration of these assets then begins the cycle anew, strengthening beliefs and encouraging behaviors that in turn enlarge that capital bundle. Each revolution of the engine helps people move further from poverty and toward prosperity.

Part I takes up each type of capital in turn. We begin with institutional capital because these macrolevel mindsets and values—and the organizations they spawn—play a pivotal role in the quest for self-reliance. We saw the negative impact on James Watt of the guild system of eighteenth-century England; institutions can preserve the status quo of poverty. Watt used other institutional elements of his time to create, protect, and preserve his invention. As you'll now see, institutions can enable development for both individuals and societies.

PART I

THE FIVE TYPES OF CAPITAL

CHAPTER THREE

INSTITUTIONAL CAPITAL

Yarn-Dyed Cloth

There is so much talk about the system. And so little understanding.
—*Robert Pirsig,* Zen and the Art of Motorcycle Maintenance

IN 1331 ENGLAND'S KING EDWARD III granted John Kempe, a Flemish weaver, formal royal protection to bring his craft and skill across the Channel to England. Edward promised physical and economic safety to Kempe in order to establish a vibrant weaving and textile trade. The "Sovereign Lord the King" would use his power to safeguard Kempe's trade secrets and [would] "grant franchises as many and such as may suffice."[1] The grant appeared in a document that legal historian William Blackstone described as a "letter . . . exposed to open view, with the great seal pendant at the bottom . . . usually directed or addressed by the king to all his subjects at large."[2] The document carried the title "letters patent," the forerunner of what we call a patent.

Letters patent served as tools of economic development: by granting talented artisans exclusivity of manufacture and, by implication, sale of their products, the British Crown sought to introduce new industries and technologies into the country's economy. Within two centuries, however, the House of Tudor twisted the purpose and administration of letters patent from public economic development to private commercial gain. Patents became gifts of patronage, rewards for loyalty, or exclusive grants available to the highest bidder. With the ouster of the Tudors in 1603, one of Elizabeth's key tasks lay in reforming the corrupted patent system.

This she did over the course of two decades; the Statute of Monopolies in 1624 laid the foundation for our modern system of patent protection.[3] The statute repealed all existing patents and monopolies, limited future patents to new inventions or "manners of new manufacture," and limited exclusive rights to fourteen years from the date of issue. Most important, however, the statute removed the granting of patents from the prerogatives of the Crown and its self-serving motives; patents once again became a tool of economic development rather than private enrichment.

Economic historians see the evolution of the modern patent system as vital for the development of technology and industrialization.[4] Patents provide one way of securing the rewards to an inventor's intellectual property. In theory, patents encourage innovation because the inventor receives a limited but exclusive monopoly to both recoup the costs and reap the economic gains of a new device or process. By the time Watt developed his steam engine, the patent system was well ensconced in English life and law. The monetary incentive created by the patent process fit hand in glove with deeply held societal beliefs about the moral value of innovation and progress.

Citizens in eighteenth-century England had a very different view of the natural world than their grandfathers.[5] Newton's mechanistic vision of the universe had fully diffused through the scientific community and larger society; in consequence, people began to see the world as understandable, controllable, and malleable rather than mysterious, controlling, and immutable. The ensuing spirit of discovery encouraged investment of time, talents, and money in the search for new inventions and processes.

Scientific progress and invention created a positive feedback loop: new inventions that harnessed and altered the physical world encouraged the next round of exploration and discovery. Watt's relationship to the Newcomen engine typifies this type of innovation. Technological progress took on an air of inevitability. Harvard economic historian Benjamin Friedman explains that the confluence of scientific discovery and Protestant theology turned economic progress from a merely social to moral good:

> More famously, scientists like Robert Boyle (of Boyle's law, which relates the volume of a gas to its pressure), Isaac Newton, and in the next century Joseph Priestley (the discoverer of oxygen, but a clergyman as well)—thought that to advance human understanding of nature was a fundamental element of religious experience, a way of seeking to know the works of God.[6]

The medieval and biblical idea that trade and commerce represented a morally reprehensible economic necessity for fallen man gave way to the idea that trade, commerce, and industry enriched people through economic wealth but also ennobled moral character in the individual and benefit for larger society. The writing of Adam Smith embodies this larger transformation. Smith, a professor at the University of Glasgow during Watt's emerging discoveries and experiments, articulated his famous invisible hand metaphor whereby commerce combines specialization, voluntary exchange, and the pursuit of economic self-interest to create social progress.[7] With a few strokes of the pen, trade and commerce morphed from the bane of a spiritual life to benefactor of moral progress.

Which of these social forces mattered more for the invention of the steam engine? Did the economic incentives available through a patent spur an anxious and financially conservative Watt on to invention and commercial success, or did the moral imperative of using his talents to create "progress" steer him to build and improve the steam engine? Was the letter patent or the spirit of the times more important?

Both mattered. Without the spirit of the times—discovery, invention, progress for both self and society—Watt probably doesn't go to London to get the requisite skill to pursue a new, high-tech profession. The patent really is central to the story of Watt's engine; historians all note that he assiduously pursued the original patent and its extension in 1775, and he and his partner, Matthew Boulton, diligently and doggedly defended the patent against encroachment well into the nineteenth century.[8]

Formal documents like patents and intangible, but widely held and accepted, beliefs represent different manifestations of institutional capital. Today both manifestations matter for development and poverty elimination, just in different ways. Economic institutions such as markets, prices, property rights, and contracts represent the regulatory structures that constrain and enable transactions. The social institutions captured in the spirit of the times—social and religious cultures, commonly held attitudes and worldviews, and specific notions of right and wrong—embody the cognitive and normative structures that encourage or discourage action by individuals, groups, or organizations to create and sustain development.

INSTITUTIONAL CAPITAL

What are institutions? Nobel Laureate Douglass North defines institutions as "humanly devised constraints that structure political, economic, and social interactions."[9] These constraints consist of formal rules (think laws and regulations) or informal norms (think customs or taboos) that organize and sustain social life. For North, institutions constitute the rules of the game, to borrow a phrase. His work in the field of economic history explains how real capitalist markets, as opposed to the abstractions of theoretical economists, grew out of a long historical process of institutional change and development.[10] Economic history portrays institutions as the foundational warp upon which actors weave the tapestry of products, services, and transactions that constitute an economy.

Dick Scott, a premier sociologist in the field of institutional theory, offers a similar, yet more precise, definition of institutions: they are "multifaceted, durable social structures, made up of symbolic elements, social activities, and material resources. . . . They are relatively resistant to change." You may recall a variation of this theme in Chapter 1, in which I draw on Scott as well: institutions consist of "regulative, normative, and cultural-cognitive elements that, together with associated activities and resources, provide stability and meaning to social life."[11]

The notion of institutions as the rules of the game serves as an excellent starting point for this chapter. Economists like Douglass North focus more on the *rules*—constraints—while sociologists like Dick Scott center their attention on the *game*, or the meaning provided by institutions.[12] Social life consists of *both* the games we play and the rules we play by, so both views of institutions matter; however, whether you focus on the rules or the game influences how you think about the role of institutional capital in eliminating poverty, especially little p poverty.

Economics, Rational Choices, and Institutional Rules

That economists would focus on the rules more than the game should come as no surprise, as the momentum of twentieth-century economic thought portrayed the game as predefined: the world consisted of atomistic, rational actors engaged in the pursuit of maximizing their utility, most easily defined as wealth. With the game largely given, the interesting story surrounds why and how people create the rules: people create institutions to more efficiently pursue their economic ends, and they use a process of rational choice to create an optimal set of institutions.[13]

North's work on the origins of modern capitalism and commercial contracts provides a nice example.[14] Medieval Europeans lived in a feudal society—an extremely hierarchical economic, political, and social structure based on land ownership; the king owned all the land of the realm, and lords, princes, or knights held a tenure that allowed them to operate tracts of that land in exchange for their loyalty. Villeins and serfs worked the land in exchange for their opportunity to profit (villeins) or merely subsist (serfs). Fealty or loyalty was defined as an obligation of days/hours of service—military for lords and agricultural for villeins and serfs—to the king or the landholder directly above one.

As crop yields increased throughout the twelfth and thirteenth centuries, the time spent in military service became a drain on the economic prospects at *every* level of the social hierarchy; time spent in military service meant less time for cultivating crops, raising livestock, or engaging in associated trade or industrial pursuits facilitated by a growing economy. Kings and lords began accepting payments from those below them in lieu of direct military service. Temporary arrangements became customary, and over many centuries they gave rise to a set of formal institutions such as contracts and courts that enabled the development of modern industrial economies.

In the rational choice model, institutions exist for instrumental purposes—they don't define our goals in life, they just help us reach them. Good institutions are *efficient*; they provide a set of opportunities and constraints that allow people to transact with others to reach their own goals. Formalized institutions work best. Rules have been openly negotiated, written down, and can be enforced by objective outsiders. Formalization encourages economic growth as it allows us to trade with strangers, firm in the knowledge that we both operate from a commonly held set of rules and subject to common penalties for malfeasance.

Rational choice advocates can go the extreme and see all economic transactions as based on formal institutions: we rely on contracts, property rights, and legal recourse to structure and guide increasingly sophisticated transactions.[15] Ian McNeil, a lawyer by training, sees in rational choice an impoverished view of economic and social life. He argues, as do many others, that economic life lies deeply embedded in and infused by the taken-for-granted norms and values of the larger society in which we live.

Tradition, Taken-for-Grantedness, and
Institutional Games

McNeil's work in the 1960s considered the state of commercial contracts a half-millennium after their formal development.[16] A lawyer by training, Mc-Neil examined manufacturing contracts, purchase orders, and invoices used by firms operating in the Midwestern United States. He found that most of these formal transactions had little hope of legal recourse: sellers would sign purchase orders and agree to one set of contractual rules and then send the buyers an invoice—which the buyers executed—specifying a different, and often contradictory, set of contractual stipulations and means for legal recourse. The institution of contracting proved far less efficient in practice than in theory.

How, then, does business get done? By relying on a set of taken-for-granted beliefs about what is appropriate, or legitimate, business practice. Business is an interpersonal, not a contractual, sport; suing over a dispute enforces the contract but usually eviscerates the relationship. I refer to this as the sociological, or relational, view of institutions. From this perspective, the important institutions aren't formally codified, nor are they rationally chosen; they get transmitted from one generation to the next as a set of taken-for-granted assumptions, unwritten but well understood principles or premises that guide our lives.

Max Weber classified relational institutions as a hallmark of traditional societies.[17] Authority, for example, rests on tradition; parents direct children not because of some rationally debated negotiation based on merit or efficiency but simply because parents have always done so. Authority rests on tradition, not a formal legal code. Parental authority—as with many other social structures—has been a hallmark of social organization since before the dawn of history, deeply and solidly sedimented into the unconscious bedrock upon which social life gets built and carried on.

The persistent power of these traditional institutional structures comes from their ability to provide meaning for individuals living under their governance. Rational institutions help us meet our goals, but traditional ones define and clarify our goals. Customs may be efficient in small settings, such as the family or community; however, they are effective at higher social levels in generating the psychological and sociological terrain that allows us to place ourselves in the world. Traditions don't usually get codified, because their power comes from their abstractness and adaptability to helping us find purpose in changing circumstances.

The traditional family—still at the center of social life in much of the developing and developed world—illustrates Dick Scott's cognitive, normative, and regulatory elements that make up an institution. These unquestioned relationships define three things: (1) how the world—natural and social—exists or is structured (the cognitive element), (2) what constitutes appropriate or inappropriate behavior as well as what is morally right and wrong (the normative element), and (3) the nature and types of rewards or sanctions that come into play for compliance with (violation of) those norms. Family stands at the center of life on the largest Native American nation, the Navajo.

The Navajo, or the Diné

The Navajo Nation—often referred to as the Big Rez by those living and working there—occupies 27,000 square miles that span Utah, northern Arizona, and northwestern New Mexico. More than 170,000 Navajos make their home in this arid desert country, for a population density of just over six people per square mile, or roughly one person for every hundred acres. I began learning with and from the Navajo in 2004. I wanted to learn about poverty and economic development but didn't have the time or resources to cross the oceans with the regularity needed to understand the context of poverty in sub-Saharan Africa, or Central or South America. In only a half-day's journey by car, however, I could engage people on the Big Rez, which has most of the characteristics of a developing country.

Unemployment on the reservation hovers above 40 percent, with 75 percent of those with jobs employed by the Navajo Nation government.[18] Just over 7 percent of Navajo hold a bachelor's degree or higher, and only 56 percent have completed high school.[19] More than 35 percent of the population lives below the poverty line, double the proportion in the surrounding state of New Mexico. They may have more money than poor Ghanaians, but on a relative basis to their neighbors (just a few miles away) they live in abject poverty. Two of every three dollars that flows onto the Big Rez flows right back off into the border towns of Gallup, New Mexico, or Winslow, Flagstaff, or Page, Arizona.

When a Navajo introduces herself, she'll tell you where she's from, which may nor may not include a geographic location. What you will get is her family background or clan membership, of which there are between 50 and 140, depending on how you count. All Navajo trace their heritage to four different clans, or people. Upon holding her newborn infant, a Navajo mother says something to the effect: "Hello, my little one. The clan you belong *to* is (her own clan), and (the father's clan) is the clan you are born *for*. (Both grandfathers' clans are then named). In this way you are my baby, and I love you."[20]

The Navajo clan structure *places* each Navajo in the universe; clan, not location, defines where one lives, and what one lives for. K'é (pronounced Keh, with a short e, as in pet) is the specific Navajo term that means a proper relationship. K'é outlines the structural relationships within the home and extended family, but much more as well. Medicine man Phil Bluehouse, whom I met early in my travels on the Big Rez, says that K'é includes one's relationships with the natural world and all human relationships.[21] To live in K'é is to live in harmony, kindness, empathy, and to follow traditional Navajo teachings. K'é articulates the rules of the game, but in a larger sense K'é is the game.

Dick Scott would say that K'é and the Navajo clan structure capture the essence of the cognitive and normative elements of institutions; the social structure, with its attendant stories of creation and separation into clans, creates a paradigm for how the world operates and the perspective from which Navajos view events. K'é outlines right and wrong, legitimate or illegitimate behaviors and goals. Unlike the instrumentalism of rational choice, K'é captures the relational view where institutions play an intrinsic role in answering the big questions of how the world works, how we fit in, and how we ought to behave.

For traditional Navajo this earth is a sacred space, prepared for and given to the Diné (the Navajo word for themselves that means simply People) by the holy ones, but already inhabited by other sacred beings when they arrived. Everything has a spirit, from the rocks and rivers through the sagebrush and native flowers to the birds, coyotes, and other animals. The world must be shared among all its inhabitants, both good and evil; conquer and control give way to acceptance and adaptation as the means and ends of existence: the Navajo seeks to live in Hózhó with the world, just as one strives to live in K'é with other people.

Navajo scholar John Farella describes Hózhó as follows: "The word is comprised of the stem -zhó and the prefix hó-. The stem refers to things like beauty, excellence, and quality. It refers to the essence, or the essential feature, of that which we regard as aesthetically positive," while the prefix refers to the "environment in a total sense—to the world or the universe as a whole." Hózhó captures the ideals of "beauty, harmony, good, happiness, and everything that is positive." [22] The moral goal for the Navajo is to live in beauty, or *the blessing way*, coexisting with (but not dominating) the natural, social, or economic worlds.

K'é and Hózhó represent two core traditional institutions of Navajo life. They regulate intra- and interpersonal conduct among the Diné by establishing a coherent worldview and resulting moral code. K'é and Hózhó provide the cognitive and normative institutional pillars of Navajo institutional life, strong and resilient in the face of serious challenges. If we look at the formal institutions at work on the Big Rez we see what many economists call weak regulatory institutions. The fact is, the strength of the cognitive/normative pillar causes the weak regulatory pillar. This is the paradoxical strength of weak institutions.

THE PARADOX OF WEAK INSTITUTIONS

A paradox is an absurd or self-contradictory statement that is nonetheless true. It appears absurd that the institutions supporting poverty, especially in developing countries, which are almost universally classified by experts as *weak*, prove quite *strong* and *resistant* to change—even in the face of compelling institutional recipes from the developed world. [23]

Weak institutions lack the capability to perform their designed and intended functions. Weak educational systems don't produce graduates; if they do, they produce ones who lack basic skills. Weak police forces can't enforce the laws on the books; indeed, police in these contexts often enforce their own private law through bribes or other corrupt actions. "Weak," in these cases, usually describes formal regulatory institutions, embodied in actual organizations that fail to achieve their stated mission.

Lant Pritchett and Frauke de Weijer both work at Harvard's Kennedy School of Government and have deep roots at the World Bank. They argue that weak institutions in the developing world have the structural *form* of their strong counterparts in the developed world but lack the internal capability to perform the same *functions*. [24] Such institutions are decoupled: the organization adopts certain outward forms to gain legitimacy from powerful actors, but the inner workings of these organizations don't produce legitimate results.

These organizational forms attack the symptoms of the problems of poverty (for example, the lack of a police force or educational system), but they don't address—and often reinforce—the causes of poverty. Pritchett and de Weijer explain why weak institutions exist from a pragmatic perspective: they have the form but can't play the function of effective organizations. This answers one valuable question about the persistence of weak institutions. But, for me, their explanation fails to answer a deeper question: why *can't* these institutions function effectively?

The answer lies in an analogy. If you buy a blue cotton shirt, its color came from one of two processes. The color, and any design, was either printed on the white cotton fabric after its weaving, or the thread (yarn) was dyed before its weaving into cloth. In a yarn-dyed process the color attaches at the molecular level to individual fibers; in print dyeing the color adheres on top of the already tightly woven cloth. Yarn-dyeing produces a deeply embedded coloration. Printed dyes stick to the surface but don't penetrate the cloth.

Pritchett and de Weijer describe regulatory organizations printed over already colored cognitive and normative institutions. Regulatory elements, embodied in tangible organizations, exist at the surface of a society; the intangible cognitive and normative elements constitute the foundation upon which those surface institutions rest. When regulatory elements align with and draw their strength from the bedrock cognitive and normative institutions of society, they function. When they don't align, they can't function.

When we couple the notion of aligning the three institutional elements (cognitive, normative, and regulatory) with the fact that we—in the Western world—know the types of regulatory structures that promote capitalism and wealth creation, we come to what seems like an obvious conclusion to the Big P poverty problem. We install—or, as Pritchett and de Weijer would say, we transplant—the regulatory infrastructure for capitalist development and wait for the power of regulatory elements to bring the cognitive and normative underpinnings of cultures into alignment, a very top-down approach.

This fails because it reverses the causal arrow; institutions survive bottom-up. We forget that institutional strengths come from a society's deeply held mental and moral models; superficial regulatory arrangements draw what strength they have from these structures, not the other way around. The mental maps people employ explain the purposes of regulatory components—they let us know where these organizations fit: which parts of the world they interact with and control. Moral values justify and legitimate regulatory arrangements by linking these arrangements to what people see as worthy outcomes. To endure and become functionally effective, the regulatory regime of a society must align with, not seek to realign, foundational mental and moral maps.

People living in Flagstaff, Arizona, formally incorporate their businesses and work on the basis of written contracts because, as they believe, the formal institutions of contract facilitate wealth creating economic exchanges, and wealth creation is valued and desirable, a desirability resting on several centuries of theology and philosophy.

Seventeenth- and eighteenth-century thinkers equated economic profit with moral progress; science, industry, and commerce became a way to fulfill God's command to Adam and Eve to "rule over the fish in the sea and the birds in the sky, over the livestock and all the wild animals, and over all the creatures that move along the ground" (Gen. 1:26). Max Weber tracked the development of this doctrine and titled it the "spirit of capitalism"; one of accumulation for its own sake; *having* more becomes a morally prized end, not merely the means for achieving other good things.[25]

Navajos living forty miles away in the town of Leupp live in a different institutional world, a world of K'é and Hózhó. Many Navajo live lives torn between two institutional worlds, the spirit of capitalism in every border town and the order set out by the Holy Ones within the sacred four mountains that demarcate the traditional lands of the Diné. Author Tony Hillerman—I read his entire series of Navajo mysteries to help learn about life on the Big Rez—captured the deep institutional tension and its tragic human consequences.

Hillerman's character Jim Chee solves crimes; he also studies to become a Navajo singer who performs many of the traditional Navajo ceremonies. Jim's uncle and mentor Hosteen Frank Sam Nakai explains the fundamental choice facing Chee: will he follow the Navajo or *bilagáana* (white American) culture. Frank reminds Jim of a trip to Gallup the two had taken and what they had seen that illustrated this choice:

Jimmy Chee remembered it very well. He remembered the woman who came out of the Turquoise Tavern and the man in the black reservation hat who followed her. They had walked unsteadily, both drunk. The woman had lost her balance and sat heavily on the dirt sidewalk, and the man behind had bent to help her. His hat had fallen and rolled into the gutter. Hosteen Nakai's fierce eyes had watched all this.

"They cannot decide," he said. "The way Changing Woman taught us is too hard for them, and they have lost its beauty. But they do not know the white man's way. You have to decide."[26]

Frank's fictional comment describes a reality Tony Hillerman understood well: nineteenth-century attempts by the U.S. government to destroy the Navajo culture and traditions failed, but the clash between Western and Navajo worldviews and moral values hobbles Navajos today. The Diné struggle to integrate the conflicting values of Hózhó with rampant commercialism and materialism, a sense of meaning derived from coexistence with nature and others or from domination and possession. The fundamental problem on the Big Rez has institutional roots: a people trying to reconcile their yarn-dyed traditions with the shifting prints of twenty-first-century America.

This institutional conflict is not limited to the indigenous Navajos in the United States; people in many developed countries face the challenge of diverging cognitive/normative and regulatory institutions. Regulatory institutional elements—even those known to work spectacularly well in the process of wealth creation—only work when those elements align with the pre-existing cognitive and normative underpinnings of a group, region, or nation. Eliminating poverty depends on creating convergence between formal and relational institutional elements.

Institutions belong in the sphere of Big P poverty. The tremendous role they play in our lives, however, means that eliminating little p poverty requires attending to the institutional cloth covering the poor. Changing the institutional wardrobe runs the risk of becoming mired in political dress balls. Without action, however, those in poverty will lack the proper outfitting for their climb to prosperity. With that in mind, let's consider some practical steps social innovators and their organizations can take to create effective institutional change.

INSTITUTIONAL CHANGE:
DYEING YARN NOT PRESSING PRINTS

Institutions act as a foundation that either encourages or discourages the development of self-reliance. The mental maps and moral virtues of a society encourage self-reliance through their effect on responsibility. *All* cultures foster responsibility because responsible actors hold societies together; the differences lie in the conception and definition of responsibility. Citizens of Flagstaff interpret this as the obligation to provide for oneself and family, to compete hard in the market place, and to enjoy the fruits of their hard work. Citizens of Leupp feel equally compelled to provide for themselves and their families, live in harmony with others and with nature, and seek the beauty inherent in a sacred world.

Regulatory structures such as business registration and insurance encourage a longer term orientation and more sophisticated economic activity because they reduce the inherent risk involved in future-oriented transactions. Contracts, and the courts that enforce them, allow people to trade with strangers, over long time horizons and significant distances. Other structures, such as financial institutions, help people create the condition of self-reliance as they can store excess quantities of physical capital.

Because institutional capital draws from, and reinforces, self-reliance, the advice in Chapter 2 about designing *in* and *for* self-reliance applies to institutional work as well. Most social innovators can't work on the regulatory structures that deeply ensconce Big P poverty in any society; however, they can—must—work on the cognitive and normative institutional structures as they exist in the minds, hearts, and lives of those working to escape little p poverty.

Institutional Change

Economists model institutions as instruments to goal attainment; sociologists see institutions as outlining what goals are worth attaining. Both views, however, see institutions developing through processes of structuration and path dependence. The concept of structuration originated with Anthony Giddens.[27] He believed that the prevailing views of human action were wrong; behavior was not solely the result of microlevel human choices, nor was it determined by the macrolevel culture in which people lived.

He rejected both the excessively atomistic view of economists and the overly socialized view held by sociologists and built a theory that incorporated both elements. Structuration recognizes human action as a complex whole; people's free choices and random behaviors fuel actions and outcomes. Those choices aren't totally free or random, however, as social norms, conventions, mores, and rules strongly influence what looks like free will. The theory sees both forces at work in creating a society that exists in homeostasis: a dynamic equilibrium of stability *and* change. Things do change, but in incremental ways.

Institutional change among the Navajo comes slowly, if at all. In 1985, under the leadership of Peterson Zah the Navajo tribal council began the effort to codify traditional Navajo law. The effort required the better part of twenty years to complete; final adoption of the *Diné bi beehaz' áanii,* or Navajo law, came in 2002.[28] Navajo law represents an interesting blend of strong Navajo traditions, a commitment to personal freedom enshrined in both the U.S. and Navajo Nation constitutions, and emerging issues facing the People.

Diné bi beehaz' áanii enshrines the Navajo worldview of the existence of the Holy People and their role in placing the Navajo as the "Holy Earth-Surface-People" in their native land. From this strong traditional base, however, the code presents an expansive and ecumenical view of religious practice. The code specifies the important roles played by elders and medicine people, but the law also provides for respect and freedom of worship of those with other beliefs, including those following the Jesus Way (Christianity) and the Peyote Way (the Native American Church).

The Navajo code speaks of new challenges as well, and acknowledges the important economic needs of the Diné. People must make a living, and they must increasingly do so in a complex and changing world; a world with many values foreign to the principles of K'é and Hózhó. The Navajo code places these values and principles as guiding stars as Navajo work toward economic development and higher standards of living. *Diné bi beehaz' áanii* represents a series of nudges, compromises, and investments of time and energy to move an oral tradition into formal legal practice.

Implications for Organizations

Four lessons can be drawn from the Navajo experience: (1) institutions change slowly, and the next step depends on the previous one in path dependent ways; (2) cognitive and normative institutional change precedes change in regulatory institutions; (3) institutional change takes a long time; and (4) the compromises and debates involved in the process reflect the real—and substantial—tradeoffs people and groups must make when the institutional structure changes.

These lessons inform organizational design, but so does the metaphor of yarn-dyed institutions. Yarn-dyeing is an old process; it's the original way human's colored cloth, and it involves human action. Yarn-dyeing is labor intensive and entails substantial expertise. For our work, that expertise lies in the principles of leadership; specifically leaders who can accomplish four specific tasks: provide vision, focus on the details, have patience, and listen to opposing voices.

Leaders who provide vision. We'll come back to the critical importance of vision in Chapter 8, but suffice it to say here that engaging in the twenty-year process of institutional change requires a strong vision of, and commitment to, the importance of what you are about. My colleague Wade Channell of USAID points out the useful distinction between law and the process of lawmaking.[29] Laws can be written easily; in a matter of days they can be implemented by fiat, or rammed through legislative bodies on a fast track in a matter of weeks or months. To print laws in books is quick and easy.

The process of lawmaking takes years. Wade estimates that it takes a decade to make a good law, one that combines form and function. The process entails heavy doses of discussion, education, negotiation, and reconciliation about the purposes, ways, and means of proposed laws. Good processes allow people and the groups to which they belong processing time to work through the emotional, intellectual, moral, and social impacts of the new institutional order. When rushed, people respond defensively and adhere to the old order on grounds of comfort; when given time, people see change as legitimate and helpful.

To yarn-dye the norms and values that support good institutions takes long, hard work; work driven by a strong vision and moral commitment (think of the responsibility you want to design into your organization) to the ultimate aim you work toward. The work of changing hearts and minds proves more time consuming and difficult than Wade's work of changing laws. Vision comes first because without strong direction from the top, innovative organizations quickly lose interest and move on to other, easier tasks.

Leaders who can focus on the details. Maintaining focus entails a very different set of skills than setting the vision. Visionaries tend to operate at 30,000 feet, articulating big ideas, grand principles, and inspiring outcomes; they usually tune out when the realities of working on the ground shift the focus to the mundane details of administration. A vision of changing the hearts (values) and minds (worldviews) of those in poverty sounds great, but that only happens as people make those changes in their daily routines.

As a young academic I heard a story about an organization that blends vision and detail extremely well. I don't know if it's true or just a legend; either way the story drives home an important point. Billy Graham was an amazing preacher; his ministry spanned the globe, his sermons captivated throngs, and he could bring thousands of people to the front of the auditorium full of a commitment to change their lives. Graham realized that those commitments to change in the moment mattered little because real change came only when people restructured their daily lives to accord with the doctrines he preached.

Part of his lasting success lay in his organization's ability to reach out to local pastors to care for and nurture those Graham had inspired long after he had moved on. Graham sketched visions of heaven and salvation for people; thousands of local ministers helped people turn those sketches into colorful and detailed paintings of a new way of living. The point of the story is this: successful organizations—ones that make lasting impact—have preachers and pastors. Inspiration matters, but so do preparation and perspiration. Preachers lift our gaze, pastors keep our feet on the ground so we can move forward.

Leaders who have patience. I have a small wooden tortoise by my computer, an ebony tortoise I purchased during a trip to Ghana. I keep tortoises handy; I have one in my home office, one at school, even one on my dresser, to remind me of a profound truth: the tortoise always wins. I love the fable of the tortoise and the hare. The hare—like many social innovators I meet—believes the race to be easy and bounds from the starting gate. The hare tires after a bit and takes a break. You know how this ends: the tortoise wins every time.

Patience may be a virtue, but it's also a practical necessity if your organization wants to play the two-decade game of institutional change. Structuration processes move slowly, incrementally, and sometimes in reverse. Entrepreneurs and organizations seeking to pick the low-hanging fruit, find the quick victories, and make what they believe are real changes often get discouraged at the first reversal, or they confuse quick wins with lasting change.[30] Organizational patience helps innovators stay in for the long haul, where the real changes take place.

How do you build in patience? First, through planning and goal setting processes that anticipate tortoise-like movement—slow and steady—rather than the rapid burst of the hare. The hare works on stretch goals that can be achieved in one period but not sustained; the tortoise chooses doable goals that can be parlayed far into the future. Remember the lesson of self-efficacy: mastery experiences build it best, and mastery takes time in execution. Reward mastery, not rapid growth or one-off big hits.

Leaders who listen to opposing voices. Institutions structure economic, political, and social life; radical change in the institutions of society threaten the stability people depend on.[31] We make specialized investments of our existing capital based on the presumed stability of the institutional structure and prefer evolutionary, not revolutionary, change. Machiavelli understood this principle many centuries ago as he explained to the potential prince: "[T]he innovator has for enemies all those who have done well under the old conditions, and only lukewarm defenders in those who may do well under the new."[32]

Change upsets existing power hierarchies, and power transfers grudgingly at best, violently at worst. If you want to change institutions, be ready to make enemies. But not all enemies are evil. Committed, visionary leaders often view opposition to their work as simple-minded ignorance, mean-spirited jealousy, or bald power plays by those who benefit under the existing rules. They may be right, but they can easily forget that opposition also comes from the pain people feel as they see the value of previous and current investments diminish. That pain, and those opponents, may suggest alternative courses of action that reach the same goals but with much less disruption. Our programs may use a hatchet when a scalpel would do.

Organizations that listen well can be built and sustained. It almost goes without saying that leadership at the top matters a lot here, the explicit and implicit ways you deal with opposition will discourage or encourage those you work with to speak up. Your actions speak louder than words. Personal commitment isn't enough, however, as two natural tendencies work against being a listening organization. First, we tend to cast our opponents as enemies; our description of their position easily moves from rational reasoning to issues of personal character. Second, our quest for success to impress ourselves, donors, or other stakeholders represents a second tendency to discount the opposition. We simply don't listen!

We remedy this by building in processes that require us to engage opponents in conversation, not conflict. Internal processes such as the devil's advocate or the creation of teams to propose conflicting alternatives can sensitize the internal organization to the need to hear opposing voices. Organizational policies may require reaching out to those disaffected, or clear opponents, as a part of planning and evaluation programs. You can always bring your detractors inside the organization through employment or alliance. This slows things down, but means you have to pay attention to what they say.

Leaders who explicitly ask for negative news, disconfirming evidence, or the views of those unfriendly to our cause invite their associates to think deeply and take seriously the potential negative aspects of our interventions. Evaluation systems, for individuals and programs, need to require the search for negative outcomes and responses among our clients, contexts, and stakeholders. The goal isn't to include merely token consideration of our detractors but rather the development of a balanced perspective that allows us to move ahead honestly and effectively with our work.

The critical role of leadership represents somewhat of a paradox. Institutional change happens in time spans that exceed the careers of individual leaders, and the actual ability of any individual to change institutions is small indeed. Good leaders work on setting the right course, a course that enables institutional change and positions their organizations to have an ongoing role to play in that process. Leadership involves the art of creating a yarn-dyed organization that can yarn-dye institutional changes, especially in the mental maps and moral sensibilities of those we hope to lift out of little p poverty.

CONCLUSION

Institutional capital matters. The cognitive and normative institutions of the people we serve provide their deepest sense of meaning; when we threaten those we create difficulties for ourselves. We must ensure that we don't do so unnecessarily; some mental maps trap their holders in constricting worldviews, and some moral compasses do point in the wrong direction. Most don't, however, and sensitivity to the yarn-dyed institutional bedrock of the people we work with can help us nudge, or structurate, long-term institutional changes. Remember, institutional change can enable progress out of poverty; it can also easily disable it.

Institutions matter in their own right; however, institutional capital also matters because it influences and impacts the four other types of capital that contribute to self-reliance. Regulatory institutions determine in large measure how physical capital gets deployed and preserved, what types of organizational capital will be available, and the opportunities for human capital acquisition and husbandry. The substantive strength of regulatory institutions determines just how far out of little p poverty people can climb; it's also the essence of the fight against Big P poverty.

Institutional capital influences social capital. We first learned the mental maps and moral compass of our institutional environment at home. We constantly update and structurate those elements through our interactions with friends and colleagues. These social interactions, and the capital they generate, go a long way in determining how self-reliant we are or can become. Watt's development of the steam engine illustrates the point; without the help of family and friends his engine would never have needed a patent, for it would never have come into being.

CHAPTER FOUR

SOCIAL CAPITAL

A Double-edged Sword

If you want to achieve your dreams, you better learn to work and play well with others.

—Randy Pausch

JAMES WATT DIED IN AUGUST OF 1819 at his Handsworth estate in the West Midlands. Six years later a statue appeared in St. Paul's chapel at Westminster Abbey; the colossal memorial features a 6-foot 11-inch James Watt sitting atop a 7-foot 10-inch pedestal and cost a hefty £6,000 (more than $1.2 million in today's dollars). An inscription on the massive pedestal reads: "The king, his ministers, and many of the nobles and commoners of the realm raised this monument to James Watt, who directing the force of an original genius . . . increased the power of man."[1]

History rightly emphasizes Watt's role in the Industrial Revolution, for the initial insight belonged to him. While Watt's achievement may have been original, a closer look reveals that it required more than just individual genius. Watt had help, lots of help. Many others provided important resources throughout the development of the engine. Some of these people helped Watt build a scientific foundation, while others filled financial gaps; they provided timely and critical resources that kept his work moving forward. Let's consider a few influential assistants in the discovery of the steam engine; some names appeared in Chapters 1 and 2, but you'll get a fuller introduction to them here as well as other influential actors in the drama of the steam engine.

Watt's father, also James, worked as a "shipwright, contractor, provider . . . a man of position and influence in the community . . . universally esteemed."[2] The elder Watt sold navigational instruments and endowed James at an early age with "a workbench, tools, and a small forge, where he made models and miniatures—tiny working cranes, pulleys and pumps, a barrel organ, a punch ladle hammered from a silver penny."[3] The younger Watt saw his father outfit mariners with navigational instruments and gained a firsthand knowledge of their various functions and what constituted quality instrumentation.

Agnes Muirhead brought Watt into the world in 1736 and, because of his sickly nature, home-schooled James until age thirteen. Her family held a tradition of learning and literacy. Watt's maternal cousin George Muirhead worked as professor of humanities at the University of Glasgow; George played a pivotal role in Watt's apprenticeship, described in Chapter 2. He introduced Watt to Dr. Robert Dick when Watt moved to Glasgow in 1754 after his mother's death. Dick, a professor of natural philosophy, recognized Watt's talent for instrument making, encouraged his pilgrimage to London, and provided a letter of introduction to James Short, an Edinburgh-born instrument maker in London.[4] Short passed Watt on to the accomplished, rule flouting brass artisan John Morgan, with whom Watt apprenticed.

Upon his return to Glasgow in 1756, Dick arranged for Watt to unpack and clean the astronomical instruments donated to the university by Alexander McFarlane, patron of the university's new observatory. Dick died in 1757, but Watt established a relationship with John Anderson, who assumed Dick's chair in Natural Philosophy. John happened to be the brother of Watt's schoolboy friend Andrew Anderson. In 1757, at John's urging, Watt was appointed as the "Mathematical Instrument Maker to The University."

The official position raised Watt's profile and helped his instrument business grow; while he proved a talented artisan, his ability to finance growth and expansion was limited. He created a partnership with local architect John Craig, who allowed Watt to finance his operations; Craig eventually lent James upward of £800 over the course of their partnership.[5] It would not be the first, or last, time Watt would seek venture partners to move his work forward.

During the winter of 1763–64 Anderson contracted Watt to repair a small model of a Newcomen engine owned by the university; others had tried, but the machine still would not function.[6] With this appointment Watt started down the path toward his remarkable engine; however, Watt did not walk alone. His relationship with Joseph Black, whom we met in Chapter 1, deepened. Professor of both medicine and chemistry by 1766 and perhaps the world's leading expert on latent heat and thermodynamics, Black, along with his former student John Robison, served as Watt's advisor on many chemical, physical, and scientific questions. Watt later admitted that from Black he learned "the correct modes of reasoning, and of making experiments of which he set me an example."[7] Watt imported the best practices from the emerging empirical method of scientific discovery.

John Craig's death in 1765 left Watt owing the estate the entire loan of £757. Lacking that kind of financial capital, James turned to Black for advice and help. Black encouraged Watt to contact John Roebuck, owner of substantial coal mines at Kinneil, about thirty miles northeast of Glasgow. Watt's double condenser would help Roebuck drain his deep mines; in return, Roebuck's money would allow Watt to clear his debts and continue work on the steam engine. They formed a partnership, with Watt holding one-third interest and Roebuck two-thirds in the development of the new engine.[8]

Through Roebuck, Watt met William Small, a Birmingham physician, friend to Benjamin Franklin, and clever intellect who played an influential role in the original patent for the steam engine. Small encouraged Watt to obtain the original patent for "some principles" by which "you intend to construct steam engines of much greater powers."[9] Watt patented a *principle* in 1769 rather than a particular machine or design, a fact that frustrated many a competitor over the years. Small's greatest contribution, however, came in 1767 in the form of an introduction to the noted Birmingham manufacturer Matthew Boulton.

Boulton took immediate interest in Watt's machine and mind, both for the direct potential at his Soho factory but also because he saw the larger commercial potential of Watt's engine. Boulton and Watt could not consummate their business relationship for six years; in 1773 Roebuck went bankrupt, and Boulton purchased his two-thirds interest in the steam engine. The new firm of Boulton & Watt incorporated in 1774.

Watt and Boulton soon realized that the 1769 patent, with only eight years remaining, would leave precious little time to commercialize and capitalize on the new principles of steam power. Rather than seek a new patent they sought to extend the old one through an act of Parliament. The Duke of Buccleuch, patron of Adam Smith, and other lawyers and engineers from Watt's days working on England's canal system agreed to assist in the effort.

Boulton had his own set of connections in "every corner" of the British Parliament. He could call in favors from many MPs from the Midlands, owed from his extensive business there. Historians Eric Robinson and A. E. Musson describe Boulton's social position: "Boulton's lines of influence . . . were so extensive that it is almost true to say of eighteenth-century society from 1760 onwards that if Boulton did not know you or did not know of you that you were probably not worth knowing."[10]

This brief history mentions thirteen people in Watt's circle who played pivotal roles in the course of events that ended with James's enshrinement as an original genius. This baker's dozen, plus a host of others not mentioned here, constituted Watt's stock of social capital—a set of relationships that provided human, physical, organizational, and institutional resources crucial to the development of the steam engine. In this chapter we define social capital, outline its key features, and consider its role in development and fighting little p poverty.

SOCIAL CAPITAL

Management professors Paul Adler and Seok-Woo Kwon identified twenty different academic definitions of social capital, from very abstract— "an individual's personal network of elite institutional affiliations"—to the very practical—"a web of social relationships that influence individual behavior and thereby affects economic growth."[11] A simple definition captures the essence of social capital: what you can get by virtue of who you know. I'll expand on this definition later, but it provides a succinct starting point because it highlights the interconnected nature of resources and relationships. Let's look at some ways relationships and resources can be structured to create social capital.

Strong, Bonding vs. Weak, Bridging Ties

It's useful to think about social capital in terms of a series of dichotomies or alternative forms. The first one cuts at the joint between strong and weak relationship ties. *Strong ties* describe the thick set of social relationships, norms, and obligations that exist within an identifiable group. The nuclear family is the archetypal strong tie, but groups also include tribes, villages, school alumni associations, churches, even fans of a particular sports team. We choose some strong tie relationships such as marriage, but many strong tie relationships are chosen for us; we didn't choose our family, ethnicity, hometown, or our religious upbringing. Harvard's Robert Putnam, in his epic work *Bowling Alone*, describes strong ties as "repeated, intensive, multi-stranded networks" that create and maintain socially exclusive groups.[12]

Strong ties help define our social identity and provide us with a deep sense of meaning and belonging. They create *bonding capital* as they transmit significant cultural resources, worldviews, and ethical values in clear and unequivocal ways. The frequency and types of interactions make up the thick details of our daily lives and provide meaning-rich exchanges where appropriate values can be displayed across a variety of situations. Strong ties create correspondingly strong obligations; what it means to be a son, for example, entails very specific behavioral prescriptions, but also very broad and expansive expectations that transcend time and location. Parents do specific things every day; good ones are also "there" for their children any day.

At the other end of the continuum we find the weak ties that describe our voluntary relationships with people from different social groups. Think of a college friend you'd call only for a business contact as a quintessential weak tie. Because they lack the basis of common blood, belief, or background, weak ties exist because of common interests and the utility the relationship offers to both parties. These relationships feature "thin" interactions—infrequent interactions with a narrow, exchange-based focus; we tend to reach out to people in our network either when we need something specific, or when we have something specific we believe others need.[13]

Putnam characterizes weak ties as "episodic, single-stranded, and anonymous."[14] The strength of these ties arises as they create access to other groups and their resources; they expand our reach and create *bridging capital*. Bridges not only connect different and diverse groups of people, bridges also create structures for information and other resources to flow between these groups. Weak ties also create a generalized sense of reciprocity: "I'll reach out and help you now in the hope you'll reach out and help me later." That sense of reciprocity lays the foundation for many business transactions; we don't negotiate the details because we depend on reciprocity, and the reputation it entails, to resolve problems that may arise.[15] We call these valuable relationships as weak only because they lack the intense obligations that arise in strong tie relationships.

Substitutes vs. Complements

University of Chicago legal scholar Lisa Bernstein examined the role of social capital in the cotton industry.[16] Trades in cotton tend to be very complex; there are forty definable grades of cotton and a number of contingencies that can affect the delivery date and quality of cotton produced. The vagaries of weather patterns, crop yields, and the logistical issues of transporting cotton on time and on price raise the potential for problems and eventual disputes.

Interestingly, traders in the cotton industry don't rely on the public legal system for contract enforcement. Judges and juries lack the type of sophisticated knowledge of the market to dispense fair justice. The industry relies on trust and social capital to facilitate cooperation and hold the industry together. Cotton traders created their own code of private law maintained and administered by formal and informal strong ties among farmers, traders, and manufacturers. Social capital very effectively *substitutes* for legal remedies in business disputes.

The industry association and regional and local groups all sponsor meetings and professional conferences to strengthen ties between individual traders. They also expend tremendous resources on social functions such as balls and cotillions that sustain a thick set of reciprocal ties among not only members but their families as well. These social events serve a dual purpose; they clearly *complement* ties that would form through geographic proximity or the regular course of business. They also complement the sanctioning power of private law as knowledge of contract violations spreads throughout a broad network that includes the traders and their families.

Episodic vs. Enduring

A final dichotomy goes to the heart of the economic value of social capital and considers whether social capital represents an enduring or episodic resource. Here we must distinguish between the relational and resource components of social capital. The bottom line: the quality of your social capital depends on how well your relationships endure and how episodic your resource demands are.

Strong tie relationships have a built-in bias toward endurance: after all, most of us don't change families or tribes. We do choose, however, whether those ties remain strong and vibrant or wither and weaken. Cotton traders have a ball every year to burnish the strength of those ties. Weak ties require more effort to sustain through time, but the better we do this the more valuable those relationships become. At one level we all feel squeamish when we call an old friend just because we need help. At another level, the value of reputation and reciprocity—helping now for help later—intimately depends on there being a later to motivate or constrain behavior now.

Resources tend to be episodic. Social capital's resources work best when they fill gaps in our own resource base; effective networks help us solve problems we can't on our own. Whether they substitute or complement what we bring, not only self-reliance but common courtesy requires that we use what we have before asking others for help. A constant call for resources makes it hard for relationships to endure, and we all know people in our networks that constantly call for our help but offer little in return. These people go by a number of names, such as deadbeat, lazy, moocher, or slacker.

At this point in the chapter you would expect me to relate a story about people who used social capital wisely and consistently to become self-reliant or work themselves out of poverty. We could talk the value of regular relationships, many with family, friends, or trading partners that provide access to resources; however, the essence of social capital is "what you get" by virtue of whom you know, and that tends to occur irregularly. Rather than relating a single story, then, let's look at a particular at-risk group for poverty: single mothers in the United States.

Single Moms and Social Capital

The U.S. Census Bureau classifies single mothers as custodial parent families: the custodial parent lives with the children while the other parent does not. Custodial parents may have sole, split, or joint custody of the children with the noncustodial parent. National data on the challenges of custodial parenting present a stark picture. *The Fragile Families and Child Wellbeing Study*, directed by scholars at Columbia and Princeton universities, tracked five thousand families formed by unmarried parents—they use the word *fragile* to describe these families—over a nine-year period.

One source of fragility lies in family duration and persistence: "[O]nly about 35 percent of unmarried couples at birth, compared to 80 percent of married couples, are living together five years after the birth." Children suffer when fragile families break down. Single mothers are less likely to engage in literacy activities with children, five times more likely to use harsh parenting techniques than married moms, and 50 percent less likely to maintain stable routines for children such as a regular bedtime. Each factor contributes to children's health and overall development.[17]

Custodial parenting does not pay well. Just over a fourth of custodial parents (28.3 percent) lived below the poverty line in 2009, *double* the percentage of the general population (14.1 percent). That number represents a 20 percent increase from 2003.[18] Crises such as the Great Recession tend to hit the vulnerable the hardest, and custodial parents are no exception. Single moms are almost twice as likely to live in poverty as single dads, 30 percent versus 18 percent. Almost half of custodial parents living in poverty were unemployed (44 percent), and 38 percent of poor custodial parents relied on at least one form of public assistance in 2009, a 20 percent increase from 2007.

Roughly half (50.6 percent) of custodial *mothers* have explicit agreements for financial support from former spouses, but less than a third of custodial *fathers* (30.4 percent) have such agreements. "Fragile Families" data indicate that only 14 percent of nonresident fathers make regular child support payments after five years.[19] The average amount of child support due was $5,960, or $500 per month, but the average amount received was $3,630, or just over $300 per month. Researchers estimate the monthly cost of raising a ten-year-old child living in a lower-income household at over $600 per month: the average custodial parent gets about half of what is needed.[20] That $300 average is deceptive, however, as an alarming 30 percent (technically 29.2 percent) received *no* child support, and fewer than a quarter (23.3 percent) received close to the full amount. Some 25 percent more custodial parents get nothing than get all they are due. These striking numbers reveal the challenges facing this group.

Several years ago I had an opportunity to facilitate a focus group of single mothers living in Salt Lake City. The Ballard Center for Economic Self-Reliance invited me to host these sessions as part of a larger research survey on the challenges facing single parents in the state of Utah. While not an empirically rigorous data set, these focus groups enhanced my professional understanding of the implications of these abstract dichotomies and gave me a unique view of how social capital impacts the life of these women.[21] My personal understanding came as a child growing up in a home led by a single mother.

The twelve single mothers who shared their stories in the focus groups put a human face on these numbers. These women identified two major challenges in their lives: having enough money to raise their children and having enough time to raise them well. Welfare policy in the United States creates a financial "valley of death" for these women: a rise in earned income cuts them off from public assistance, but the increased wage level won't offset the loss of public support. The valley of death creates a perverse incentive for these women: since they can't make up for the lost public support with private wages, they're better off not trying to improve their earning capabilities and become trapped in either low-wage jobs or chronic unemployment.

Time is as constrained as money. One single mom described her day: leave the house at 6:30 a.m. to get to work by 8:00, split the day between work and school, return home about 6:30 p.m. to get her son in bed by 8:30, then study until the wee hours. Wake up the next day and do it over again. This woman noted that "if my mom wasn't there to take care of him [her son] there's no way I could have done it." Strong tie social capital filled the gap for her; family members and close friends rotate care giving; they substitute for parental supervision and they complement her deep desires to get ahead.

Other gaps prove less constant or taxing. Nuclear and extended family members, friends, neighbors, and church associates provide money to help pay rent, or skill in home and auto repair, or emotional support, including the occasional opportunity to get away from it all and spend a little time on themselves. Community resources may exist for some of these services, such as help with rent, but social capital provides a quicker, closer, and usually more targeted bundle of resources to supplement a single mother's resource base.

Friends and family complement the resources available to single mothers, as they often provide strong male role models for their sons. Uncles, grandfathers, fellow church members, neighbors, or friends help these women show their sons, and daughters, male behaviors usually lacking in their former spouses, such as compassion, courage, and commitment to responsible behavior. These role models become increasingly vital as children enter puberty; an uncle, grandfather, or pastor usually gives a much better talk about the birds and the bees to their sons than the mothers could.

While they may not fit the typical profile of poverty in Ghana or on the Navajo Nation, these women share some characteristics with those in the developing world: they struggle to make ends meet, let alone get ahead, in the face of limited capital accounts. Social capital makes a difference in the lives of these single moms. Social capital can make a huge difference in helping women out of poverty; unfortunately, social relationships can also drain their resources and enervate their efforts at becoming self-reliant. The web of resources and relationships that constitutes social capital represents a double-edged sword that creates gain or pain for these women.

SOCIAL CAPITAL AS A DOUBLE-EDGED SWORD

"What you get through who you know" serves as a nice starting point to think about social capital, but it gives no hint of the powerful dark side. A more accurate definition reads: "Social capital: how you grow from, and what you owe to, who you know." Adler and Kwon, whose twenty definitions of social capital I mentioned earlier, get at the heart of the dual nature of social capital: "[I]ts source lies in the *structure* and *content* of the actor's social relations. Its effects flow from the information, influence, and solidarity it makes available to the actor."[22]

Positive relationships enhance information quantity and quality, amplify influence, and strengthen solidarity. They also add valuable resources to the recipient. Negative ones squelch information, mute influence, and sustain perverse versions of solidarity, and they extract resources. World Bank economists Michael Woolcock and Deepa Narayan describe social capital as both a blessing and blight in the lives of those trying to work themselves out of poverty.[23] Their alliteration provides a nice framework to examine the bipolar impact of social capital.

One Edge: Social Capital as Blessing

As an MBA student I didn't have a lot of discretionary income; most of my money went for rent, groceries, tuition, books, and supplies. I attended a church with a number of other students, almost all of whom could tell the same story with only slight variations. Each month we'd come together and have a pot luck dinner; everyone brought a dish to share, and the assorted meal always left us very satisfied. The meals were good, better than most of us could do on our own, and the sense of belonging and fellowship we shared lightened the load we all carried as graduate students. When social capital blesses lives, it plays a similar role.

Information. Our relationships with others allow us to tap into information flows we wouldn't normally have access to. The fall of the Iron Curtain dismantled many institutional structures and organizational arrangements in Eastern Europe and created opportunities for entrepreneurial action. Successful entrepreneurs in this highly fluid environment used their informal, social contact networks to reduce uncertainty about the direction of changes, gather information, and identify potential opportunities they could exploit. Social capital facilitates the transfer of finely grained and specific information about opportunities and conditions rather than general statements and prescriptions offered in more formal channels.[24]

A single mom's social capital may help her find a job (or a better one), community resources, or other information she lacks. During our focus group several women shared websites or contact information about available resources with the others; even this very brief bridging network led to information transfers. More valuable than just the information, however, they also shared stories of their experiences, good or bad, that allowed the group to *evaluate* both the availability and fit of different resources to their needs. They could share detailed information, for example, about how willing different employers have been to accommodate the unique needs of single parents.

Influence. Max Weber preferred formal to informal institutions, as I noted in Chapter 3.[25] Bureaucracy—a very formal institution—works on merit and transparent procedures that should prove more efficient and effective than reliance on opaque personal relationships that typify traditional social organization. As a country like Ghana continues to develop and bureaucracy becomes the dominant form, we would expect social capital to become less important. Researchers found the opposite: social capital held by managers increased their ability to gain information as the economy formalized; it also helped them exert sway within government ministries to win projects that improved their organization's performance.[26]

One single mom in the focus group described how building social and reputational capital with her boss allowed her the flexibility in her schedule to get her kids to school, or to leave suddenly when real emergencies happened. Single mothers who have climbed up a couple of rungs on an organizational ladder provide both direct and indirect help to others; they will occasionally go to bat for their colleagues to solve problems, but they'll far more often teach effective strategies or use role plays to allow the recipient to build her own credibility and influence.

Solidarity. Social capital blesses lives by providing solidarity and the sense of belonging that comes along with being embedded in a social network. Solidarity comes from strong, bonding ties. Solidarity, the sense that our goals have value and that others stand with us, allows all of us to face difficult challenges and circumstances. As Emile Durkheim noted decades ago, deep relationships help us keep the anomie of modern life at bay and make life rich and meaningful.[27]

Single mothers talked about feeling outside the major social groups; they were unattached to an adult partner, but they had strong attachments to children. They fit with neither their married nor single friends. Two single moms described how they struggled to fit in and how their relationships meant that someone recognized their struggles and "that we exist," said one. The other agreed: "Yeah, or just recognizing us at all!" Anomie can be a biting, constant companion for these women; I noticed that our recognition of their struggles benefited them as much as the information they gave to us.

Resources. Social capital expands the amount and quality of resources available to the poor as it bestows resources otherwise unavailable, or available at much higher cost, on members of a network. Immigrant enclaves in Miami and New York provide ethnic entrepreneurs with preferred access to financial capital (through rotating credit associations), local suppliers, and customers for their business. Social capital plays an insurance role as well, when it eliminates search and bonding costs for financing, vetting efforts with suppliers, and marketing and advertising expenses to customers.[28]

More than a few single moms lived with their parents, most temporarily. Parents provide an effective substitute for rental housing, allowing the women to allocate their meager financial resources to more productive ends, such as school books or clothing for their children, health insurance premiums, or simply being able to save money. Moving in with parents gave single moms an escape route when relationships turned abusive, or when spousal abandonment or death made their current situation unsustainable. Friends or work colleagues who contribute expertise, money, or time to help out in medical or education emergencies strengthen a single parent's resilience during difficult times.

Social capital helps the poor instrumentally through information, influence, and resources; it also contributes to an intrinsic sense of belonging and meaning that contribute to mental health and a good life. That's the blessing part; social capital is not all light and truth, however. There can be a very real and very dark side to social capital.

The Other Edge: Social Capital as Blight

Allow me to share another story from my own past. When I was a kid, my sisters and I spent a summer living with my Uncle Ed and Aunt Lillian, some of it at their beach house close to the Chesapeake Bay. One day we went crabbing. You tie a string around a raw chicken leg and drop it off the pier. After a while you pull it up and find one or more blue crabs trying to gnaw the meat. You put the crabs into a bucket. The first crab in the bucket is quite feisty; the crab can easily climb out and works hard to do it. But get a second crab in the bucket and, as soon as one crab tries to escape the other one pulls the escapee back into the bucket.

The phenomenon, known as the crab mentality, refers to the pervasive problem of "If I can't have it, neither can you."[29] The crab mentality is a social behavior—it exists only in groups and perfectly describes the dark side of social capital. Just like crabs in a bucket, social networks can very effectively keep people from escaping poverty; instead of capital assets, social relationships become capital liabilities as they distort information, twist influence, and extract resources.

Information. Negative social capital means that ties that bind also blind.[30] The price of entry into a group includes adopting the mental maps and moral values of the group that filter, sift, and reject important information. This filtering gives rise to groupthink and the not-invented-here syndrome (NIH), whereby groups think that their own solutions must be inherently better than ones developed outside. For single moms the price of some assistance, particularly from family, may mean adopting a destructively antagonistic and militaristic mindset for problem solving with former spouses or noncustodial parents.

Influence. Harmful social capital subjects us to coercive influence by others and creates a corrosive dependency on them. One woman in our focus group went to prison to protect her spouse. That's negative influence! Many of these women would hardly call themselves angels; however, alcohol or drug use, gambling problems, theft, and infidelity on the part of their noncustodial partners exerted tremendous influence over their choices and opportunities to move forward. Several women indicated how lucky they were not to have any contact—they willingly left child support on the table; however difficult life would be without their spouse, it was certainly easier than with him.

Solidarity. Educator Ruby Payne uses a case to illustrate the cost of avoiding anomie and finding belonging:

> You are a 32-year-old [widowed] female [with one child]. You work long
> hours as a domestic for a doctor. You go to the Missionary Baptist Church

every Sunday where you lead the choir. Your employer treats you well and you take home about $300 every week. Your employer gives you a $400 Christmas bonus. You thank the Lord at church for the gift. After Church, three different people approach you privately. One asks for $50 to have the electricity turned on; one asks for $100 to feed her brother's family; one asks for $60 to replace a pair of broken glasses. You were hoping to save some money for an emergency.[31]

Payne provides this debrief: "[O]ne of the hidden rules of poverty is that any extra money is shared . . . . Oprah [the woman's name] will share the money; she has no choice. If she does not, the next time she is in need, she will be left in the cold. It is the hidden rule of the support system." Community sharing really means community taking.[32] Solidarity comes at a high cost, as the unwritten rules of poverty allow friends to act like the crabs in the bucket; they tug and tear away resources and prevent people from getting out of the bucket.

Resources. Destructive social capital dissipates, rather than accumulates, resources. Former spouses would renege on joint credit agreements such as car loans or mortgages, leaving the single mom on the hook for the entire amount, creating crushing financial hardships. Legal haranguing over child custody or other terms of a divorce decree allows embittered or unstable former spouses a formal mechanism to extort resources—most often cash payments or adjustments to support agreements—from the limited capital held by the custodial parent.

These negative relationships often engender negative complementarities. Several moms noted the negative impact after their children return from weekends or visits with the noncustodial parent. Rather than modeling compassion, courage, and responsibility, a number of these men view their children as pawns in an ongoing battle. Lavish gifts, a lack of rules, and exposure to inappropriate situations leave the custodial parent to pick up the emotional pieces of their children's manipulated lives. This uses up precious emotional and intellectual stores in the moms.

Social capital acts as a double-edged sword. Positive, productive, and healthy relationships can help the poor cut poverty out of their lives. Their opposites prove toxic; they cut the poor out of progress and carve away important resources. We must handle sharp swords carefully in our work; the concluding section considers how you can design your organization and efforts to cut at the joints of little p poverty in ways that eliminate it, not perpetuate it.

SOCIAL CAPITAL AND ORGANIZATION

Social capital contributes to self-reliance because our relationships act as the conduits through which the elements of self-reliance move from institutional values to personal disposition. We learn the moral virtue of responsibility at home, first and foremost. In my interviews with more than twenty Ghanaian entrepreneurs I found that the most successful learned the principles of hard work and moral responsibility for their own well-being from their parents.[33]

Self-efficacy comes best through mastery experiences, coupled with reinforcement and feedback, and these best occur at home or through other strong tie relationships. Think of Watt in the workshop his father set up for him. He had plenty of opportunity to experiment and build on his own, plus he had the benefit of feedback from his father and associates to hone his skills and develop self-confidence. Friends and colleagues all along our way teach us new skills, watch us practice, and coach us as we master them.

We inherit our first worldview from our parents, preachers, and teachers. Watching our parents scrimp and save, or spend and squander their money, endows us with our first sense of the importance, or lack thereof, of planning for the future. That worldview will be strengthened or weakened by each relationship we cultivate as children, youths, and adults. We learn and teach the mechanics of a long-term view in social settings. The importance of families, close friends, and others can hardly be overstated; social capital captures the world in which we, and our clients, live. With that in mind, here are some suggestions for strengthening your work.

Understand the social context of your clients. Steve Gibson runs the Academy for Creating Entrepreneurs in Cebu, the Philippines. His experience illustrates how easy it is to overlook social relationships and the resources and restrictions they engender when trying to eliminate little p poverty. Steve, a successful entrepreneur in his own right, carefully designed the course curriculum and related field training experiences to help his students start and grow their businesses.

He discovered *after* he enrolled his first class that his students' families would view the hard-won profits from their children's business ventures as an entitlement; they could literally eat success. Steve spent time understanding the institutional environment and larger, macro culture of the Philippines before setting up the academy, and he knew the profiles of his target clients. But he overlooked the powerful restrictions family norms and social relationships could exert on his students.

To avoid Steve's error, draw a map. Put your client in the center of a piece of paper and draw three other circles around the client, one each for primary, secondary, and tertiary relationships. Map the familial, friendship, and work relationships that create the social context your client lives in. I draw positive relationships in blue and negative ones in red and use thick lines to signify stronger relationships. Map resources with arrows, with resource gains as arrows pointing toward your client and drains pointing the other way. You want to capture strength of relationships and directions of resource flows. This is social capital.

Drawing such a map isn't as easy as it sounds. The hours you spend drawing should come after days or weeks of interviews and observations if you really hope to understand the social context. Setting people in their social context has both a design and implementation element. As we design interventions we need to be continually aware that, while we work with individuals in many cases, those individuals live in a web of deeply embedded relationships. Strong program implementation leverages social capital; poor implementation allows social actors to leverage away your resources and capital.

Avoid being the "big chief." I met Craig Cardon during my travels in Ghana. Craig served as a high-level minister for his church, shepherding a number of pastors and congregations in West Africa. He taught me the "big chief" problem of dependency.[34] In many traditional societies the chief has the responsibility and obligation to care for tribal members; the chief gets to be chief as long as he takes responsibility for meeting the needs of the people. We must pay careful attention so we don't lift people out of one set of dependent relationships and put them right back into new ones. We must avoid the temptation to become a big chief.

Craig described how the social and economic development programs of his church, without intending to, often perpetuated the big chief mentality. Individual pastors had funds and resources to provide emergency help to members of their congregation; and the social services arm of the church offered help with employment placement, literacy training, marriage counseling, and other forms of assistance. The church became a new big chief; many members joined or remained active to access the resources available through the pastor.

How do we avoid the big chief problem? Two design principles help. For Craig the solution lay in engaging people in reciprocal relationships. While his Christian faith precluded the pure quid pro quo of market type exchanges, Craig worked to link assistance and program participation to reciprocal efforts on the part of parishioners; those who expected the church to act as the big chief, and not contribute their own work, would not receive further aid. In short, Craig's church had created the incomplete organization described in Chapter 2; participants actually had to participate in their own rise from poverty.

The second principle involves seeing our work as a temporary intervention in the lives of individuals and families. On the one hand, programs and organizations must provide mastery experiences that develop self-reliance. That takes time. On the other hand, the longer people stay in our orbit, the greater the potential for dependency; they can easily become dependent on us, but we can just as easily become dependent on them. We must stay long enough to do our work, but not so long that we destroy self-reliance. Systems that notify us when people need to exit our programs become an essential element of organizational success.

Many social innovators I've met struggle with the big chief problem, mostly because they want to be the big chief. They think they really want to help, but what they often want is for people to move out of poverty along *their* trajectory, and they want to be appreciated for what they do. The problem is they'll never admit to either of these desires; both desires tend to stifle self-reliance and a true exit from poverty.

Build your organization's social capital. Brian Uzzi is an expert on social capital.[35] He taught me about how we can effectively build our bridging capital base. Much of this fits with our preconceived ideas: identify the people with resources we want access to and create a relationship with them. Working on common projects—whether business or community-based—proves an excellent way to expand our social network without having to schmooze or falsely ingratiate ourselves with others.

Brian also taught me about a major pitfall we encounter as we create social networks and capital: the trust-diversity paradox. Our natural instincts and unspoken reservations lead us to seek out social contacts and relationships with people like us; we share many things in common with those like us, and it's easy to trust them. High trust social networks are great, but they can be poor sources of resources, particularly expert advice or contacts with others. You see, people like us think like us, and that means their advice won't differ much from our own thinking. Their contacts tend to be our contacts; their resources look strikingly similar to our own: strong networks but weak capital.

Strong capital requires diversity in the network, or including people who aren't like us. This fights against our natural inclinations; we have to work harder to build trust and learn new languages, customs, and norms of behavior. The increased cost pays off when we need different resources; we now get advice from people who don't see the world as we do, so we get a more robust and accurate assessment of our plans. We don't share the same contacts, or maybe even the same skills, so diverse networks give us greater leverage for our own resources: strong networks and strong capital.

We can overcome the trust-diversity paradox in our own efforts and organizations by adopting an inclusive orientation; hiring and engaging people based on merit rather than social status, ethnic group, or religious affiliation presents one way. We build our own network, but we also model a behavior valuable to our clients. Our own diverse networks offer a natural diversity to our clients; we can plant the seeds for them to create their own diverse networks of bridging capital.

Creating diverse networks of social capital may prove particularly difficult for those in poverty, but more important than for us. Those closest to them have the most similar resources, and if the name of the game in social capital is access to resources, then diversifying their social capital becomes a key step in climbing out of poverty. Years of war, long simmering ethnic tensions, strong cultural ties to those closest to them, and a history of being burned by strangers create almost instinctive barriers to bridges with diverse others. Our efforts at reaching out to create diverse networks can act as a strong counterweight to their experience.

CONCLUSION

James Watt's baker's dozen served him well; these individuals substituted for things he lacked, such as connections in Parliament or contacts in London's instrument making guilds. People like Joseph Black provided complementary scientific knowledge that leveraged Watt's innate skill and intelligence. A more correct statue in Westminster Abbey would have been truly colossal and included Watt's social network as codevelopers of the modern steam engine. History evens things out, however, and the newest British £50 note includes both Watt and Matthew Boulton, in recognition of their powerful friendship/ partnership.

My mom became a single mom in 1966 with the death of my father. Looking back now, I see how she marshaled and used her social capital to fill her own resource gaps, but also to benefit my sisters and me. My grandparents, aunts, and uncles provided child care and family support so she could return to school to earn her master's degree in nursing. She went on to enjoy much professional success. My two sisters and I had a powerful example in our mom. My oldest sister is an M.D., my other sister has a Ph.D. in public health, and I have a Ph.D. in business. The strong ties of our family relationships produced benefits that spanned generations; social capital begets human capital. It is to the human capital account that we now turn.

CHAPTER FIVE

HUMAN CAPITAL

The Heart of the Matter

Poverty would fall faster and the distribution of income would become less skewed if the volume and quality of human capital could be raised.

—*Shahid Yusuf,* World Bank Economist[1]

BY THE SPRING OF 1765 James Watt had assiduously puzzled over steam power and the problem of how to improve on Thomas Newcomen's engine for the better part of two years. One Sunday in 1765 Watt went walking through Glasgow's College Green, which for most of the week served as a public laundry. On the Sabbath the good Scottish Presbyterian would find a peaceful park. Watt recollected the event a half-century later:

> I had entered the Green by the Gate at the foot of Charlotte Street—had passed the old washing house. I was thinking on the engine at the time and had gone as far as the Herd's house when the idea came into my mind, that as steam was an elastic body it would rush into a vacuum, and if a communication was made between the cylinder and an exhausted vessel, it would rush into it, and might be there condensed without cooling the cylinder. . . . I had not yet walked further than the Golf-house when the whole thing was arranged in my mind.[2]

The sudden realization "flashed on his mind at once, and filled him with rapture." The design suggested by that fundamental insight would not change, but Watt's rapture would ebb and flow over the next ten years as the engine moved from inspired design to installed machine.

Watt began the next morning by building the first of many models to test his design. His knowledge of mathematics and the principles of instrument making moved the idea toward reality, as did his ability to build meticulous models. His intellect and craftsman's skill would prevail in battles with his darker tendencies: a sickly nature, a pessimistic outlook, and a maniacal fear of poverty that led him to abandon work on the engine for long periods while he worked to support his family. These tendencies diverted Watt's attention from the engine and resulted in extra years in bringing the engine to market.

In 1775 Boulton and Watt produced their first engines for commercial use. November 1776 brought orders for engines to pump mines in eastern England, and by 1779 the order book was filling briskly.[3] James saw safety, security, and prosperity, but Boulton saw opportunity. In 1781 Boulton shifted his gaze toward what he considered the bigger prize: rotary engines. Boulton saw limited potential in the land-locked mining industry but a vast market if steam could power England's mechanizing cotton mills and eventually all of British manufacturing.

Watt, like Newcomen before him, designed a reciprocating engine. Steam drove a piston that moved an attached beam up and down; the beam operated a pump to lift water out of the mines. Boulton realized the potential of a rotary engine: the ability to power wheel-driven machinery, be they looms, dyes, lathes, or eventually moving carriages. The results would be stunning, as historian Lewis Mumford noted: "[T]he technical advance which characterizes specifically the modern age is that from reciprocating to rotary motion."[4]

While revolutionary in its consequences, the advance from reciprocal to rotary motion represented a feat of science and engineering that would require Watt's substantial intellectual and practical prowess. Rotary motion meant replacing up and down (back and forth) energy with circular (spinning) motion. Watt and his assistant William Murdock engineered a set of gears known as the sun and planet scheme: a toothed gear (the sun) attached to a wheel and another toothed gear (the planet) articulating with the sun on one end and attached to the beam at the other. The up and down beam stroke "rotated" the planet around the sun and spun an attached belt to power looms or other machines.

Another challenge centered on the chain that connected the piston and beam.[5] The piston moved up as steam filled the cylinder and released tension on the chain and beam; the counterweight at the other end of the beam pulled its end down (just like a teeter-totter). As the steam exited the cylinder the resulting vacuum pulled down the piston, and the connecting chain and beam up. Piston-down was the powerful stroke; power and efficiency would both increase *if both* piston-up and -down strokes had the same force. Watt used a series of valves and pipes to inject steam at both the bottom and top of the piston to produce this double-acting engine.

Double action could power the cycle but the chain remained a problem: it would easily pull the beam down but couldn't push it back up (you can pull something with a string but not push it). The chain assembly was valuable, however, because it moved straight up and down and minimized wobble on the piston as it moved. Wobble wore out pistons faster, reducing efficiency and adding cost. Watt devised a complex set of rods and joints to maintain the strict vertical plane essential to the longevity of the piston. This "parallel motion" arrangement presaged the branch of engineering known as kinematics. Watt always felt that parallel motion represented his greatest achievement.[6]

Two other innovations would make Boulton & Watt machines the world's premiere engines.[7] Watt adapted a set of existing technologies to equip the engine with a governor—two balls attached to a rod that would open or close a valve that allowed hot steam to escape as they rose or fell. As the engine accelerated, centrifugal force pushed the balls up, lifted the rod, and opened the valve; the reverse occurred as the engine slowed. The governor made the engine self-regulating, and that saved customers time and money through stable, predictable operation.

Watt also invented an indicator mechanism that continuously determined the pressure and volume of steam in the cylinder; this provided a measure of available power. The indicator helped with engine operation and maintenance, and it allowed Boulton & Watt to assess royalties due the firm more accurately.

"The work of James Watt forged an epoch":[8] the epoch we call the Industrial Revolution. We've already seen the role Watt's country (institutional capital) and colleagues (social capital) played in the revolution; the story above illustrates Watt's unique contributions, based on his human capital. His dexterity, intellect, and passion all played important roles in his inventive activities; Watt employed his head, hands, and heart to change the world. This chapter takes up the third type of capital, human capital, and considers how to improve what's in the head, hands, and hearts of the poor we work with.

UNDERSTANDING HUMAN CAPITAL

Gary S. Becker won the Nobel Prize in economics in 1992 "for having extended the domain of microeconomic analysis to a wide range of human behavior and interaction."[9] His substantial early contribution centered on the phenomenon of human capital. Becker defined human capital in simple terms as resources embedded in people. His work was a tough sell: "[We] were really dealing with virgin territory in the early days; I suffered a lot of criticisms for applying the notion of capital to people, to human beings. We had to overcome a lot of initial opposition." Admirers claim that "for all practical purposes [Becker] first put the concept on the map as a subject worthy of economic discussion."[10]

As with most things economic, the roots of human capital trace back further than the 1960s; the concept owes to the profession's founding father, Adam Smith. He spoke of the "useful abilities of all the inhabitants or members of the society" and noted that "the acquisition of such talents, by the maintenance of the acquirer during his education, study, or apprenticeship, always costs a real expense, which is a *capital* fixed and realized, as it were, *in his person*."[11] Gary Becker and Adam Smith both linked broad societal prosperity with investments in the narrow development of individual citizens.

Recent work in human capital recognizes that "human capital is rather complex. The concept includes, not only the role of education and on-the-job training, but also the importance of differences in ability, attitudes, and outlook that individual human beings bring to the production process as they attempt to improve their economic lot and, by extension, that of society at large."[12] Differences in human capital stocks may help explain differences in economic performance for individuals and nations alike. Becker divided human capital into two components, general and specific. We'll look at other types, but these provide a nice jumping off point.

Types of Human Capital

General. General human capital includes skills and knowledge used to perform a broad set of activities; literacy and numeracy stand as excellent examples. The ability to read, write, and do basic calculations enables people to perform a variety of value-creating functions, from communicating orders for products and services to pricing and then tracking them through the course of the transaction. General capital creates value, just not very much because most people have these skills. As a consequence of its ubiquity neither individuals nor firms get any competitive advantages or extra returns from this type of capital.

With few opportunities for profit, Becker reasoned that firms had little incentive to incur the costs of providing general human capital to workers. Why spend money on workers who could take these skills to competitors? The state fills the void, and general human capital becomes a very public good as general human capital increases social welfare. Put simply, everyone benefits through investments in public education that implant a set of platform cognitive abilities in the heads of each citizen.

Specific. Specific human capital, as its name implies, involves specialized and localized knowledge or skills. The knowledge required to operate heavy construction equipment, play the piano, or perform complex eye surgery all represent specific human capital. Specialized knowledge creates value for both society and individuals; we all benefit through eye surgery, and eye surgeons capture some of that benefit for themselves in high compensation. The drawback: specific human capital creates value only within those particular contexts (eye surgeons don't operate heavy equipment, and vice versa). Investments in specific capital entail risks, but they can also produce big payoffs for individuals and companies.

Becker argued that firms, and their employees, had substantial incentives to develop specific human capital because each party would benefit from such investments. Specialized knowledge creates stickiness, another benefit for both firms and individuals. Businesses and employees willingly risk investing in advanced training and development because the acquisition of these skills makes the employee more valuable to that business; the more specific the knowledge the more sticky (and valuable) the employee becomes.

Hidden. Becker's distinction between general and specific human capital laid the foundation for how economists think about, and measure, human capital; however, both types focus solely on cognitive or mechanical skills and omit attitudes and beliefs. Ruby Payne, whom we met in Chapter 4, helps us categorize and understand some of these complex attitudes and outlooks. Payne's unique life history allowed her to understand the game of life from the perspective of the poor (through her husband Frank's family), the middle class (her own upbringing), and the wealthy (as a principal at an affluent elementary school).

Consider the differences in human capital captured in the following statements: "I know how to move in half a day (poverty); I know how to decorate the house for different holidays (middle class); I know how to hire a decorator (wealth)."[13] While these skills are clearly specialized by social class (instead of occupation), they are also hidden. People in poverty may be unaware that decorators work for hire, and the wealthy can't conceive of having to move on very short notice. Payne believes that getting out of poverty requires the poor to jettison much of their veiled human capital and acquire a very different stock.

Public states dispense general human capital, private businesses generate specific capital, but no one actively teaches the hidden rules of class; we learn them through experience. Hidden rules look like general capital in that they are widely held and diffused within a social class. They create stickiness, just like specific capital, because they make it hard for people to move successfully from one class to another, in that we can't act appropriately for the group we want to join. For Ruby Payne the key to moving people out of poverty is to reveal the hidden rules; when we know *what* the rules are it's easier to learn *how* to follow them, and how to replace them with more productive ones. Let's look at a social innovator named Martin Burt and his innovation, the San Francisco School, to see how to successfully make the hidden plain.

The San Francisco School

The San Francisco Agricultural School sits on 7,000 square meters of beautiful land on the edge of Paraguay's Chaco region, 46 kilometers from the capital city Asuncion.[14] The World Bank classifies Paraguay as a lower middle-income country; it's $2,720 GDP per capita in 2010 bested neighbor Bolivia's ($1,810) by almost 50 percent, but represents only 31 percent of neighboring Argentina's per capita GDP ($8,620), 29 percent of Brazil's ($9,390), and just over 25 percent of Uruguay's ($10,590).[15] The country gained its independence from Spain in 1811; however, a stable parliamentary democracy has been in place only since 1989.

The San Francisco School is owned and operated by Fundacion Paraguaya and its leader, Martin Burt. Martin's vision for a better Paraguay and his abiding commitment to poverty alleviation has deep roots, as he explained:

My parents formed a group to set up a private bilingual American school
in Paraguay so that we would have access to a bilingual, U.S. type educa-

tion. It quickly became apparent to my brothers and sisters that we were among the very privileged in Paraguay, a poor country, and so we always heard from my parents and my grandparents that we had to take advantage of the opportunities we had but to also give back. So giving back became a very honorable thing to do, at least in the ethos of my family. That is, I suppose, what influenced me.[16]

After receiving his master's degree in public policy at George Washington University in 1983, Martin founded Fundacion Paraguaya, Paraguay's first microfinance organization. Since its inception, Fundacion Paraguaya has provided technical assistance, management training, and loans totaling $18 million to more than forty-five thousand Paraguayans and has reached over twenty thousand youth through its entrepreneurship and educational programs. Martin also served as the mayor of Asuncion, Paraguay's capital city, from 1996 to 2000.

In 2002 a group of Roman Catholic priests, The Congregation of the La Salle Brothers, approached Martin about assuming ownership and control of the San Francisco Agricultural School. Political unrest in 1999 brought funding and administrative uncertainty to Paraguay's education system and by 2002 left the San Francisco School in an unsustainable situation. The La Salle Brothers saw in Fundacion Paraguaya an organization with the financial resources to run the school, the ability to offer courses in business and entrepreneurship to students, and a clear mission of helping youth escape poverty.

Fundacion Paraguaya took control of the school on New Year's Day 2003, with a lofty set of objectives: to ensure that students graduated ready to succeed as rural entrepreneurs, obtain midlevel jobs in modern agriculture, teach at other agricultural schools, or attend the university. They hoped to run a school that would enable youth to lift themselves out of poverty, create new jobs, and contribute to their communities' economic development through entrepreneurial activity. Moving from vision to reality required a fundamental shift in the nature and type of education the school provided.

Martin redesigned the curriculum and organization of the school to create a number of small, independent businesses. The objective for each business: to become self-sufficient, then profitable within five years. The school's dairy operation served as the test case. In early 2003, the dairy's output could not even cover the needs of the school dining hall; rather than generating revenue, the ineffective dairy drained cash. School leaders increased the herd size, and the foundation made capital investments to upgrade both the quality and capacity of the Planta Lactea (milk processing plant and cheese factory) to safely and efficiently produce milk, yoghurt, and cheese for internal use *and* sale to local markets.

Over the next year, production tripled and Martin had his first victory in the quest to make the school profitable. The ensuing years saw similar changes in the six other business units at the school: the Huerta (organic garden and fruit trees), Chacra (cash crops such as corn), Cerdos (pig farm), Cabras (goats for both dairy and slaughter), Forraje (animal feedstock and silage), and a Parador or small retail shop at the edge of the school along the main highway.

Martin organized each as a separate business unit expected to produce and sell goods to generate income for the school. These on-campus businesses could sell to one another or to third parties, but always at market prices. This structure allowed students to participate in activities along the value chain (for example, from waking at 4:30 a.m. to milk the cows or feed the pigs through working in the Planta Lactea and on through the actual packaging, marketing, and sale of the final products), thus providing a more complete, practical, and entrepreneurial education.

In September of 2003 Fundacion Paraguaya began its most ambitious move yet—the transformation of the Spiritual Retreat House into a Rural Hotel. The Spiritual Retreat House had been, as its name implies, a place for the La Salle Brotherhood to find solace and refuge. The size and layout of the building accommodated an easy remodel with a spacious lobby, rustic private rooms and simple yet technologically sophisticated conference and meeting rooms. Martin envisioned a venue designed not as an escape from Asuncion but rather an immersion into the life, goals, and mission of the school.

Students worked the front desk and check-in facilities, cleaned and maintained rooms and conference facilities, and handled payments by guests. The hotel provided not only a needed source of income but also, consistent with the broad mission of the school, another training ground to prepare students for meaningful careers. Because of its conference facilities and its proximity to Asuncion, the hotel marketed to local business, not-for-profit, and government organizations needing retreat, training, or conference space, emphasizing the connection with the school and its overall social mission of student entrepreneurship. Guests not only enjoyed a quiet and rustic retreat, they also contributed funds and support to the broad social mission of the San Francisco School.

Martin wants to develop three types of human capital in the school's graduates: traditional intellectual skills and knowledge students need to succeed, a set of practical skills and abilities to engage in value-creating economic activities, and a body of attitudes and beliefs the students hold about themselves and the world they live in. The San Francisco School hopes to influence and shape *Heads, Hands,* and *Hearts.* Changing heads, hands, and hearts provides a better way to think, and to act, in ways that can eliminate little p poverty.

HUMAN CAPITAL: THE HEAD, HANDS, AND HEART

The head, hands, and heart metaphor locates human capital where it belongs: in people. It provides much more than just a visualization of the different elements of human capital; the metaphor also provides a sorting mechanism for categorizing and prioritizing the types of human capital necessary to eliminate poverty. Just as the head, hands, and heart all play vital roles in physical life, these different types of human capital contribute to our economic well-being. Getting people out of poverty requires clear heads, strong hands, and full hearts. We'll consider each element in turn; however, we'll spend less time on the head and hands, since these have been the focus of development specialists for decades.

Heads and Hands

The head captures the cognitive knowledge and intellectual resources. Watt's knowledge of mathematics, particularly geometry, Martin Burt's degrees in public policy, and his students' work in the classrooms at the San Francisco School all represent cognitive capital, or a set of (primarily) abstract concepts, theories, models, and sets of generalized relationships that allow people to do many important things. The 3 R's: Reading, wRiting, and aRithmetic constitute the platform knowledge needed for prosperity.

The ability to read allows individuals to communicate with others, and to tap into the collective knowledge of experts, both past and present. Reading represents one form of the vicarious experience that enhances self-efficacy. Writing also allows us to communicate with others, whether they be next door or across the world. Writing underlies contracts—fundamental instruments of commerce that facilitate complex economic transactions in time, across space, and over time. Numeracy, whether basic or advance, plays a similarly important role in value creating economic activities.

The hands represent the tangible, tactile, and concrete skills required to work as a craftsman, artisan, or laborer. Watt's ability to craft the fine instruments of his day enabled him to design and build the many models, of various sizes and materials, of his steam engine that helped bring the machine to fruition. Students at the San Francisco School work outside the classroom with their hands to milk cows, feed pigs, or weed gardens. If the head represents abstract concepts, then the hands give us the complementary concrete experiences.[17] We need both to succeed.

Formal education occupies a central place in theories of economic growth and Big P poverty approaches: universal access to primary education is the second of the UN's millennium development goals. Schooling works best when it combines the head and hands; academic work increasingly includes practical components; conversely, vocational or technical work relies more and more on conceptual knowledge foundations. We all know that formal education makes a difference in lifetime earnings, but just how much? More than you might think, according to economic researchers.

Economists like pristine, controlled experiments to test something like the value of education; identical (maternal) twins yield the perfect test population. The basic model of individual performance includes three factors: genetic or innate abilities, family influences, and education. Differences in earnings among twins should arise solely from differences in education (plus luck) because they have the same genetic makeup and the same family environment. The best estimates of the increased returns to schooling show that the twin with more schooling earns between 5 and 16 percent more *per year* of additional schooling than the sibling.[18]

To calibrate that difference, consider the following financial benchmark. Experts estimate the annual, long-term return in the U.S. stock market to be about 9 percent.[19] Put simply, staying in school an extra two years, based on the lowest benefit of additional schooling, beats investing in a stock index fund. If you believe the 16 percent number, then those extra two years earn 3.5X what you'll get investing in stocks. Not a bad return on your educational dollar.

Education in many developing countries divorces the head and hands. The abstract concepts useful to the head stand apart—figuratively and literally—from the concrete capabilities the hands use to turn concepts into products and services. The genius of Martin Burt's model lies in marrying, rather than divorcing, the head and hands in his fight against rural poverty. Agricultural science undergirds the school; geography and cultural studies help students frame the markets; numeracy—basic and advanced—allows them to track their businesses and spot trends and patterns.

The hand-driven work Martin's students do in the fields provides both a powerful application of and context for many of the head-driven skills that separate San Francisco graduates from both the poor peasant farmers and the typical school graduates. Students understand, for example, the *what* and *how* of market trading and negotiating; this allows them to earn good returns. They also learn about the larger *why* of markets and economic systems. They can leverage this knowledge in either a practical, technical, or academic career.

Hearts

For me, Martin exemplifies the power of the heart. Consider his passion and motivation for the work he does:

> I had an early sense of wanting there to be social justice in Paraguay . . .
> not from a position of resentment, but with joy; how can we amplify what
> "the haves" have, and extend it to the poor? How can we give back? How
> can we expand prosperity to everybody?
>
> My vision is to develop social innovations to alleviate injustice in the
> world, that's what I want to do. . . . I don't feel guilty that the poor are
> poor—I don't feel responsible. I don't feel a burden because of the injustice in the world at all.
>
> In fact I think that working from a position of guilt is a problem.
> My strategy is to unleash the energy, happiness, and motivation of the
> members of the target population. So throughout these 25 or 27 years of
> working with very, very poor people, when I deal with them I have an
> equal-to-equal conversation and this is very good because I don't have a
> paternalistic feeling towards them, nor do I allow them to take advantage
> of me.[20]

The heart of the social entrepreneur determines, in large measure, the direction of the work. Martin's heart, personal outlook, and drive enable him to focus on educating the heads, hands, and hearts of his students. The curriculum at San Francisco aims for a gestalt, or bundle of attitudes and outlooks, that creates an entrepreneurial heart. To catalog these into a list would be a fool's errand; such a list would falsely prioritize some over others, omit more than a few critical variables, and atomize what must be a holistic set.

One gestalt that captures these values is the collection of beliefs, values, and virtues known as the Protestant work ethic. While it may seem impolitic to bring religion into the science of development and the fight against poverty, the Protestant ethic provides us with a powerful shorthand to think through the attitudinal component of human capital. We would be in very good company to do so.

In April of 1999 Harvard University's Academy for International and Area Studies convened a conference to consider the role of culture on economic development. Guru Lawrence Harrison organized the conference that included a panel of academic luminaries and industry heavy hitters: New York *Times* bureau chief Barbara Crossette, sociologist Francis Fukuyama, economic historian David Landes, business scholar Michael Porter, development economist Jeffrey Sachs, and a host of others. The proceedings of that conference appeared in book form a year later with the title *Culture Matters: How Values Shape Human Progress*.[21]

The Protestant work ethic appears enough times in that work to have fourteen separate index entries. Even more surprising, the importance of the Protestant work ethic was mentioned by developing country participants almost as often as by developed country ones. John Calvin's brand of Protestantism held that salvation in the world to come was predetermined by God, but an individual's life and livelihood in this world gave strong signs of one's election by grace. The Protestant ethic validated several attitudes, and their consequent behaviors: "industriousness, discipline, honesty, sobriety, patience, thrift," specialization, excellence, pride of workmanship, self-sufficiency, and attention to family and social duties.[22]

At one level the Protestant ethic represents a form of cognitive/normative institutional capital; when that ethic finds its way into individual behaviors it becomes a powerful configuration of human capital that Max Weber equated with the spirit of capitalism.[23] Martin's work at the San Francisco School and his work with Fundacion Paraguaya more generally hope to catalyze the students (clients) with the spirit of capitalism, as he explains:

My experience is that poor people have great wealth and resources inside of them. This is sort of it—I know it's corny—but I really believe that the poor have the wealth inside of them. It's almost like Aladdin's lamp; our work is to rub the lamp, like rubbing off tarnish, and to make the lamp shine, to motivate the poor to "let the genie of wealth and resources" be released.

This is the only explanation that I can find for all of the people that I have seen lift themselves out of poverty. Where was that money before? Where was that strength before? It was inside of them. So I have a very strong sense of this, even when working with the most vulnerable groups. Because they are human beings, they have wealth and a human spirit that just needs to be unleashed so my work is really easy, that's because I know that the power is in them. "Hey I'm just going to go and stroke the lamp!"[24]

The bedrock philosophy of Fundacion Paraguaya structures and organizes activities in a way that encourages the "spirit of capitalism attitudes" to flourish in their clients. They don't teach industriousness, or discipline, or honesty; they expect it of their students. They offer no class in patience or pride or workmanship; the students develop these character traits as they go about their daily work in the classroom, the fields, the hotel, or the market. The spirit of capitalism gets unleashed as an almost natural consequence of everything else that gets done. That spirit changes how the poor view their world, as a fascinating event proved.

Property Ownership in Argentina

Harvard economist Rafael DiTella and his colleagues Sebastian Galiani (Universidad de San Andres, Argentina) and Ernesto Schargrodsky (Universidad Torcuato Di Tella, Argentina) illustrated how the spirit of capitalism emerges from other activities in another rare natural experiment. The problem with measuring attitudes like the spirit of capitalism lies in the endogeneity of attitudes; if we correlate success with attitudes we can't sort out which came first. Did success create the attitudes, or did the attitudes create the success?

DiTella and his colleagues described the setting for their research:

More than 20 years ago [the early 1980s], a large number of squatter families occupied an area of wasteland in the outskirts of Buenos Aries, Argentina, thinking it was State property. In reality, the area was made up of different tracts of land, each with a different legal owner. An expropriation law was subsequently passed, ordering the transfer of land to the state (in exchange for monetary compensation). The purpose of the law was to allow the state to later transfer ownership to the squatters. However, only some of the original legal owners surrendered the land, while others chose to contest the expropriation law.

Given the slow functioning of the Argentine courts, the dispute between the state and the owners who challenged the expropriation law has not been settled to this date [2004], resulting in weak property rights to squatters who happened to settle on a parcel of land on these tracts. Thus, a group of squatters obtained full property rights, while others are currently living on similar parcels but without legal titles. Since the decision to challenge the occupation was orthogonal to the characteristics of the squatters, the allocation of property rights amongst these squatters is exogenous.[25]

The natural experiment controlled for the endogeneity of attitudes, as the assignment of property rights was random: some with the spirit of capitalism received title, while others did not. The team could study what happened to attitudes after some squatters gained property rights and what happened to those who didn't. In 2003, some twenty years after the initial assignment of land titles, the team surveyed residents of the area.

They found significant and substantial differences among those who held property and those who didn't. Those who gained property rights were far more likely to place importance on "materialist and individualist" beliefs: the association of money with happiness, people can succeed through their own hard work, rewards should follow efforts, and other people are basically trustworthy. DiTella collapsed these four variables into a "pro-market" index that contains character traits held dear in the Protestant work ethic.

Rafael and his colleagues concluded that bestowing property rights on the squatters facilitated the development of the spirit of capitalism. Martin's efforts with his students seem to have the same effect. I sensed a strong sense of ownership, pride in workmanship, discipline to detail, and a willingness to work hard among the students I met. That spirit motivates and energizes the work students do with their head and hands. Given the importance of the heart, and human capital generally, we'll now consider implications for organizations and programs that create the type of human capital that eliminates little p poverty.

HUMAN CAPITAL AND POVERTY ELIMINATION

Whether the head, hands, and heart lead to the triangle of core beliefs that constitute the disposition of self-reliance depends on how individuals exercise their free will. Living in a knowledge-based society won't automatically make people knowledgeable without active effort, nor does the Protestant work ethic infuse every individual who lives under its influence. Individual choice and diligent effort define whether these types of capital become embedded within us and thus truly human capital. We all know people who are academically gifted but with little sense of self-efficacy or confidence, skilled but irresponsible, or industrious and hard working people with no long-term view or vision.

Human capital contributes directly to the asset configuration that defines the *condition* of self-reliance. The data on the returns to schooling (both head- and hands-based) shows that higher levels of human capital lead to higher income: human capital helps accelerate the acquisition, husbanding, and leverage of assets. Knowledge and behavior that lead to budgeting, insurance, investment, and savings represents a powerful bundling of the head and hands that complements the long-term view fundamental to self-reliance. To create the organizations and interventions that create human capital that eliminates little p poverty consider the following suggestions.

Reveal what's hidden. The hidden rules of poverty often stymie our best efforts to help people lift themselves out because exiting poverty means not just earning more, but living differently. Payne describes differences in how the poor and the middle class tell stories. One hidden rule of poverty involves telling stories in a roundabout fashion, adding lots of rich detail and circling back many times to repeat and expand key plot lines. These stories almost always have a moral component; they teach how principles of morality and justice operate in life.

The middle and upper classes, on the other hand, tell linear stories. Clarity takes precedence over detail, and our descriptions move in a chronological fashion. Stories tend to have a more instrumental focus on what to do or how things can be most efficiently done; moralizing occurs rarely, and only in the right contexts. Payne notes that the middle or upper-class people often demean the poor as missing out on essential features and wasting time in getting to the point; we get frustrated because they don't communicate as we expect them to.

We must work to *discover*—literally dis- or un-cover—the hidden rules that drive clients in their life conditions and contexts. Otherwise we become frustrated because we believe they don't understand how to act, or they missed our instructions. We fail to see that they operate on a different set of rules and assumptions. Asking them to describe the hidden rules may be akin to asking a fish to describe the water it swims in. We can get at those rules through focused observation, active listening, embedded participation in the lives of our clients, and asking them pointed questions about why they do what they do. Time in the field proves essential as well; Payne discovered her set of hidden rules after years in a variety of schools.

If we want linear stories, then we need to teach people to tell them. The other side of the hidden rules coin involves making explicit our own hidden rules. We frustrate our efforts partly when we don't understand our clients, but also when we make it hard for them to understand why we do what we do. How can we discover the water we swim in? Again, it's not easy, but commitments to transparency and openness around our programs, core assumptions, and values represent a good starting place. A culture that constantly asks, "Why did he/she/we do that?" will eventually uncover many, if not all, of the hidden rules, unstated assumptions, and taken-for-granted beliefs.

Remember the heart is the heart of the matter. The postmodern realities of pluralistic societies and an ever encroaching moral relativism make it difficult and somewhat politically incorrect to talk about attitudes and values. After all, for the majority of the world that isn't Protestant talking about the Protestant work ethic seems parochial and antiquated, at best, and at worst risks alienating them and demeaning their faith traditions. It may be politically incorrect, but it's economically and morally necessary to teach people the values that underlie the Protestant work ethic and how they create economic value.

Efforts in the very secular public arena of American education illustrate how this can be done. New York's elite private Riverdale Country School and the public charter schools in the KIPP network now focus on character as well as cognitive education.[26] The idea for character education originated in the work of Martin Seligman, father of the movement known as positive psychology; Seligman argues that character is a crucial ingredient in human flourishing and that schools have a responsibility to give students the tools to flourish. Values-driven education builds competence as well as character.

Traditional coursework and grades still drive the students' GPA, but these schools also track their students' CPA, or character point average. CPA measures value-based behaviors such as zest, grit, self-control, gratitude, optimism, and curiosity. Two of my children attended a public charter school that provides traditional grades in each of their subjects, as well as a CAB grade. CAB stands for Cooperation, Attitude, and Behavior. My daughter, for example, received a grade for her performance in math—how many questions she answered correctly—but also for her enthusiasm during class, her willingness to take risks in solving difficult problems, and her kindness and consideration of others in the class.

The administration and faculty all preach the values in the CAB profile, in a very secular way. The curriculum doesn't teach kindness, risk taking, or zest; however, the larger school environment allows these latent qualities in children to find both voice and recognition. The CAB, or the CPA used in other schools, provides students with incentives to engage in behaviors that allow them to flourish, and they get useful feedback on their performance. The key to the program lies in allowing students to practice and develop their character actively, rather than having lectures about character education.

The implication for our organizations should be obvious; we need more than just speeches about the values underlying the Protestant work ethic; we need measures that can track and reward the behavioral manifestations of these abstract values. Further, if an environment as constrained by tolerance and fear of religious or moral education as the New York City school district can focus on critical values, then so can you. Sensitivity matters, but so does focusing on the elements of the heart that lift and elevate people in their economic and social lives.

Take your own pulse. Martin Burt's list of accomplishments is long, much longer than his growing list of awards and accolades. You've read above about the values, virtues, attitudes, and outlooks Martin brings to his work. These things motivate him to action, but they also guide that action. A deep respect for the capacity of people everywhere means that Fundacion Paraguaya is hypersensitive to ensuring that its clients' autonomy and freedom of choice won't be encroached by their programs.

It's more than just offering a hand up rather than a hand out, a cute phrase that often trivializes very important things. Fundacion Paraguaya presents its clients with real opportunities to grow and options around different ways to move out of poverty. Their clients must choose, and then act for any of the opportunities to become real. Underlying Martin's vision and work is a deep sense of humility. I asked him how he dealt with increasing worldwide attention to his successes and invitations to events like the World Economic Forum.

> At a personal level I treat everybody the same, and I am not impressed by titles. Growing up, my parents had many people over for dinner, from ambassadors to ministers to foreign dignitaries, and we were all raised in an environment of not being impressed with titles. I mean in my family you didn't impress anybody with your title or with your money.
>
> I don't expect anybody to be impressed with me either when I go to a slum or to a rural village. My title is just my position. I may drive the truck, but the mechanic is as important or the person who helps load the truck is as important as I am. I'm not that impressed with titles although I am impressed by some people's merits.[27]

Martin's humility, I believe, acts as a compass that points his efforts toward moving people out of poverty, not massaging his own ego. This makes his work sustainable. Since you are a leader in your various causes and projects, knowing and assessing your own heart will allow you to gain better focus and direction in the work you hope to accomplish. Success in your endeavors brings attention, and even accolades, for the work you and your organization perform. The sweet elixir of recognition brings an initial euphoria but easily becomes a distorting intoxicant.

How do we keep track of our own hearts, to make sure we're living the right values? I've found that two things help. First, maintain contact with the field. The poverty you see has a sobering effect, and the smiles and genuine thanks of people emerging from poverty provide a reward for efforts unmatched by fancy dinners, plaques, or titles. Second, remember those who work with you. Be quick to praise and note their accomplishments. I'm not suggesting false humility or self-deprecation, but rather a willingness to recognize the honest and excellent work you didn't do, but others did. Only after we've got our own heart right can we hope to influence the hearts of those we hope to help.

CONCLUSION

Western medicine views the heart as the physical source of life, and many Eastern meditative traditions see the heart as a crucial source of spiritual energy. For those interested in eliminating little p poverty, the human capital captured in the heart may be just as important as the physical heart is to life and the spiritual one to flourishing. Real progress in the war on poverty requires that we give the heart the honor and attention it deserves.

One lesson of the barrios of Buenos Aires is that human capital develops in unexpected ways. Our programs may target the head or the hands, but if done well they'll influence the heart. Conversely, programs that target attitudes may or may not succeed. In helping people unleash the spirit of capitalism they innately possess, we need to be prepared for the unexpected. We can teach, train, and help people become more self-reliant; we can't control how they use what we've taught them. There will be mistakes, false starts, and unexpected twists. That shows a healthy respect for individual choice and agency.

Human capital development encourages specialization. The specific human capital that Gary Becker considered really does create more value for its owners. Becker's analysis showed that firms had the incentive to invest in developing this unique human capital. Specific human capital, and the specialization of labor that it engenders, creates more value when combined with other specialized human capital. The best venue we know of to leverage specialized human capital is formal organization. As you turn the page you'll see how James Watt's impressive stock of human capital became more valuable through the firm of Boulton & Watt.

CHAPTER SIX

ORGANIZATIONAL CAPITAL

Power from Simple Machines

Any darn fool can make something complex; it takes a genius to make something simple.

—*Pete Seeger*

MATHEW BOULTON ENTERED THE WORLD on September 3, 1728; he shared his father's name as well as the name of an elder brother who died at age two in 1726. The senior Matthew Boulton made toys in Birmingham, a rising manufacturing city described by noted historian Edmund Burke as "the toy shop of Europe."[1] These weren't your children's toys however; today we'd call them household and clothing accessories: "Trinkets, Seals, Tweezer and Tooth Pick cases, Smelling Bottles, Snuff Boxes . . . Cork Screws, Buckles, Draw and other Boxes: Snuffers, Watch Chains, Stay Hooks, Sugar Knippers &c and almost all these are likewise made in various metals."[2]

Matthew Boulton adored his son, and it seems natural that just as the younger Matthew carried his father's name he would carry on his father's business. The son exhibited a substantial talent for the craft of both toy and profit making; by age seventeen "he is said to have produced an enameled or inlaid buckle which helped greatly to enlarge the output of his father's business."[3] The younger Matthew loved business, and his life's work sought to increase the success of his business.

The early success of the Boultons' business in Birmingham resulted from their technical and business skills as manufacturers, aided by the emergence of a nascent middle class in eighteenth-century England that fueled an explosive growth for the accessories and trappings of wealth that "toys" represented. By 1749, when the father made his son a partner in the business, the Boultons' contract manufacturers occupied most of Birmingham's Slaney Street to satisfy a seemingly endless demand for mass-produced goods. Business was brisk, and one biographer described the young partner as "neat, dark and dapper . . . a man on the make."[4]

The year 1749 was very good to the younger Matthew. He cemented two key partnerships: one in the family business and the other with his new wife, Mary Robinson. Boulton didn't marry solely for money—he seemed to love both his first and second wives—but money came through his unions. Mary, his distant cousin, would inherit £3,000 (about $700,000 today) upon her father's death; however, she died prematurely in 1759. In 1760 Boulton married her sister Anne, and their life together indicates a marriage full of love and devotion. Anne survived her brother Luke and became the sole heir to the family's £28,000 (roughly $6 million) inheritance.[5]

Boulton would leverage that £28,000 inheritance to create the Soho Works—a model of British manufacturing. Soho would capitalize on three major changes in eighteenth-century England: the rise of a middle class and an explosion in demand for mass-produced goods; technical improvements in machinery and new innovations that made standardization and higher quality possible (we'll return to this topic in Chapter 7); and the factory method of organizing production. This new structure allowed businessmen (and they were all men in the eighteenth century) to exploit the opportunities created by market expansion and technological innovation.

Factory production broke "with the old practice of 'putting-out' work, whereby a manufacturer received an order and then delegated the work to different craftsmen—to one man who made button 'shells,' another who made the thread rings, a third who made the decorated tops."[6] Manufacturers set up specialized workshops that linked these processes, yielding standardization, scale, and control over inventory and delivery schedules. Boulton's Soho Works brought the emerging factory system of production together under one roof:

> Everything was done on a grand scale. The warehouse, which was known as "the principal building," was nineteen bays wide, on three floors, with a Palladian front, a clock tower and a carriage drive worthy of a stately home. Clerks and managers and their families lived on the upper floors, and on each side were wings enclosing a great yard. . . . The production was arranged in different workshops according to the objects made or the techniques used.[7]

The factory system transformed the nature of business. The amount of capital required to compete increased exponentially; Boulton would struggle well into the 1790s to find the cash to fund his expanding business empire. Business became a complex endeavor. Josiah Wedgwood, the porcelain maker and friend of both Boulton and Watt, created sophisticated systems of cost accounting and the precursor to the diversified corporation centered on product lines. The relationship between capital and labor shifted tectonically; wage labor—the object of hatred for Karl Marx—replaced the contract model prevalent under the putting-out system. The factory altered politics and political economy for the next two-plus centuries.

Shrewd capitalists hired "fatherless children, parish apprentices, and hospital boys, which are put to the most slavish part of [the] business."[8] They worked long hours. In the summer the workday ran from 6:00 a.m. until 7:00 p.m.; in the winter the schedule shifted an hour later in each direction. Workers had a half-hour for breakfast and an hour for lunch. Soho violated many common practices. Boulton hired from the same labor pool but differed in training and work assignments. Rather than consign his workers to "slavish" conditions, Boulton developed their skills as craftsmen or draftsmen. Boulton seems to have been a progressive employer.

Boulton kept Soho well ventilated and clean, and he paid his workers well. A skilled craftsman earned £1 ($200) a week, and mangers could rent apartments at Soho for between £5 and £8 ($1,200 and $1,800) per *year*. The boss sponsored an insurance club, a prototype of modern workman's compensation, and traditional benefits. Workers contributed a small part of their wages that would assist others in the case of accident, sickness, or death.[9] The Soho Works to which James Watt would come in 1768 epitomized the marvels of eighteenth-century British industry.

The Soho Works represent the power of organization; the organizational capabilities developed at Soho allowed Boulton and Watt to manufacture, sell, install, and maintain enough engines to change the face of manufacturing forever. The importance of Soho to the Industrial Revolution is easily overlooked and largely forgotten. It shouldn't be. Organization, and organizational capital is the topic of this chapter; good organization turbocharges people's efforts to leave poverty and travel toward prosperity.

ORGANIZATIONAL CAPITAL

Organizational capital captures the power, energy, skill, and capabilities that come to individuals through their affiliation with formal or informal organizations. What is an organization? Textbooks emphasize three features of organizations: they are social, composed of many people; deliberate or goal-directed; and discrete, or have clear boundaries with other organizations.[10] More simply, organizations are purposeful sets of relationships among people that allow them to accomplish their own goals. We look around and see a world filled with complex, sophisticated organizations that create equally complex and sophisticated products or services; however, you'll learn that Pete Seeger's wisdom applies: the genius of complex organization stems from a combination of very simple elements.

Organizational theorist Max Weber parsed the complex organizational world into two basic forms: formal and informal.[11] Weber described formal organizations as rational-legal entities. They incorporate many tools of rationality, such as conscious and deliberate goals, explicit roles, and structured processes for action. Legitimacy and ethical moorings come from law and legal standing; incorporation or registration is an active process that unambiguously recognizes the existence of the entity and bestows well-specified rights and privileges. The coercive power of the state enforces contracts, and law provides the ultimate sanction for individual or organizational malfeasance. Boulton's Soho Works existed as a formal organization.

Weber labeled informal organizations as traditional. Goals, roles, procedures, and processes arise implicitly from the cognitive and normative institutional background of the group; goals tend to be generally understood and taken for granted by all, but precisely articulated and consciously accepted by none. Generalized roles replace the specialization and division of labor found in formal organizations. Control and authority both come through time-honored norms or customs such as patriarchy or matriarchy. The ultimate sanction in informal organization comes through exclusion from the group and its monopoly on membership. The putting-out system that the Soho Works replaced operated with many features of informal organizations.

Formal and informal organizations both play important roles in the economy and society. Formal organizations encourage the specialization and advancement of knowledge, standardization of products and services, and the ability to scale activities and transactions to deal with strangers—people with whom our only contact is economic. On the other hand, informal organization allows flexibility and increased adaptability when conditions and contexts change. Informal organization fills the gaps where formal organization falters; interestingly, informal organization continues to proliferate in very advanced economies as a response to the pervasive rigidity of formal organizations.[12]

Whatever form they take, organizations provide tangible answers to two bedrock questions that determine their effectiveness and viability. Who does what? (In economic terms how does value get created?) And who gets what? (How does that value get apportioned?) Similar to the pattern we saw in Chapter 3, sociologists have thought long and hard about the former question while economists have focused on the latter.

Who Does What? Organizing to Create Value

Why people organize has a simple answer: human beings are limited creatures.[13] Our vision has limited range, as does our hearing. Strength varies substantially among us, but even the strongest can lift or move no more than a couple hundred pounds. The reason our ancestors chose to cooperate, or organize? They realized that they could accomplish more if they worked together. Cooperation vastly extends our human limitations and creates value we could not realize by our own efforts; however, working well together requires that we overcome the dual problems of coordinating and controlling effort.

Coordination. Humans pool their efforts to amplify their abilities, but if everyone does the same thing, or if what they do doesn't fit together, then organizing yields few gains. Coordination answers the questions of how we divide up tasks. In the organizations in which many of us work (universities, firms, even the Stanford University Press, for example) we find the answers to these questions by looking at individual job descriptions. The modern job description embodies one key source of organizational capital: it divides tasks in ways that capture gains from specialization.

Adam Smith thought hard and wrote extensively about the gains from specialization.[14] When people focus on a single task, or a few related ones, their knowledge of that task deepens, their dexterity improves, and they find new ways to accomplish tasks more quickly and with higher quality. Matthew Boulton's Soho Works exemplified the division of labor as "each button passed through at least 10 hands" during its production.[15] Boulton didn't found the assembly line, but work was laid out at Soho in sequence so that material naturally flowed from start to finish.

We also find evidence of coordination in the typical organization chart. The chart tells us whom we work with—what other specialists we interact with in order to create value. The boxes horizontally next to ours on the chart represent the people, and the tasks, most essential to our own success. The closest vertical boxes (both up and down) identify key lines of communication: people we coordinate with to accomplish our work. An organization's structure emerges over time as a response to the challenges it faces and the solutions it generates.[16] The ability of an organization to accomplish its purpose depends on how well individuals execute according to the plans captured in job descriptions and organization charts.

Control. The organization chart also helps to answer two important questions surrounding who does what: how do we make sure people *do* what they should and *don't* do what they shouldn't? The lines on the organization chart define more than lines of communication; they also delineate authority, or the power to direct the work of others. Authority optimizes the gains from specialization and the division of labor, as those with it ensure that the knowledge, skill, and innovation that characterize specialization remain focused on the overall organizational purpose. Authority acts as a governor that keeps specialization from spinning out of control.

Authority exists in both the job description and the organization chart. As a professor I have the authority—in my job description—to organize and direct my classes as I see fit; the job description gives me discretion. The organization chart of the college defines who has authority to direct my work (my department chair tells me which courses I have to teach) and whose work I get to direct (my poor teaching assistants). My formal authority empowers me to utilize my expertise in designing and executing what I hope are meaningful courses.

The other side of the authority coin is responsibility. Sure, I have the authority to choose what, and how, to teach, but I'm the one responsible for the success or failure of the effort. That responsibility motivates me to work well, but so does another facet of authority: the responsibility doesn't rest just with me but also with those who have authority over me, such as my department chair and dean. Organizations work effectively when those in authority hold those they manage accountable for the actions they are empowered to perform.

Chester Barnard, a pioneering American management theorist, noted that "in fact, successful cooperation in or by formal organizations is the abnormal, not the normal, condition."[17] He highlights the difficulty of creating effective organization: while cooperation and control sound easy, and even look easy on paper, in practice successful organization is the exception rather than the rule. The problem of symbolic organization described by Lant Pritchett and Frauke De Weijer in Chapter 3 illustrates the difficulty: these types of organization look great, but only on paper. One way to make organizations *substantively* effective is to set up reward systems to encourage desired behaviors.

Who Gets What?
Organizing to Distribute Value

Rewards for coordinating work matter because, at the end of the day, organization depends on individual action for goal accomplishment. Economic theory, and our own practical experience, indicates that people won't work unless they receive adequate rewards. Chester Barnard succinctly described this inducements-contributions challenge: people won't contribute to organizational success unless the inducements (payoffs) they receive exceed the cost of their contribution. Also important, however, what people do depends on what they will get; rewards drive behavior.

Wages, piece rates, or commissions serve as the most typical organizational rewards, in part because of their simplicity. Ownership of organizational assets, from tangible tools and machines to intangible knowledge, designs, or patents, represents another way that the gains from organized cooperation, or inducements, will be allocated. The legal traditions in most countries—developed and developing—recognize the right of asset owners to claim the gains from the employment of those assets. Economists Michael Jensen and William Meckling revolutionized organizational and corporate governance in the United States with their observation about the incentive problems between those who own assets (principals) and those who employ them (agents).[18]

Principals want agents to work hard and maximize the value of their investments, but agents want to maximize their own welfare or utility. As long as agents care more about money than, say, relaxation, everyone's interests remain aligned. After a point, however, principals still want more work but agents want more free time, what economists call on-the-job consumption.[19]

The goals of each party now diverge and agents rebuff efforts by the owners to encourage more work.

Owners have two ways to solve the problem. They can set up organization control mechanisms that establish authority and responsibility for tasks and then monitor for compliance. This works to some extent; however, it tends to be quite expensive and begs the question of who monitors the monitors when they find enforcement distasteful. Jensen and Meckling suggested an alternative control mechanism: share the gains from cooperation in a way that gives the agents the same incentives as the principals. The stock option package that many businesses offer reflects the belief that sharing ownership with employees encourages them to think and work in ways the principals desire. Employees think like owners because they are owners.

The Jensen and Meckling model of incentive alignment transformed the compensation landscape in American capitalist organizations. Supervision, especially of top managers, by boards of directors became secondary to the incentives and supervision of the stock market. People would act as their own monitors because now they had greater incentives to do what they should and forego what they shouldn't. The incentive alignment problem, and the Jensen and Meckling solution, teaches us that answering the "who gets what" question can help answer the "who does what" question as well.[20]

This short primer helps us remember the importance of organization in creating real cooperation and reminds us that this doesn't happen automatically. Organization, particularly complex formal organization, requires active effort in its design and management. Let's turn our attention to a social entrepreneur, Greg Van Kirk, who's mastered the power of organization in the fight against little p poverty.

Community Enterprise Solutions

Greg Van Kirk and his partner, George "Buckey" Glickley, founded Community Enterprise Solutions (CE Solutions) in 2004 after both had completed Peace Corps tours in Guatemala. CE Solutions implements the MicroConsignment Model.[21] Greg explained the origin of the MicroConsignment Model (MCM):

> The MCM first emerged when I donated profits . . . to a wood-burning stove project in La Pista, a village 40 minute walk from Nebaj. Like mil-

lions of Guatemalans, these families had always cooked campfire-style on their dirt floors. Cooking this way is extremely energy inefficient, harms the health of family members, and destroys the local environment. Pulmonary illness is a top cause of death in Guatemala and deforestation is ubiquitous.

Relief agencies had determined that locally manufactured concrete stoves could immediately and dramatically reduce energy costs and improve the health and safety of Guatemalan families. But once that money was spent, no one else would get a stove. I realized that many more people could obtain a stove if distribution was built on a sustainable model. In response I developed what I then called "the stove model," which would later become the MicroConsignment Model.[22]

Even if the poor in the villages had money to buy the stoves, finding entrepreneurs willing to assume the risk of selling such a big ticket item would be difficult. Most of these individuals can't afford the cost of inventory to start their own business, nor can they shoulder the risk of a microcredit loan. Ownership is out of reach. Rather than relying on selling or giving stoves away, CE Solutions bridges the divide through consignment. The organization or one of its partner groups advances inventory to a small entrepreneur. At the end of the month, the entrepreneur pays only for the goods actually sold.

Consignment brings immediate profitability to the entrepreneur, and reduces the burdens and risks of product financing. As a community and economic development tool, the MicroConsignment Model works as a hybrid ownership mechanism to fill the space between philanthropic donations (asset gifts) and business credit (asset purchases).[23] CE Solutions is built on the premise that ownership matters; CE Solutions wins only when the entrepreneur does—selling products to pay for the consigned goods. The entrepreneurs have incentive to sell, and CE Solutions has the incentive to help them sell. Incentives and interests align.

Candidate entrepreneurs receive their first consignment only after they survive seven training sessions: four classroom sessions and three in-field sales experiences. The training teaches selling skills among other things (targeting the head and heart), but the sessions allow potential entrepreneurs to self-select. The training attracts women, age twenty to fifty-five, who are motivated, professional, literate, willing to travel, entrepreneurial in orientation, and exhibit high character standards (targeting the heart). Six of ten people attending the first training won't be around at the end of the course. This process begins with many and ends with a select few.

CE Solutions uses the tools of organization to eliminate poverty. Their recruiting, training, and ongoing management of entrepreneurs defines who does what. Financing through consignment creates the type of incentive alignment of which Michael Jensen and William Meckling would approve; CE Solutions doesn't lend money or grant it away. They try to create a cadre of co-owners in their business model. They also artfully craft a blend of informal and formal organization that has led to real success in Guatemala and now expansion throughout the region. Greg Van Kirk has tried to build a holistic organization, combining formal and informal responses to the needs of who does and gets what.

ORGANIZATIONS AS SIMPLE MACHINES

Most of us don't put simple and machines in the same phrase; the machines we use often complexify life rather than simplify it. For engineers and physicists, however, simple machines have a clear definition: tools that make work easier, in terms of making outcomes possible that could not happen without them or making things happen more efficiently than by hand. Levers, screws, inclined planes, and wheels are all simple machines. The principles of formality, informality, distribution of effort, and distribution of rewards function as simple machines in creating organizational capital. From these four simple elements an incredible variety of complex organizations emerge.

Development economists miss the mark because they focus on the most complex organizations rather than the simple machines. They overlook actual organizations and the principles that create them and instead focus on large, complex, and high-level combinations of organizations such as educational systems.[24] Measures like the "ease of doing business" also receive attention: a set of institutional measures from the difficulty of starting a business (measured in the number of days to incorporate), dealing with construction permits, registering property, paying taxes, enforcing contracts, to bankruptcy protections.[25]

Those at the other end of the spectrum advance "micro" solutions to fight poverty. My experience with this crowd reveals an unwritten article of faith that the poor have been, and will continue to be, shut out from organizations. Somehow the simple tools of organization lie beyond the grasp of the poor. Attention centers squarely on the individual, and not much effort goes toward creating organizations or teaching organizational principles. By failing to take the power of organization seriously, many of these micro efforts in fact condemn the poor to living on a subsistence income because they won't ever realize the real advantages of scale and specialization that come through organization.

Let's take for granted that you accept the premises of this chapter: that organizational capital plays a real role in eliminating poverty. Consider yourself an organization designer, trying to use the simple tools to create organizations that help eliminate poverty; better yet, think of helping the poor establish their own businesses. You've got two simple questions to answer: Who does what, and who gets what?

You can answer these questions using formal, legal-rational machinery, or you can rely on informal, traditional, and custom-driven methods. This gives you four fundamental organizational forms: a pure informal organization where traditional mechanisms answer both questions; a purely formal one where you employ only rational-legal tools; a hybrid with traditional answers to who does what and legal answers to who gets what; and a hybrid with rational-legal tools defining roles but an informal distribution of gains.[26] Each type has advantages and disadvantages that we'll consider below.

Pure informal. The Guatemalan women that CE Solutions recruits to the MicroConsignment Model have, at best, informal organizations. CE Solutions does not require that they register their businesses with the local authorities—probably a good thing, considering that Guatemala ranks 165th out of 183 countries for ease of starting a business.[27] CE Solutions provides training and direction for the entrepreneur; however, if they hire their own employees there are no rules, regulations, or standardized procedures they must follow. The work will be loosely organized to ensure maximum flexibility to deal with nuances in individual markets.

The pure informal organization represents the archetype for many of the world's poor. Registering businesses with the state provides few benefits. States often lack the infrastructure to collect registration fees or taxes, with the result being few public services that enhance the environment for business. The operation uses traditional methods to organize; the small numbers involved mean that trust and mutual adjustment resolve most issues, and the simple nature of the work requires little sophisticated coordination.

Pure informality maximizes the values of flexibility and adaptability but minimizes any advantages to scale, legal protection, complex trades, or trades with strangers. These organizations proliferate in states with dysfunctional institutions and the political, economic, and security uncertainty it invites. Informality also works in very small entities or ones that trade in small circles rich in cultural and relational capital. These organizations face difficulties in growing as members acquire few skills regarding the processes of substantive organization. Pure informality generates an organizational capital that helps leaders get things done through persuasion and negotiation, without any formal power or authority.

Pure formal. CE Solutions exists as a formal organization, legally registered in the state of New Jersey and organized with explicit job descriptions and roles because Greg Van Kirk worked in several bureaucratic organizations before founding CE Solutions. The logic of bureaucracy and formality permeates the air in the developed world; all of our role model organizations tend to be set up this way. If we want to form an organization we naturally gravitate toward a formal one. Formality grants CE Solutions legitimacy among the myriad networks of donors who finance the nascent MicroConsignment Model, and government officials in both countries that support and regulate the firm's operations.

The institutional structure of advanced economies and societies privileges formal organization. The law provides tangible benefits and sanctions that induce organizations to formalize. Organizations compete in complex environments and face definable risks, the type of environments in which tools such as written contracts function efficiently and effectively. Complexity engenders specialization that in turn yields definable advantages to clear and explicit operational roles. The grand appeal to formal organization is the ability to scale operations, whether for profit or social impact.

As the opposite of pure informality, formal organization maximizes stability, scalability, and standardization. The downside to formality comes in the form of diminished ability to identify and adapt to rapidly changing conditions or to innovate and try new approaches. Formality generates lots of organizational capital that fosters impersonal power and authority; think about how much you know about dealing with bureaucracy and complexity. This capital tends, however, to be fairly narrow in scope, with limited applicability beyond the organization.

Formal rewards, informal organization. The prevailing global template for who does what is the family, specifically the family business. Even in the developed world! In the United States, for example, 90 percent of all businesses are family owned; they generate almost two-thirds of U.S. GDP and, interestingly, they outperform nonfamily businesses by better than 6 percent in return on assets.[28] Some family businesses in the United States look like bureaucracies; however, many do not. Like many in poor environments, most businesses operate along family lines. Patriarchy or matriarchy but not hierarchy defines who does what, and family structures favor generalized work assignments to highly specialized ones. Who gets what depends on a mix of explicit rewards or contracts *and* family tradition, birth order, or custom.

Cultural inertia and the dominance of the family, or larger clan, as a social organization mean that attempts to formalize (legalize) organizations stop short; the business registers and creates formal ownership rules, but these principles end where day-to-day business begins. Work roles, processes, and procedures arise from tacit, taken-for-granted ways of working. Boulton's Soho drew on the law of the eighteenth century to define ownership and rewards, but the craft-based traditions of individual toy makers by and large defined how work got done.

This hybrid form maximizes neither informality's adaptability nor formality's security. It blends both. As such, this organization works well in environments with two features: fairly robust legal institutions and public infrastructure create real benefits to formalization but endemic uncertainty. Developing countries such as Ghana feature a number of these organizations, as do faster growth emerging economies such as Turkey or Brazil. This "legal" hybrid leverages the best of legal registration and informal organization, and leaders acquire organizational capital about how to balance formal, impersonal processes with informal, personal ones.

Informal rewards, formal organization. Matthew Boulton's dealings with his partners reveal a clever, shrewd businessman with sophisticated acumen for risk management. He created several companies in his vast empire, among them Boulton & Watt, and thirteen different partnerships over his lifetime. The terms of each partnership were clearly understood by all parties; however, Boulton never formalized these partnerships through written contract.[29] If his partners suffered a reversal of fortune (read bankruptcy), Boulton would not be saddled with their debts; he leveraged formality while avoiding its dangers.

When pure informal businesses begin to grow they add workers to handle increases in business. This increases complexity within the business and naturally spawns a division of labor and specialization. Operational formality—a protobureaucracy, if you will—is born as things that look like job descriptions and a hierarchy emerge. Legal formalization yields few benefits, and many smart entrepreneurs mimic Boulton; they avoid the costs of legal formalization in terms of tax payments, obligations to employees, or compliance with ill-fitting government regulations. Legal registration always brings costs but occasionally benefits such as police protection, infrastructure, or other government services.

The "operationally formal" hybrid, like its sibling discussed above, seeks to leverage and capitalize on the advantages of both formal and informal organization. This form works well in growth markets where scaling up creates substantial and sustainable advantages but where there are onerous legal climates; they don't score well on measures such as the ease of doing business. Entrepreneurs running these firms, just like the other hybrid, create a rich source of internal organizational capital around balancing formal and informal processes.

CE Solutions offers an interesting example of how an organization can help people move from informality through semiformality and on to formality. The MicroConsignment Model proved to be quite successful, and by 2005 the CE Solutions operations in Guatemala were growing well and extending access to a basket of goods in the country. CE Solutions organized Soluciones Communitarias (SolCom) to create a formal ownership opportunity for some of its successful entrepreneurs. SolCom is an independent legal organization and partner that buys inventory and consigns it to local entrepreneurs.

SolCom collects the sales revenue, which it then plows back into more inventory as well as salaries for the SolCom owners and staff. SolCom fits the vision CE Solutions has for eventual scaling and expansion. SolCom should become the implementation partner for all of Guatemala, freeing up CE Solutions financial, human, and organizational capital to focus on new potential markets. SolCom also provides an upward career path for successful MicroConsignment entrepreneurs to help them move from often unstable informal to more stable formal organizations.

You've played the role of organization designer and seen four different templates for creating firms and leveraging organizational capital. Each form has an appropriate environment where it works best, and each generates different types of advantages. What happens when we move from theory to reality? In the next section we'll consider some practical implications of organizational capital in the quest to eliminate poverty.

ORGANIZATIONAL CAPITAL AND POVERTY ELIMINATION

Organizational capital influences each element of the disposition of self-reliance. When we participate in an organization we tend to become more responsible; the dedicated relationships we form engender obligations and provide strong incentives to meet them. Organizational tasks provide individual mastery experiences that enhance self-efficacy; as we watch others execute their tasks we gain vicarious mastery experiences. Accountability for performance allows people to get feedback, and when training accompanies accountability we gain the skills to help us succeed.

The operating assumption of any organization is that it will persist into the future—that's why accountants label firms as "going concerns." Formal organization, and particularly things like hiring people or incurring debt, naturally makes us think about the long term. The dedicated relationships that allow us to achieve our goals exist *in* time (what we need to do today) and *over* time (our commitments that extend into the future). The bedrock assumption of organization is that the costs and hassles of coordinating with others, often incurred up front, pay off in the long run. That is the essence of the long-term view fundamental to self-reliance.

In terms of the behaviors that lead to the condition of self-reliance, organizations and organizational capital contribute here as well. Membership in CE Solutions allows Guatemalan entrepreneurs to acquire products and services to then employ and sell. The essence of MicroConsignment is leverage that makes each party's scarce resources go further. The organizations that help us create value also preserve that value by establishing and maintaining the mix of context, skill, and physical assets for the long term, perhaps into perpetuity. Organizational elements such as culture or training and development encode capital (human, social, physical, or even institutional) in the heads, hands, and hearts of members. Once encoded, it remains.

Each of the previous chapters focused on recommendations to help you create effective organizations, to build your own stock of organizational capital. What follows contains less, albeit some, about how you can *build* your own organization and more about how you can *share* what you have with those you work with. Building and sharing organizational capital allow clients to look past the apparent complexity of your organization to its fundamental simplicity.

Organization begets itself. Organizations, particularly formal ones, don't automatically appear, much to the chagrin of many development economists and microfinance providers. The small, poorly coordinated markets that characterize many Big P and little p environments mean that large, formal private organizations (such as multinational business corporations) may be few and far between, and when you find them they may be focused as much on export as building in-country capabilities. Your organization may be one of the few formal organizations your clients deal with—or maybe the only one.

Once formal organization gets a toehold in a community, however, it tends to perpetuate itself. Nobel Laureate Douglass North recently observed that the one important characteristic of advanced economies is the plethora of formal organizations and different organizational forms for solving economic and social problems, and the first organizations provide models for others to observe and templates for them to replicate.[30] The poor live in organizational poverty: a paucity of organizational forms and recipes for collective action.

The predominant recipe in many environments lies in the family; it becomes the default business structure because corporate or bureaucratic structures aren't there to copy. Bureaucracy is not in the air! You can use two powerful tools you many not know you have to overcome the dearth of organizations and build organizational capital: your organizational histories and current organization. If you're reading this book, chances are you have more experience living in, dealing with, and using the tools of formal organization than you realize. Our experiences in organizations can help those we work with design their own work systems, both in terms of operations and ownership.

Ours may be the only organizational template those in poverty interact with—or one of only a handful; let's not waste the opportunity to give them firsthand experiences with the principles and realities of organization. CE Solutions takes entrepreneurs to a new village and lets them watch, and participate in, the initial marketing and sales pitches to village leaders. The regional, and sometimes country, directors move from abstract organizational roles and become real people, potential partners get firsthand experience with organizational specialization and a chain of authority. We need to employ and leverage our own organizational capital so that others may build theirs.

When do our clients *see* our organization? When they observe how we deal with the realities of organizational membership. This probably means that you'll have to have more formality inside your own camp than you may care to; however, if your field personnel don't have job descriptions, coordinating relationships, and a line of authority in their work, it proves doubly difficult to give your clients a recipe for creating their own organizations. This formalization needs to complement and supplement, not choke or substitute for, the principle of incompleteness described in Chapter 2.

Focus on the formal, private middle. Development economists, when they think about organization at all, tend to do so at the most *macro* level in the public domain. Social innovators fascinated with all things *micro* neglect all but the smallest forms of organizations; their focus lies at the individual level. It's time to pay attention to growing the middle, or *meso* level, of private sector organizations. Firms like Boulton & Watt drove the processes of industrialization; small and medium firms provide a huge source of growth, innovation, and development in the world's economies, developed or developing.[31]

I attended a conference several years ago at which I presented an early version of the five capitals model. At lunch I sat next to a former Ghanaian minister dealing with a basket of development projects. We talked about what his country needed; he was quite explicit that they didn't need more microapproaches. Ghana would leap forward, he believed, when development led to organizations capable of creating jobs and employment opportunities. Microcredit, whatever else it's done, has failed to grow firms capable of hiring nonfamily members.[32] Similarly, large development projects tend to provide few jobs, and fewer jobs at the skill levels prevalent in the country.

Admitting the need for, and creating a focus on, small and midsize private firms gets us "well begun" as the old saying goes. We want to get more than merely "half done." Helping our own clients create firms entails three interrelated processes. First, our own organizations have to be fully registered within the countries and regions we operate in; it's about leading by example, but it's also about learning the process of registration. When we register we learn about the time delays, paperwork requirements, and even the potential for facilitating payments or outright corruption.

Second, formalizing our clients must be an explicit goal, and we have to have the skills in place to help them do so. Navigating the byzantine and complex processes of business formalization challenges the best of us with a bureaucratic background—pity those trying to fly blind.[33] The fundamental principle of incompleteness applies here as well. We can, metaphorically, show people which lines to stand in and what forms to fill out; standing and filling out, however, should be done only by our clients.

Finally, once our clients form their own organizations, they need to understand some basic principles of management to answer for themselves the questions of who does what and who gets what. Business training often focuses on the technical details of the business, from accounting and record-keeping through merchandizing to wholesaling. What is lacking is management, the softer, nontechnical skills of leadership, delegating responsibility and then holding people accountable, or creating and implementing some type of strategy.

Formalization matters, pure formality may not. Chester Barnard worked in the early twentieth century's biggest bureaucracy, the telephone company. Barnard spent the better part of his career as president of New Jersey Bell, an AT&T regional operating company. He witnessed the complexity and power that comes when individual cooperation becomes formalized and leveraged in a very, very formal organization. His writings clearly focus on the power of formal organization, but he makes an interesting observation: formal organization can't exist or survive without an accompanying informal organization.

Formality standardizes work, scales production and sales, and creates real economic value for the firm and the larger society; it also alienates people. Max Weber noted that one characteristic of bureaucracy was the depersonalization of work; Karl Marx labeled it dehumanization. Barnard saw a host of informal organizations, groups of people held together by friendship, common customs, and shared norms embedded throughout the formal structure. These organizations blunted many of the dehumanizing effects of bureaucracy and gave AT&T a measure of flexibility and creativity.

Concern with the pure types of formal or informal businesses diverts focus from the immediate, and potential long-term, power of the hybrid forms. Operationally formal organizations can enhance productivity and profitability by making work roles and rules—that is, who does what—clear; specialization adds value and leverages the skills in the cooperative effort so that everyone wins. Legal registration may not be possible or advisable to register and regulate the business. In many countries, for example, formal organizations are more prone to requests for bribes or other corrupt actions by officials.[34]

Conversely, organizations that become formal, legal entities may continue to benefit from informal work roles. Legal formalization can generate benefits that exceed the cost—enhanced police protection or the ability to contract with other formal organizations. Within that formal structure, the reality of change, uncertainty, and volatility advantage informal work arrangements, as they provide businesses with added flexibility and responsiveness to deal with these uncertain and evolving environments. In both cases the hybrid forms allow entrepreneurs to capture the best of both types.

The hybrid forms will, in my opinion and experience, create the most valuable organizational capital. The poverty we want to eliminate occurs within contexts marked by either insecure, ineffective legal regimes or highly uncertain, tenuous market conditions. Hybridization builds organizations that can navigate these treacherous waters. They can get things done and leverage individual efforts. A final implication of organizational capital deals with what types of rewards businesses can provide for joining the organization.

Think of ownership broadly. Greg Van Kirk and his partners at CE Solutions created SolCom for two reasons: one material and the other not. Owning their own consignment company would certainly allow his Guatemalan partners to increase their earnings and equity. These rewards have been slow in coming. In 2010 SolCom revenues amounted to about $6,200 per month, with $2,400 being shared among the eleven employees as wages. That's about $218 per employee, about half the $433 monthly per capita GDP for Guatemalans. Further, the company itself lost about $1,500 per month, which CE Solutions subsidized through its donation network.[35]

Growth in 2011 appeared to put SolCom on the verge of financial self-sustainability, but that's six years after its creation. SolCom's role in the CE Solutions vision involves more than income, however. SolCom provides its owners with substantial nonmaterial rewards: the pride of ownership, the challenges of knowledge development and personal growth, and the opportunity to be a part of a solution and help others like themselves lift themselves out of poverty. SolCom employees had trained more than two hundred new entrepreneurs and marketed their products in eighteen hundred villages by 2010.

Organization theorists and management gurus from Chester Barnard in the mid-twentieth century, to Jim Collins in the early twenty-first, all point out the power of nonmaterial rewards in creating effective organizations. Monetary rewards and material inducements play a valuable role in motivating people to contribute effort and energy, but these elements suffer from rapidly diminishing marginal utility. Once some basic set of physical needs have been met people tend to focus more on the nonmaterial benefits that come through organization; beyond a subsistence wage nonmaterial benefits become increasingly important—even decisive—in eliciting organized cooperation, even in very low wage situations.

Nonmaterial benefits include praise, reputation, opportunities for learning, and importantly, participation. Organizations that give employees or clients a voice in the development process—for new products, services, or production techniques—share ownership in that process, whether or not they share ownership of the outcome. Participation has the powerful side effect of reinforcing each element of a self-reliant disposition. Participation engenders responsibility and a sense of obligation toward what one has co-created; it equips individuals with another opportunity to manifest self-efficacy, and participation encourages a long-term view as people witness the effects of their effort over time.

CE Solutions offers a model of how we can think broadly about creating ownership opportunities along the value chain. Social innovations often begin and grow with entrepreneurs plugging holes in the supply chain and finding the resources needed to deliver services and meet objectives. Many of these "holes" represent important, but at best, supplementary activities to our core mission and purpose; they represent fertile ground for the creation of new organizations, like SolCom. These intensely local organizations can offer our clients another ladder out of poverty.

CONCLUSION

The confluence between radical changes in two sectors of society, technology and organization, ushered in the Industrial Revolution. James Watt and his steam engine represent the first sector; Matthew Boulton and his Soho Works the second. When Watt's rotary motion steam engine propelled the massive looms of the British cotton industry, looms powered by wage laborers in a true factory system of production, the Industrial Revolution took off. Steam-powered machinery accelerated the spread of the emerging factory system—the precursor to today's formal, bureaucratic corporation. Technological invention *and* an organizational innovation drove industrialization.

This chapter considered the importance of what went on *inside* the Soho Works. The true marvel was the organization of work and capital, more so that than the grand building itself; however, the *outside* of Soho mattered as well, its machinery, technological advances, and the financing that brought it into being. The next chapter takes up, metaphorically, the outside of the Soho Works or the role of physical capital in the fight against poverty. You'll see that physical capital matters, just in a different way than you might have thought.

CHAPTER SEVEN

PHYSICAL CAPITAL

The Last Puzzle Piece

First we shape our buildings, thereafter they shape us.

—Winston Churchill

THE YEAR 1485 BROUGHT significant political change to England. Henry Tudor (Henry VII), Welsh rebel and leader of the "red" faction, defeated the sitting king Richard III of the "white" faction to end the war of the roses. Eleven years later, in 1496, Henry was still occupied with securing his tenuous rule; to fend off a potential Scottish invasion Henry turned to a new, emerging technology for help. He commissioned England's first cast iron foundry at Newbridge, located southeast of London in a heavily wooded area known as the Weald, an Old English word for forest.[1] Cast iron offered the promise of better cannon to buttress the king's forces and repel enemies.

Cast iron represented a substantial advance in the technology of war. Medieval engineers constructed cannon by welding iron rods together and creating a cylinder reinforced with iron hoops. These crude cannons had limited range, could be fired only a few times each day, and were prone to explode and kill those using them. No general could count on cannon as a reliable, sustained force during battle.[2] The new technology allowed cannon to be cast, or poured into a mold, to make a one-piece weapon. Henry's new cannon could be cast from a single cylinder of iron, producing stronger, larger, and more accurate cannons for use in repelling his Scottish invaders and other threats.

The Weald proved an excellent location for producing cast iron, as the heavily forested area provided a rich source of a prime material for making cast iron—charcoal. Like other winning innovations throughout history, iron found its way into other uses, and the production of cast iron took off. Over

the next two centuries the country's appetite for iron products would deci-
mate the forests; 10,000 tons of iron consumed 100,000 acres of forest. By the
eighteenth century timber was scarce and expensive; a huge opportunity existed for anyone who could find a new fuel source for the cast iron foundries.[3]

England abounded with coal, but the black substance had never found
its way into cast iron; smelting iron with raw coal transferred sulphur into
the iron, making it extremely brittle and hence worthless. In 1709 Abraham
Darby, a Quaker living outside of Birmingham, pioneered the large-scale use
of coke, the remains of coal baked at high temperatures to remove most of its
impurities. Darby's process radically changed the economics of making cast
iron: coke produced a higher quality iron (with fewer impurities, because of
the higher blast temperature of coal) at lower cost (the physical properties of
Coke facilitated much larger blast furnaces).[4]

Abraham's son Abraham carried on the family business and began casting
cylinders for, among others, Thomas Newcomen and his massive steam engines. As a part of their expanding empire the Darbys built a foundry, the Bersham Furnace, across the Severn River from their home in Coalbrookdale. In
1753 Isaac Wilkinson acquired the Bersham operation from the Darbys. Four
years later Isaac combined the Bersham works with other foundries in the
area and created the New Willey Company, with his son John as cofounder.
John Wilkinson would be known by the moniker "Iron Mad" during his lifetime and forever after.[5] The New Willey Company focused on armaments—
namely, the production of cannons.

Cast iron cannons were an advance over their medieval predecessors, but
the technology of cast iron created its own problem: noncircular holes. You
load cannon by putting powder down the hole, followed by a spherical cannon ball. When the powder ignites the resulting explosion propels the ball
down the barrel and downrange. If the spherical ball seals well with a circular
hole it maximizes the propulsive energy from the explosion and minimizes the
wobble of the ball. If the ball doesn't seal well then, at best, the ball doesn't fly
as far or as straight; at worst the cannon explodes and kills its operators.

Iron Mad developed a process to bore a perfectly circular hole into a solid
cast iron cylinder of almost any diameter. Wilkinson patented his invention
in 1774. New Willey cannon had almost perfectly circular holes, to within
one-thousandth of an inch; the accuracy and effectiveness of British cannon
improved dramatically.[6] So, what does the history of cast iron, and the unique

invention of Iron Mad Wilkinson, have to do with James Watt and his steam engine? Cannons and steam engines share two common features: they are both, at the core, cylinders with holes, and the effectiveness of the machine depends on the precise circularity of the hole.

In 1775 Boulton and Watt were busily constructing two demonstration engines based on Watt's unique design, an engine for the Bloomfield Colliery outside of Birmingham and one for the Wilkinson's New Willey Works in Shropshire. Watt was concerned about the quality of the cylinders; escaping steam around the piston dissipated the energy of the new engine and lessened its advantage over the Newcomen Engine. Escaping steam also created a serious safety risk to those operating the engine. Dissatisfied with the quality of the cylinders produced by the Darbys and his old partner Roebuck, Watt contracted with Wilkinson to make the cylinders.

Wilkinson's boring technology created tight seals on the 38-inch-diameter engine for his New Willey Works, as well as the 50-inch cylinder at Bloomfield. Iron Mad Wilkinson would become the sole supplier of precision cast cylinders for Boulton and Watt Engines for the next two decades. Boulton observed in 1776 that "Wilkinson hath bored us several cylinders almost without error, that . . . doth not err the thickness of an old shilling."[7]

Cast iron, and the accurate machinery of Iron Mad Wilkinson, exemplifies the role of physical capital in creating wealth. This chapter takes up this last capital. Physical capital can be thought of as an important piece of the puzzle of development and poverty elimination. The analogy works because the effectiveness and value of physical capital depends on how it fits and connects to the other types of capital. A good fit makes physical capital a useful tool in the fight against poverty; a poor fit results in useless artifacts that drain other capital accounts.

PHYSICAL CAPITAL

Economists see three types of resources in a production function, a description of how goods and services come to market. The three resources, or inputs, are land, labor, and capital.[8] We've talked about labor and human capital and its value in Chapter 5. Land may be nature's endowment, but without the capital, the machines, equipment, and tools that economists speak of, land doesn't produce much, unless you live as a hunter-gatherer. The important types of capital for economic activity, and poverty elimination, represent artifacts, objects designed and constructed by humans. Much of what we mean in common parlance by "technology"—tools for accomplishing tasks—falls under the rubric of physical capital.

That physical capital, or technology, comes from human hands has two powerful implications that guide any thoughtful discussion of technology. First, artifacts are designed by humans to meet their needs within the other systems they live in. That means that newly designed artifacts or technologies fit within one or more existing type of capital: institutional, social, human, technical, or organizational. The QWERTY keyboard we all use provides an excellent example. Human hands could create more keystrokes than the mechanical system could at the time handle; QWERTY slowed human skill so the machine wouldn't jam up. QWERTY may not make much sense now, but it did in 1866 when the modern machine emerged.[9]

Second, once in place, technology feeds back onto those systems; in the language of Chapter 3, physical capital structurates the other capitals in an ongoing relationship.[10] QWERTY improved the performance of the typewriter, which helped it become the standard for formal organizational but not social communications (the formal letter vs. the handwritten note). QWERTY altered the institutional fabric as generations of students learned to type, or keyboard using today's term, according to the QWERTY method. All technologies exhibit both of these properties.

The field of accounting provides us with a systematic way to think about the types of physical capital, or assets.[11] The first cut is made based on whether an asset has physical substance or not. Cash, inventory, property, plant, and equipment all have physical substance; patents, brands, and goodwill exemplify assets without physical substance. Assets with physical substance subdivide into two more general categories: liquid assets such as cash, receivables, investments, and insurance policies; and illiquid assets such as buildings, factories, machines, and tools. We'll replace the word illiquid with an easier surrogate: solid.

Solid assets create economic value through *transformation*. Land provides a platform, buildings shelter and safety, machines and tools the capability to combine or convert raw materials or other inputs into economically valuable outputs. Liquid assets generate income and wealth through *transaction*. Money allows us to trade for things we need now; saving money lets people trade for things later while credit allows them to pay later. Insurance acts as a type of saving in that it guarantees our ability to trade when the potential risks of life become real. Let's consider each type in greater detail.

Solid capital. The defining feature of solid capital is its ability to enhance human capabilities, to allow us to do things we can't otherwise do. Think for a moment about a CAT scanner, one of the most complex pieces of equipment we know of. CAT scanners create value because they allow doctors to see what's going on inside our bodies in ways their eyes could never see, even if they open the body during surgery. For a lower-tech device, think about a forklift; anyone who ever worked moving heavy things can appreciate the forklift's ability to move very heavy objects using fine instead of gross motor muscles.

For people in the developing world solid capital is usually far less sophisticated but, in the context in which they live, equally valuable. We met Freddie in Chapter 2. His set of simple, small knives allow him to transform branches, logs, or cut lumber into finely crafted carvings, representations of African animals, traditional masks, or wooden jewelry targeting a more modern audience. For Warner a key piece of solid capital would be a motorcycle that could extend his reach in selling cigarettes in and around Accra.

It's important here to keep the notion of capital in mind. Solid things only become capital when they enhance human abilities *over time*, without being used up. That means that the motorbike is capital, but the cigarettes aren't because Warner can only sell them once. Inventory isn't capital, either for accountants in the developed world or for subsistence entrepreneurs in environments of poverty. Inventory is a true expense; both its cost and value-creating ability get used up in a single transaction.

This distinction matters because inventory and capital can easily be confused. One problem with giving money to help the poor—the problem identified at the beginning of this book—is that money often gets used to provide inventory rather than capital goods.[12] Financing inventory has immediate appeal, and impact; it also costs less than longer-term investments in capital goods. The old saying about teaching a man to fish, rather than giving him one, applies here; give a man a fish and he'll eat for a day, a fishing pole and he'll eat for many days.

Liquid capital. Liquid capital—money and its derivatives—also enables people to do things they couldn't do without it. Money enhances our ability to do things, not by allowing us to act on other physical objects but by exchanging it for other things we need. A basic economic truth about money is that its value lies in exchange; unless you want to paper your walls with money its worth comes when we use it to purchase other things. Money beats barter because it represents a universal unit of exchange. Warner's customers exchange money for his cigarettes, and then he can use that money to exchange for other things he needs. Freddie's customers pay dollars in New York, and he converts them into Ghana cedis in Accra.

When used well money is capital, when used poorly it's an expense. The wise use of money lies in exchanging money for other types of capital—in effect exchanging one store of value for another. Tuition, for example, exchanges liquid capital for human capital in the form of education. Savings and available credit each represent the ability to trade for value tomorrow; insurance protects our ability to exchange even when we can't earn. Even exchanging money for food preserves some of its capital value; we exchange money for, literally, stores of energy that allow us to work.

Money gets used unwisely when we exchange it for immediate consumption with no lasting value. While buying food exchanges one type of capital energy for another, buying junk food or alcohol represent empty calories. These diversions provide pleasure, either in the very moment of use or shortly thereafter; however, they fail to provide pleasure on a sustainable or ongoing basis. Many other forms of entertainment, from movies or rented video games (popular in many pockets of poverty) to tickets to sporting events dissipate the capital value of money.

The philosophy of consumerism, then, becomes a potential deterrent to poverty alleviation. Management guru C. K. Prahalad opened an important conversation about fighting poverty by pointing out the potential for business to reap, according to the title of his book, a "fortune at the bottom of the pyramid."[13] Businesses, and the poor, would both win as the poor became better consumers of the world's goods.

His colleague at the University of Michigan, Aneel Karnani, rightly criticized this approach.[14] Development activities that focus on creating consumption among the poor provide little sustainable value; the poor are just allocating their income in different ways. Activities that enhance the abilities of the poor as producers, improving their income, skills, and other types of capital will result in the elimination of poverty. The difference between the two approaches? One involves trading money for consumable goods, the other focuses on investments in other forms of capital.

Three stories, one from the Navajo, one from the lives of single mothers, and one from Fundacion Paraguaya help illustrate the ways in which physical capital and technology work (or not) in the fight against poverty. As you'll see in the next section, the success or failure of these technology solutions to the problems of poverty depends on how well these last pieces of capital fit with the other four types.

Corn Grinders, Cars, and Chapels

The Navajo corn grinder. I took my first trip to the Navajo Nation in the spring of 2005 with an MBA student assistant. We traveled to an area of the Big Rez north of Winslow, Arizona, in the Painted Desert to meet the leader of a local NGO working on the reservation. He wanted to teach us about agricultural outreach to traditional farmers; one specific project involved a corn grinder that his group had purchased to help the Navajo grind their own corn. This individual and his organization have helped hundreds of Navajo by providing education and agricultural training and support services to hundreds of residents.

Unfortunately, the corn grinder would not count among those successes. The grinding operation was consistent with the goals of the organization to reinvigorate traditional Navajo farming practices; they wanted to allow Navajo farmers to avoid the large milling operations in Winslow and keep the grinding fees on the reservation. The corn grinder failed to contribute to a well-intended vision.

We saw the corn grinder later that day. It was a small machine, at an appropriate scale for the size of farms and harvests found on the reservation. The NGO had purchased a trailer to haul the grinder to individual farms or to the small towns that dot the Big Rez. Because the corn grinder was grant funded, the group estimated that they could grind corn at $7 per bushel, about a third the cost of grinding in Winslow. The $7 fee covered the cost of the operation: gas and the operator's wages. The most striking feature of the grinder we both noticed: it sat idle inside a trailer with a broken axle. No corn would be ground that, or any ensuing, year.

The corn grinder, a piece of solid capital, might have helped the NGO in its efforts to encourage Navajos to engage in what they term traditional agriculture. It seemed mission consistent and scale appropriate; the technology was simple enough that it could "plug and play" anywhere on the Navajo land. The lack of liquid capital, however, stymied this effort, and the grinder sat inactive, its value reduced to a platform for spider webs and its trailer a source of shade from the hot Arizona sun.

Single moms and their cars. A car may be a true luxury in many developing countries; in the expansive American West a car becomes an economic necessity. Cities in the Western United States are geographically dispersed; the Salt Lake metropolitan area where these women lived and worked covers about nine hundred square miles. Public transportation systems, while improving, still lag their counterparts in the large cities on the East Coast or the Midwest. Some single moms traveled twenty-five to thirty miles each way to work or school; others traveled half that distance each day; a rare few had commutes of a couple of miles or less. The geography of living in the West makes a car an essential economic asset for these women.

Automobiles enable these women to live in the suburbs, where housing and childcare costs are lower, and commute to better paying jobs or to the universities and colleges in the urban center to retool their skill base. Automobiles also provide flexibility in meeting their children's needs for day care, doctor visits, or days at the park. Last, but by no means least, having a car gives these women a deep sense of worth and meaning. The car frees them from dependence on public transportation, but also from reliance on family and friends to get to work or school. Cars give single moms the pride of ownership.

Cars, in addition to a huge upside, consume enormous amounts of liquid capital. Few single moms we interviewed own new cars, and fewer still understand or have the resources to lease cars. They tend to drive older cars with higher fuel and regular maintenance costs; these cars also tend to break down more than a new car would, another drain on cash. Fewer still have an extensive—or even basic—knowledge of auto maintenance or repair; they either have family, friends, or neighbors work on their cars or they pay to have the work done. Given their limited incomes, auto expenses absorb a large share of their income. Whether the car helps or hinders these women depends, in large measure, on having liquid capital, or effective substitutes.

The Chapel Hotel. Martin Burt transformed the old chapel of the LaSalle Brotherhood from a wellspring of spiritual renewal into one of sustainable revenue.[15] The layout of the old chapel facilitated an easy remodel to create a rustic hotel. The building has a large main area that now serves as a very welcoming lobby. The long hallways of the old chapel mean that the guest rooms array like a typical hotel with rooms lining both sides of long hallways. Visitors enjoy plenty of peace, quiet, and opportunity to rest. The original square footage of the chapel proved adequate so that Martin avoided expensive additions to the building; the project became a cost-effective remodel rather than an expensive new build.

During our visit to Paraguay in 2010 we traveled to a new school site in the Mbaracayu, a forest preserve about 350 kilometers (240 miles) north and east of Asuncion. Fundacion Paraguay had partnered with the Nike Foundation to establish a school for girls in this forest preserve and its surrounding communities.[16] The new school would replicate the San Francisco model of a self-sustaining school, with a hotel targeting ecotourists as the centerpiece. Building a hotel in the Mbaracayu would be a very different operation than at San Francisco, however, as there was no chapel to use as a shell. Replicating the physical capital that fueled the San Francisco model would take time, energy, and substantial amounts of liquid capital.

In each of these cases creating effective physical capital requires both solid and liquid resources: cars and corn trailers require fuel, repairs, and maintenance, and chapels need money to become hotels. These stories hint at another important principle about physical capital, one that highlights the core premise of the book: in each case physical capital matters but in no case was it the decisive factor. When physical capital works to eliminate poverty it does so only in concert with the other types of capital. We now turn our attention to exploring those relationships.

PHYSICAL CAPITAL AS A PUZZLE PIECE

The analogy of physical capital as the last piece of a puzzle vivifies when we remember the two important realities of physical capital as an artifact: it has to fit with the other pieces in the beginning, and it then shapes the entire puzzle over its lifetime. Winston Churchill was right: we shape our houses and then they shape us. We often forget these fundamental lessons, however, because of our own cultural bias toward being enamored with physical capital and the tendency we have to view technology as a savior in our distress.

Viewing physical capital as the savior, or rescuer, of the poor is a variation on this common theme. Other popular variations include seeing the market, government, or private philanthropy as playing the role of savior; the debate between William Easterly and Jeffrey Sachs outlined in Chapter 1 embodies two renditions of this tune. Why do we look for saviors, white knights, silver bullets, wonder drugs, or other cure-alls for our ills?

The existence of a rescuer is one of the oldest motifs in literature, and that role plays prominently in one of psychology's deeply held structures: the victim-perpetrator-rescuer complex or drama triangle.[17] Victims are those hurt, perpetrators those inflicting the hurt, and rescuers the ones who relieve or eliminate the hurt. From our view, the poor play the role of victim in the drama; an easy role for them to play because they have been oppressed, suppressed, and victimized far too often. Something plays the perpetrator, be it oppressive dictators, evil corporations, devastating natural disasters, or any other thing that creates and perpetuates poverty.

The rescuer provides relief for the suffering victim, but also, if they are really good, a way out of the victim-perpetrator cycle. Artifacts have always played a prominent role in rescues, from the silver cross that finally kills Dracula, to the silver bullets that take out werewolves, to Hermione Granger's time turning talisman of more recent vintage. These artifacts have some mystical, supernatural quality that humans don't really understand but can readily employ. A moment's reflection reveals how most of us view technology in very similar ways: powerful objects endowed with powers we don't truly understand that magically solve problems or create opportunities.

The corn grinder, cars, and the San Francisco chapel all fail the test of magical objects; they are very mundane and very real. Whether they solve the desired problems depends less on their innate qualities and more on how they work with, and within, the other capital accounts we've discussed. A more detailed look at each example illustrates these powerful interdependencies; we can see why the corn grinder failed, why a single mom's car can go either way, and why Martin Burt's new school will most likely succeed.

Failure

The corn grinder stands as a clear example of technology not making a difference. When we first saw the machine, it was gathering desert dust on the rangelands of a Navajo's expansive ranch. The obvious failure was technical: the axle on the accompanying trailer broke. An apparent suspect here was the lack of liquid capital to provide repairs. The deep cause, however, lay in the failure of the corn grinder to leverage organizational and institutional realities successfully.

As my research assistant and I saw the broken corn grinder, we listened to the NGO leader and his Navajo assistant talk about the delay and difficulty of obtaining a new grant to fix the corn grinder. They repeated this same refrain a few times during our visit; each time my assistant just looked at me and we both rolled our eyes; we saw the irony in the underlying premise of the entire endeavor. The *promise* of the corn grinder was a low-cost service to Navajo farmers. The *problem* was that they priced those services too low.

The $7 fee to grind a bushel of corn did in fact cover the gas and labor costs associated with the operation, but the $7 left no reserve to maintain or replace the assets as they wore out. My assistant and I realized that the true cost of corn grinding, including capital recovery costs and an adequate incentive for an entrepreneur to undertake the work, was somewhere close to the $21 per bushel charge for grinding corn in Winslow—a price Navajos willingly paid. The failure to price services correctly is organizational; the NGO's operating model clearly included administrative overhead as an *organizational* expense, but they never saw that repairs and maintenance count as a *project* overhead expense.

I learned the second failure of the corn grinder long after our visit. I related the story at an economic development conference on the reservation a couple of years later. A Navajo woman came up after my remarks and told me the rest of the story. She agreed with my assessment of the organizational problem, and she told me she knew of that organization; however, for her that was not the real story. The real story was one of a failure of a technology to fit within the institutional system of the Navajo.

She related that when the purchase of the corn grinder had been proposed, none of the tribal leaders favored of the idea. No one was actively opposed to the project, and no one raised a voice against the NGO's work; however, no one really saw much merit in the purchase either. The majority of Navajos farm corn as a hobby, not cash, crop. Very few farmers (I've met only a handful) produce more than a bushel of corn. Even those who grow corn for money tend to focus on corn pollen as the cash crop. Corn pollen fetches about $150/ounce for its ceremonial and religious value, while the corn itself garners far, far less. Plus, corn pollen needs no grinding.

As the last piece of the program's puzzle, the corn grinder interlocked with the NGO's internal mission and goals, but it failed to link with the other four types of capital among those served by the NGO. The grinder lacked institutional support among those who would use it, didn't meet the organizational needs and realities of Navajo farmers, and may have even run counter to social norms that welcomed a trip to Winslow to meet with others and do other business.

Failure or Success

Whether a car works as an asset or a liability for a single mom depends on how well it fits with her human and social capital stocks. The cost of ownership of a car depends greatly on knowledge of the automobile ecosystem, a system based on the total lifetime cost, including sales price, financing expenses, regular maintenance, and irregular or crisis repairs. Those who understand these costs lower their overall automobile outlays by buying the "right" (one they can afford) car in the right way. Those who plan for regular and unanticipated maintenance and repair costs create and preserve the capital (human or liquid) they'll need to keep their machine running.

Few of us, and fewer of the single mothers we met, have the knowledge (head), skill (hands), or desire (heart) to repair a car. That said, knowledge about regular maintenance such as tire rotation and oil changes can dramatically lower the lifetime cost of a car; these scheduled activities cost a little but prevent more costly, unscheduled repairs later on. If we don't have the knowledge, we have to rely on either our wallets to afford someone with the knowledge or friends or family who can help.

Social capital plays a role in the automobile ecosystem. It begins when we get recommendations from friends about good cars, and good dealers. It continues when church members, coworkers, or other colleagues inspect a potential purchase with a knowing eye. It concludes when our networks help us locate reputable mechanics, or even better help do the work themselves. Social capital can complement and extend our own knowledge and may substitute for our financial capital. The automobile and its ecosystem fit into a larger system for all of us, and single mothers in particular.

Transportation options determine the range and viability of work and school opportunities single moms can take advantage of; however, for single parents transportation pales in importance when compared with child care. Without adequate child care things like full-time work or school become monumentally difficult for single moms. Child care tends to be the decisive issue and bottleneck constraint on many opportunities for single moms. Child care very often depends on the institutional and social capital account balances.

When institutional (public initiatives such as all-day kindergarten), organizational (on-site employer-sponsored day care), or social (willing friends and family) capital accounts are well stocked, the constraint of child care disappears. When that bottleneck opens up physical capital, like having car, can become decisive in opening educational and vocational opportunities. It's easy for us, as observers of their lives, to see the criticality of the auto puzzle piece; however, we too easily overlook the other pieces the car has to fit in order for real progress to occur.

Success

The hotel at the San Francisco school represents the power of alignment between physical and other capital accounts. The hotel aligns with institutional objectives at several levels. At the national level the idea of a self-sufficient private school does not conflict with systemwide goals; it may even garner appreciation because it frees up resources for use elsewhere. Locally, the school provides education and opportunities plus positive exposure to key communities and stakeholders. Organizationally, the idea for the hotel fits with Fundacion Paraguaya's overall mission of self-reliance and economic opportunity.

The hotel also fits the business model in many ways. The hotel provides another venue where work toward the goals of revenue generation, empowerment, and capability development occurs. In the early days of the school, the microcredit arm of Fundacion Paraguaya funded the investments in and operating costs of the school; the idea of cross-subsidizing organizational units was already in place. The San Francisco hotel follows that pattern, except that now it's one unit of the school subsidizing others. The hotel, one of more than a half-dozen business units, provides 25 percent of the total revenue for the school.

The hotel aligns with Fundacion Paraguaya's, and the school's, human and social capital stocks as well. Running the hotel trains service-oriented heads and hands, but it also reinforces an entrepreneurial heart in both the students and faculty. Simply put, the hotel *leverages* and *is leveraged by* the human capital in place at the school. The success of the school, of which the hotel is a key contributor, allows Martin to take that model to his global network of social entrepreneurs, academics, executives, and public policy-makers.

The challenge for Martin lies in replicating that success with another school in the Mbaracayu and beyond: finding a piece that fits into a new puzzle. When my students discuss the success of the San Francisco school and the challenge of replicating it elsewhere, the discussion often turns to the outsized role the hotel plays at both locations. For many, the original hotel is a truly decisive element; an idiosyncratic physical asset that supports the school but, because of its physical uniqueness, difficult and expensive to replicate in the Mbaracayu preserve. Such an analysis, while highlighting a real challenge, misses a critical point.

The hotel was not the decisive resource or capital account in the success of the San Francisco school. The hotel, the school, and the capital accounts of Fundacion Paraguaya exist in a symbiotic relationship. The hotel originated from the genius and capabilities of the institutional, organizational, human, and social capital held by the foundation. For example, the reputation of the foundation (a form of social capital) enabled a purchase price well below the replacement cost of the hotel. As it succeeds, the hotel contributes back to those capital accounts and modifies them through its success. The hotel and its unique features are indeed important; however, the hotel would not be decisive, nor would it exist, without the other capital stocks.

The new school in the Mbaracayu will likely succeed, but it will prove more difficult and more expensive than its predecessor at San Francisco. This optimism stems from the fit, alignment, and positive relationship between both hotel projects and the other capital accounts of Fundacion Paraguaya. Martin should succeed for the same reason the corn grinder failed; physical capital, just like the blanket term *technology*, accelerates, as management guru Jim Collins notes.[18] Fundacion Paraguaya's other capital accounts provide a strong foundation for success and give efforts clear direction; physical capital just accelerates movement along that path.

These examples build on a firm, yet simple theory of physical capital and technology as both social and mechanical elements that, once implemented, become a part of a living, complex whole. They represent the pieces of the puzzle of poverty elimination. In the next section we'll consider some implications of this simple theory for your organization and its work.

MAKING PHYSICAL CAPITAL EFFECTIVE
IN POVERTY ALLEVIATION

At one level physical capital represents the condition of self-reliance. At a deeper level, however, physical capital contributes to the dual benefits of self-reliance, bouncing back and bounding forward. Physical capital may or may not help us bounce back from a negative shock. Houses, cars, and tools and equipment contribute to bouncing back when they allow us to be productive. However, when large houses, cars, tools, or other equipment consume our resources—as they do when they engender indebtedness—then they hinder our ability to bounce back in crisis. Sometimes the peril of indebtedness even increases the speed of our downward spiral. Debt derails our deliverance from adversity.

Similarly, physical capital can help us bound forward; think of the role that a car plays for a single mom going to school. Other physical and liquid assets play similar roles; housing provides a stable platform, savings the means to pay for schooling or other improvement, and so forth. Just as with bounding back, however, excessive physical capital can impede our bounding forward, primarily by reducing our willingness and desire to move forward. A focus on consumption-centric physical capital easily distracts us from the need to move forward and destroys our motivation to engage in the hard work of personal development.

Physical capital matters, but only the right types of physical capital engender self-reliance and help people exit little p poverty. Your organization and programs should consider the following items.

Good puzzles are ones where all the pieces fit. Cooking is a universal need, and poor stoves are a common problem throughout the developing world, as we saw in Chapter 6. Solar stoves have long been seen as a rescuer: a clean technology that would cook villagers' food while preserving their health and local forests.[19] Why hasn't this win-win-win device caught on worldwide? First and foremost because solar-powered stoves, a real engineering marvel, don't mesh well with the institutional, organizational, and social capital stocks among those who need them most. Solar stoves work only in the middle of the day, not when people *actually* cook.

People cook in the morning, often before dawn, and the evening, often after dusk. We cook in the early morning and evening for several reasons.

Traditional patterns of community and family life are probably the main ones, but having to work outside the home during the sunlight hours may be just as common. The sun generates heat; cooking during the heat of the day becomes oppressive in its own right, and few of us enjoy eating during that time. The problem should be apparent by now: the sun isn't up when most people want to use the device.

Making solar stoves valuable in villages and towns introduces at least two complexities. The stove needs to get hot to cook—200°C (almost 400°F), and, if people cook when the sun's not up, the unit must be able to store sufficient heat for use later. Getting a stove hot enough adds cost and complexity, but the heat storage problem has proven particularly vexing. The stoves aren't traditional solar-panel collectors that generate enough charge for a battery, so engineering teams have been looking at using solar energy to heat complex combinations of water, sand, and different plant husks.

Cooking with solar stoves would be much easier if the societies would change their patterns of life! Solar stoves or any other physical capital-based solution to poverty will gain widespread use when the technology fits, like a piece of a puzzle, with the other types of capital that generate and permeate poor communities. Kudos to Climate Healers, the nonprofit working to redesign the stoves, for recognizing that technologies alleviate poverty only when they prove consistent with, or only mildly disruptive to, the complex patterns of life found in real families and communities.[20]

New capital replaces old capital! Technologies always displace other technologies, but they also displace and change other types of capital as well. The new puzzle piece never fits exactly—it's not supposed to—and so the other pieces have to change as well. An instructive legend from Africa illustrates how this happens. Well-meaning development specialists watched people walk several miles round trip to haul water from the nearest source; either individuals (usually women) gathered their own, or commercial water vendors would gather water for a price.[21] Turns out lots of people paid for their water, and being a water merchant was good work.

Saving all that wasted time and money carrying water entailed digging wells to tap an aquifer that lay near the village. New pipes and well heads completed the installation, and the installers departed pleased with how much time and money they'd saved the villagers; accessible drinking water is a very worthy goal. The villagers enjoyed water delivered to their homes, and the water merchants either left in search of other parched communities or took other jobs. Everything went well until the well heads broke; these were, of course, high-tech well heads that weren't supposed to break.

Now the villagers had no easily accessible water. They knew how to deal with that situation: either gather water themselves or pay the commercial haulers. Except that the merchants were gone. So the villagers all hauled their own water until a new market developed for commercial water hauling. The legend should not engender pity toward the villagers or the water merchants; the story helps us realize that the wells altered the local economy in ways that became quite disruptive when the wells no longer worked.

A fundamental principle of economics holds that when prices go up, consumers lose but producers win. An economy, when it works well, acts as a wonderfully balanced system. In closed economies, like rural villages that don't generate much trade with outside communities, one man's gain is another's loss. An easy and cheap supply of water comes at the expense of thriving merchants willing to haul water. Effective use of technology doesn't mean don't install the wells, it tells us to think about the economic displacement the new intervention will initiate.

Displacements can be social as well as economic. In one Navajo community a church runs a model farm to encourage Navajos to engage in agriculture. The farm produces corn, beans, onions, tomatoes, squash, and a host of other great vegetables. The church usually gets retired *bilagáana* farmers to come and run the model farm. They run it like they know how: with fertilizers to provide nutrients in the highly alkali desert sand, and copious amounts of water in either sprinklers or drip irrigation systems.

Many Navajos use the church's farm as a model, but many do not. Traditional Navajo farming, the way they learned to farm from their parents, grandparents, and relatives far into the past, eschews processed chemical fertilizers, irrigation, and many techniques that markedly increase crop yields. Navajos dry farm, planting their crops in low lands where rain and groundwater collect, and irrigate maybe once a year during the spring runoff when water is plentiful. Adopting *bilagáana* farming techniques would almost certainly increase farm yields, but at the cost of traditional farming practices.

This isn't just some knee-jerk reaction to new technology: farming and the corn it produces play a primary role in traditional Navajo religious beliefs; most Navajos growing corn do it for the pollen to use in ceremonies.[22] Farming with processed fertilizers and more intensive irrigation would provide some economic gains—gains more than offset, for many, by the threats to the theological and social fabric of the nation. Navajo elders look with a wary eye at new farming techniques and technologies not because they don't want to grow food but because they fear the displacement of their culture and values that these technologies invite.

As you design programs, there's more here than just a call to be culturally sensitive. Drawing on a metaphor from Chapter 2, be very careful about "counting the cost" of your technological intervention. Design reviews and planning processes need to encourage a consideration of how physical capital may affect people tomorrow, not merely the advantages of implementing it today. Project reviews, much like the approval process for new drugs, should be sensitive to unexpected outcomes and developments.

CONCLUSION

Physical capital, or technology, plays a role in helping people out of poverty. In fact it plays a vital and important role; what it never plays, however, is a decisive one. Iron Mad Wilkinson's ability to bore precise holes in cylinders of cast iron certainly helped James Watt craft an efficient steam engine; it accelerated the advance of the double condenser. Watt's invention, design, and the unique piping and valve system that made the double condensing engine work were decisive; a perfectly cylindrical fit for the piston in the cylinder maximized the energy produced by the engine. Technology accelerates.

So it is with the other manifestations of physical capital we've dealt with in this chapter. We've focused mostly on solid capital, but liquid capital behaves in very similar ways. Early microcredit programs targeted women because lending to men tended to subsidize their drinking habits. Whether the poor transform or transact their way out of poverty, the decisive elements in that process will be found in their stocks of institutional, social, human, and organizational capital. The physical and financial resources and tools at their disposal will help greatly in this process; however, the stock of physical capital rarely, almost never, atones for deficits in the other capital accounts.

This chapter concludes our discussion of the five types of capital and part one of the book. Each chapter has concluded with some implications for building the types of organizations and programs that can leverage each capital account in the fight against poverty. Part two of the book focuses more on building those organizations.

The next three chapters take up very practical and detailed issues that will determine your performance. Remember that it will take upward of a decade to see real progress in some areas. Chapter 8 argues that a strong mission and vision will give you that sustainable focus. Fighting poverty requires attention to each of the five types of capital, a very tall order and one best done in concert with others. Chapter 9 outlines the systemic nature of poverty and how you can create effective alliances to fight it. Chapter 10 takes up the issue of measurement. How will you know if you've succeeded? Winning the fight and really eliminating poverty means that we have to be able to measure our results. The five capital accounts are the means to fight little p poverty, but what is the end goal? Chapter 11 concludes the book by considering this important question.

PART II

CREATING EFFECTIVE ORGANIZATIONS

CHAPTER EIGHT

MISSION AND VISION

Leading the Fight with Values

Management is efficiency in climbing the ladder of success; leadership determines whether the ladder is leaning against the right wall. . . . If the ladder is not leaning against the right wall, every step we take just gets us to the wrong place faster.

—*Stephen R. Covey*

JAMES WATT FIRST VISITED Matthew Boulton's Soho works in 1767 with Dr. William Small, friend to both men. The Soho impressed Watt; however, Boulton had been away on business and the first meeting of the men took place in the late summer of 1768. Watt was in transit from London to Glasgow, having just secured the patent on his new steam engine concept. Watt spent two weeks at Soho and "the two men took an immediate liking for one another, Boulton recognizing that Watt's diffidence concealed a keen intelligence in need of encouragement, whilst Watt marveled at the organization, skill and ingenuity displayed at Soho and the beautiful work done there."[1]

Watt returned to Glasgow to continue work on the engine but maintained an active correspondence with Boulton. On 7 February 1769 he received the following from his new friend (italics added):

Dear Watt

By this time I dare say you have fully concluded that I am a very queer fellow, I having never answered your friendly letter of the 20th October nor your last of the 12th December—in truth 'tis a shame, and I ask you ten thousand pardons, . . .

I note what you say in respect to your connection with Dr. Roebuck from whom I received a letter dated the 12th of December offering me a

share of his property in your Engine as far as respects the counties of War-
wick, Stafford, and Derby; I am obliged to you and him for thinking of
me as a partner in any degree *but the plan proposed to me is so very different
from that which I had conceived at the time I talked with you* upon that subject that I cannot think it a proper one for me to meddle with, as I do not
intend turning Engineer. I was excited by two motives to offer you my assistance which were *love of you* and *love of a money-getting ingenious project.*
. . . to produce the most profit, my idea was to settle a manufactory near
my own by the side of our Canal, where I would erect all the conveniences
necessary for the completion of Engines and from which Manufactory *We
would serve all the World with Engines of all sizes;* . . .

It would not be worth my while to make for three Counties only, but
I find it very well worthwhile to make for all the World. What led me to
drop the hint I did to you was the possessing an idea that you wanted a
midwife to ease you of your burthen, and *to introduce your brat into the
world* . . .

Your affectionate
humble Servant
MATTHEW BOULTON[2]

Mathew did not lack for vision, and within a few short years the firm of
Boulton & Watt began to serve "all the world" of the English manufacturing.
Such a grand vision proved vital to bringing Watt's "brat" into the world, and
without Boulton's vision the potential of rotary motion might have remained
a pipe dream for another generation. Only in the last decade of the century
did the firm realize the "money-getting" part outlined in the letter. Boulton's
vision and values supplied the energy and focus that helped the partners acquire, husband, leverage, and preserve their own capital stocks. The vision of
engines for "all the world" kept the pair going through the decades of development and formed the core of the strategy for the venture we know as Boulton
& Watt.

Part I of the book introduced you to the power of the five types of capital and a nuanced understanding that should guide your efforts to eliminate
little p poverty. Part II builds from the foundational assumption that the fight
against poverty is at its heart an organizational one. We *know* how to create and sustain organizations that can win this war. Part II details some best

practices so that you can build an organization capable of helping individuals move from poverty to prosperity.

Watt's vision of the double condenser enlightened his work, and Boulton's vision of making "engines for all the world" enabled a true industrial revolution. We'd have a hard time separating Boulton's vision from his core values—a love of others, in this case Watt, and a love of money, business, and commerce; values and missions go together hand in hand. Successful organization begins with mission. This chapter takes up the importance of mission in creating organizations that not only alleviate but also truly eliminate poverty. We'll consider the vital role values play in the fight against poverty, provide a framework for understanding what constitutes a good mission, and discuss the role of a mission in more practical terms.

THE IMPORTANCE OF MISSION

People often use the terms *mission*, *vision*, and *values* interchangeably, which results in confusion. Look again at Boulton's letter to Watt. His desire to "serve all the world with engines of all sizes" may be seen as a vision of the future—a world full of steam engines—or a mission—to build an organization that would serve the entire world by bringing these engines to market. I view mission and vision as essentially the same thing, and I'll use those terms interchangeably throughout this chapter.

Boulton's vision rested on two values: a love of Watt (friendship) and a love of money-getting projects (profit). Friendship, love, or sympathy for others stood as a signal moral virtue in eighteenth-century England. Benevolence, mutual affection, and kindness represented the moral glue that held the good society together for none other than Adam Smith.[3] Money-getting, profit, or gain represent similarly strong moral values; Smith recognized that the self-interest of the butcher or baker resulted in a better society.[4] Boulton's vision, one that would truly change the world, illustrates the subtle interplay between values and vision.

Strong missions build upon well-articulated values. The sustainability of your vision rests on the strength of your values; real commitments to principles matter more than flowery descriptions of possibilities. Mission, vision, and the values that undergird them provide your organization three essential tools, described below.

Values as a compass. Values help you navigate the moral spaces that envelop those in poverty. Poverty is, at its root, a moral not a practical problem. Poverty, deprivation, or the absence of opportunity certainly creates pragmatic hardship in terms of blight and human outcomes such as sickness and suffering. Poverty, at its core, however, represents a deeper dearth—a dearth of human dignity and justice; it disables people's ability to reach their full potential, a disability neither earned nor equitable.

The denial of justice to the poor may originate in familial, group, or larger cultural norms, power structures that elevate some while oppressing others, or moral evaluations of outside circumstances (from natural disasters to genetic disabilities). Poverty survives because injustice claims the false status of a moral good; the arrival of justice—explicit or implicit—in your work collides with injustice and that contact produces conflict. The fight against poverty takes place in two spheres, the practical and the moral, the secular and the sacred.

We resolve practical conflicts through processes of consensus or compromise; however, the moral conflicts of justice do not yield to Solomon-like splits that accommodate competing visions. Justice and morality represent hard, unyielding walls that require clever, measured, and patient work to scale or penetrate. Resolution happens at the level of values and principles, not tactics or strategies. Knowing your own values prepares you to deal with these difficult conflicts; your values help unearth potential landmines and clarify sometimes obscure opportunities for convergence.

The core message of both Chapters 3 and 5 centers on the role of moral maps (cognitive social institutions) and mental models (individual attitudes) that build on very basic and fundamental notions of right and wrong held by the groups you serve. The invitation to change deeply held values carries a danger of reprisals, such as physical violence or expulsion from neighborhoods or countries, and smacks of a "Western" moral imperialism. Understanding your own values—the reasons why you do what you do—helps to blunt these negative aspects of your work. Finding common core values with those you serve provides you with a healing salve to assuage those who see your work as dangerous and a powerful antidote to impose imperialistic solutions to their problems.

Mission as a map. Once you understand why you want to eliminate poverty and identify your core values, you can focus on the where, what, how, and when that a strong mission statement captures. Diversions and distractions can easily derail your quest to eliminate poverty; poverty exists safely ensconced within the social systems that spawn it and spans social sectors and problems, from education and illiteracy to religion and intolerance. Each societal touch point represents an opportunity for effort, or a distraction that dissipates your energy. Mission allows you to optimize your efforts in a few areas rather than satisfice in many.[5]

The entrenched poverty we fight, both Big P and little p, bridges generations, usually becoming more obstinate with each turn of the generational wheel. The abstract cultural milieu of poverty, as well as very real grandparents, parents, aunts, and uncles all play the role of crabs in the bucket I described in Chapter 4. The path from poverty to prosperity involves a long-term journey for your clients as they abandon sedimented mindsets and family or community values. Changing deeply engrained behaviors takes time and may ultimately require a generation to become sustainable.

Being involved for the long term requires both strong grounding values and a clear mission. Missions help organizations persist when the going gets tough—because it takes a clear sense of direction for the tough to get going. You can persist only toward a clear and meaningful goal; otherwise you will merely subsist until you run out of resources. Mission also drives and directs the resource allocation process, both inbound and outbound. Values and vision enable effective pitches to donors, but, more important, they help constrain and channel revenue generating activities toward ultimate ends.

Mission consistency acts as a powerful filter during program design and development, budgeting processes, implementation, and eventually evaluation. Programs designed to last a decade need more than an annual budget review; they require a set of clear interim milestones to measure progress toward the future state defined by the mission. Just as going on a long hike without a good map invites folly and failure, so does engaging the war on poverty without a clear and sustainable long-term vision.

Vision as a set of binoculars. A well-developed vision helps you see the people you work with clearly. In Chapter 9 I'll take up the topic of seeing your partners, but here I want to focus on your associates (or employees) and clients. Let's consider the latter first. We can become deeply involved in the lives of those we hope to help, sometimes beyond the point where we actually help. This is due to the complexity of the problems we tackle, but quite often it results from the actions, mostly inaction, of our clients. Vision helps us remember our most valued goals and can tell us when our clients need to move on. Simply put, our vision tells us when to stop working with some people and start working with others.

In terms of our associates, a strong vision helps balance conversion to the mission with the competence needed to realize it. Our passion for our work leads us to seek out and hire those with similar values and commitments. That is good. Unfortunately, hiring on passion proves problematic when we hire those who share our beliefs but can't enhance our organization's ability to fulfill the mission. It helps to employ a CFO who believes deeply in the cause; it helps more to engage one who knows the rules of accounting, can track our financial position, and work well with others in the financial world. Belief in the mission matters; the possession of competencies that help realize that mission matter more.

THE ELEMENTS OF A SUCCESSFUL MISSION

Humorist Dave Barry captures what many of us feel when he concludes that a mission statement is just a "slab of words" that diverts attention from the fact that most organizations accomplish little of value.[6] Dilbert creator Scott Adams once helped develop a mission statement for the Logitech Corporation—one of the world's largest makers of computer mice at the time. With the addition of some strategically placed buzzwords he turned what could have been a useful guide to the company moving into a new business segment into a jumbled, jargon-rich sentence with no meaning.[7]

Most of us who have lived and worked in organizations have seen a mission statement and we have an intuitive feel for what one should be. If we've founded an organization, or been around at one's founding, we likely helped develop the mission statement. For those of us who work in one place long enough, we've probably seen or taken part in the development of a new mission. This will be particularly true when we've lived through changes in executive teams. Few of us could articulate our organization's mission if our lives depended on it, and so we laugh with Dave Barry and Scott Adams; they seem to capture something real about the value of mission statements.

Cynicism aside, however, the premise of a mission, vision, or values statement is quite sound: an organization will perform better when it articulates its core and enduring purpose. Organizations are groups of people and bound up in, defined by, and working toward, a set of common goals. The mission statement articulates those goals and aspirations. As we'll see below, a good mission answers three fundamental questions about the organization.

The Elements of a Mission Statement

Mission statements go by other names as well: company visions, vision statements, and mission, vision, and values being the most common synonyms. Whatever the moniker, this phrase, sentence, paragraph, or passage communicates the biggest issues of the organization; issues of identity, purpose, shared values, and superordinate goals. Superordinate goals are those broad objectives around which internal and external stakeholders can coalesce and shared values, the common priorities and principles that bind members together.[8]

When done poorly a mission will functionally be little more than Dave Barry's "slab of words," but when done well a mission, and the strategies it gives rise to, can permeate an organization and give direction and meaning to day-to-day activities. The difference between a jumble of jargon and an artfully crafted credo lies in attention to the structure of the statement. Good missions answer three fundamental questions: What business (activities) do we engage in? What goals and objectives drive our actions? And what values and principles guide our decisions?[9]

Business definition. Defining the business begins by identifying the organization's key stakeholders; the people or groups served such as clients or customers, and those who enable the work such as suppliers, owners, donors, etc. Which needs of those stakeholders do you aim to meet? Good organizations focus their efforts and realize they can't meet all customer needs; meeting too many needs quickly outstrips resources and diminishes effectiveness. A clear mission helps avoid attempting to do too much. The mission should also address how these needs will be met. Consider the following two missions from for-profit FedEx and non-profit Catholic Relief Services:

> FedEx will produce superior financial returns for shareowners by providing high value-added supply chain, transportation, business and related information services through focused operating companies. Customer requirements will be met in the highest quality manner appropriate to each market segment served. FedEx will strive to develop mutually rewarding relationships with its employees, partners and suppliers. Safety will be the

first consideration in all operations. Corporate activities will be conducted to the highest ethical and professional standards.[10]

Catholic Relief Services carries out the commitment of the Bishops of the United States to assist the poor and vulnerable overseas. We are motivated by the Gospel of Jesus Christ to cherish, preserve and uphold the sacredness and dignity of all human life, foster charity and justice, and embody Catholic social and moral teaching as we act to:

- Promote human development by responding to major emergencies, fighting disease and poverty, and nurturing peaceful and just societies; and
- Serve Catholics in the United States as they live their faith in solidarity with their brothers and sisters around the world.

As part of the universal mission of the Catholic Church, we work with local, national and international Catholic institutions and structures, as well as other organizations, to assist people on the basis of need, not creed, race or nationality.[11]

FedEx identifies its key stakeholders as shareholders, customers, employees, partners, and suppliers, and their order in the mission appears to rank these in order of importance. Shareholders want, and will get, financial returns, customers their packages moved and tracked, and employees rewarding relationships. FedEx articulates three facets of how those needs will be met: They *safely* and *ethically move* stuff.

Catholic Relief Services (CRS), by contrast, calls out three stakeholders as central for them, the U.S. bishops, the "poor and vulnerable overseas," and lay U.S. Catholics. Unlike FedEx, it's harder to see a clear rank ordering among these groups. CRS identifies five major needs they hope to meet: disaster relief, disease, poverty, injustice, and solidarity between the prosperous and poor. They do their work in concert with networks of national and international, Catholic and non-Catholic organizations; they also promise nondiscrimination among the poor they serve.

Superordinate goals. A mission also defines goals and objectives the organization hopes to accomplish and ways to measure success. These are superordinate goals. When we've done our work, how will our stakeholders' lives be different? How will we know? At FedEx customers will get their packages through the *highest quality* services, shareholders should receive *superior* returns, and employees *mutually rewarding* relationships. The extent to which these subjective goals become objectified through processes and specific measures determines how meaningful FedEx's mission may be to its stakeholders.

CRS, consistent with its expansive group of primary stakeholders, lists as its major objectives two very broad superordinate goals: to uphold the *sacredness and dignity of human life* and to *promote human development*. When they have done their work, the poor should have a sense of their dignity and divine heritage, but they should also be developed in some way. That's a tall order for CRS and, as we'll see in Chapter 10, creating measures that capture human development, or some important aspect of it, will prove critical to the CRS mission.

Shared values. The final element of a good mission is a clear sense of values and priorities that ground all we do. Values delineate our priorities; our values tell us what we prefer. While values can have clearly moral components such as honesty, integrity, respect, justice, or love, they may also be quite pragmatic. Whether we prefer to hire from without or within, or whether we plan for the long term or the short term are also expressions of our values.[12] Values play a decisive role in a mission statement, as they should inform choices among competing alternatives, and perhaps most important, when to say no.

FedEx's core moral shared value comes straight from the first phrase: shareholder capitalism. With shareholder wealth as the top priority, FedEx expresses its solidarity with a vision of corporations and business where social welfare and economic profit are linked; maximizing the latter maximizes the former as well.[13] This value arches over other company values, given its primacy in the mission. FedEx has a statement that lays out other core values:

- People: We value our people and promote diversity in our workplace and in our thinking.
- Service: Our absolutely, positively spirit puts our customers at the heart of everything we do.
- Innovation: We invent and inspire the services and technologies that improve the way we work and live.
- Integrity: We manage our operations, finances and services with honesty, efficiency and reliability.
- Responsibility: We champion safe and healthy environments for the communities in which we live and work.

- Loyalty: We earn the respect and confidence of our FedEx people, customers and investors every day, in everything we do.[14]

We see here a mix of moral and pragmatic values. Promoting diversity, the championing of safe and healthy environments, and a commitment to honesty each have a clear moral component built on a foundational respect for human beings. Other values speak to purely pragmatic concerns such as inventing and inspiring technologies, working efficiently and reliably, and gaining the confidence of stakeholders.

CRS grounds its values in what Catholics understand as the Gospel of Jesus Christ and its call to action. New Testament teachings about the role of charity lie at the root of CRS; when Catholics stand in solidarity with and serve the poor they serve their Lord (Matt. 25: 25–40). CRS, like FedEx, appends the mission to specify some guiding principles:

Sacredness and Dignity of the Human Person

Created in the image of God, all human life is sacred and possesses a dignity that comes directly from our creation and not from any action of our own.

Rights and Responsibilities

Every person has basic rights and responsibilities that flow from our human dignity and that belong to us as human beings regardless of any social or political structures. The rights are numerous and include those things that make life truly human. Corresponding to our rights are duties and responsibilities to respect the rights of others and to work for the common good of all.

Social Nature of Humanity

All of us are social by nature and are called to live in community with others—our full human potential isn't realized in solitude, but in community with others. How we organize our families, societies and communities directly affects human dignity and our ability to achieve our full human potential.

The Common Good

In order for all of us to have an opportunity to grow and develop fully, a certain social fabric must exist within society. This is the common good. Numerous social conditions—economic, political, material and cultural—impact our ability to realize our human dignity and reach our full potential.

Subsidiarity

A higher level of government—or organization—should not perform any function or duty that can be handled more effectively at a lower level by people who are closer to the problem and have a better understanding of the issue.

Solidarity

We are all part of one human family—whatever our national, racial, religious, economic or ideological differences—and in an increasingly interconnected world, loving our neighbor has global dimensions.

Option for the Poor

In every economic, political and social decision, a weighted concern must be given to the needs of the poorest and most vulnerable. When we do this we strengthen the entire community, because the powerlessness of any member wounds the rest of society.

Stewardship

There is inherent integrity to all of creation and it requires careful stewardship of all our resources, ensuring that we use and distribute them justly and equitably—as well as planning for future generations.[15]

Each of these values has a rich history in Catholic traditions and concern for social justice; theology perfumes both the mission and values. As a religious organization CRS believes that adherence to the core moral tenets of Roman Catholicism provides ample guidance for pragmatic, day to day action. The explicit values of Roman Catholic doctrine also provide a set of boundaries for potential action by CRS.

Psychologists of all stripes use the Diagnostic and Statistical Manual IV (DSM-IV) to assess mental illnesses. Positive psychology pioneers Christopher Peterson and Martin Seligman sought to create a rigorous and defensible categorization of character traits and virtues. Table 8.1 presents a cafeteria-style list of these virtues and traits for you to consider as you articulate your values and vision. Work on little p poverty focuses either on individuals or the proximal communities in which they live, so I've arranged the table to illustrate this.

TABLE 8.1. A Typology of Virtues

Individualistic ◀—					—▶ Collectivistic
Courage	Temperance	Wisdom	Humanity	Transcendence	Justice
Deal with opposition	Balance and harmony	Use of knowledge	Foster relationships	Meaning & Purpose	Healthy communities
• Bravery	• Forgiveness	• Creativity	• Love others	• Gratitude	• Loyalty/duty
• Persistence	• Prudence	• Curiosity	• Accept love	• Admire beauty	• Fairness
• Integrity	• Self-control	• Perspective	• Kindness	• Hope	• Leadership

Source: Virtues and character strengths taken from Christopher Peterson and Martin E. P. Seligman, *Character Strengths and Virtues : A Handbook and Classification* (Oxford University Press, 2004).

Dave Barry or Scott Adams may look at the FedEx mission as a cover for a corporation trying to make as much money as possible, or see in CRS such lofty hopes that they are sure to end in disappointment. Both missions work to balance a description of the organization with some lofty aspirations for performance. Description connects the mission to reality, grants legitimacy, and helps prevent cynicism; aspiration provides members with meaning and motivation to continually improve. That's one purpose of a mission, but there are others as we'll see below.

THE ROLE OF MISSION/VISION

A well-developed mission defines, as management guru Stephen Covey noted, the "wall" of our success and each step on the ladder. A solid business definition, statement of superordinate goals, and declaration of values serve three purposes for leaders and their organizations. They *communicate* to all stakeholders what the organization does, where it's going, and a fundamental sense of identity, or how the organization answers the question of who we are. Missions *motivate* long-term commitments by various stakeholder groups, and they offer a way to *evaluate* potential courses of action.

Communication and motivation. We'll discuss these together because in practice the first begets the second; the more clearly we communicate, the deeper and more solid the motivation. A well-crafted mission is *consightful*—it speaks concisely but insightfully. Potential stakeholders can quickly and clearly choose whether they want to interact with us; whether they buy off on the mission—to use a catchphrase. They'll get a realistic sense of *what* we do and *whether* that's consistent with their own models. Is it value adding for them to get involved with us?

Our mission should tell others *why* we do *what* we do and *how* we think about successful outcomes. Clear objectives provide an honest look at our purposes and motivations. Stakeholders can stack this against their own superordinate goals to look for fit; commitment proves superficial at best when we engage in activities for different reasons. Finally, our mission writ large should give potential participants an accurate sense of our identity or constitution, a set of principles we won't violate as we act. The commitment level of various stakeholders will correlate with the number of mission elements they agree with. Clear communication begets sincere and sustainable motivation.

Evaluation. Bain and Company is a hard-nosed and fact-driven strategy consulting firm. Their most recent study of effective management practices indicated that mission statements rank as the third most popular management tool in their kit. In fact, of their top ten strategy tools, mission statements had the *highest consistent* rank of any tool over the eighteen years that Bain has done the survey.[16] Why does a tool so pilloried by humorists continue to be so well liked and used by executives? I believe the answer lies in the role of missions in evaluating potential courses of action. Missions help us decide what to do, and what not to do.

In late September 1982 tragedy struck Chicago. A twenty-seven-year old man died unexpectedly; two of his relatives, shocked at his death, took some Tylenol in the house to relieve their headaches and died shortly thereafter. During the next few days four others would die in the area from cyanide-laced Tylenol.[17] The product led the nation in market share, with a 35 percent share, and made up about 15 percent of its parent company Johnson and Johnson's profits. The threat became clear almost immediately, as J&J's shares lost $1 billion in value when the giant brand was identified as the culprit.[18]

CEO James Burke had to decide how to respond. Marketers wanted to limit the damage to the brand, and the lawyers encouraged a strategy to minimize legal liability. Each position argued for a small-scale response. Burke turned to an internal document known as the Credo for guidance. Penned in 1943 by then CEO Robert Wood Johnson, the Credo stood as J&J's expression of its core mission and values.[19] The first line identifies J&J's primary stakeholders, goals, and values, and reads, "[We] believe our first responsibility is to the doctors, nurses, and patients, to mothers and fathers and all others who use our products and services." Burke found in those few words the guidance he longed for; the mission provided a clear set of criteria to evaluate what to do.

Burke ordered a large-scale response: the recall of all 31 *million* bottles of Tylenol on the market at a cost of $100 million. Market share plummeted to 8 percent. That was the immediate action, but Burke didn't stop there; company engineers and managers worked to design the first triple-tamper-resistant packaging for over the counter drugs. The product established the benchmark for packaging safety. By the spring of 1983 the product regained its leading position in the market. Missions matter when the stakes are high and the way forward may not be clear.

A good mission statement helps us make important decisions through the same three core mission elements. When faced with decisions about how to proceed we need to ask ourselves, How will this decision fit with what we do and the activities we are currently in? J&J didn't just sell drugs or make profits; they saw their core business as helping people. A good mission cuts to the chase and helps us calibrate forward motion consistent with our true value-creating activities. Missions help us avoid drift by keeping us focused on the right *What*.

Is the decision consistent with our goals and objectives? How will different directions influence our superordinate goals? J&J's primary goal was to be a responsible, trusted partner in health care. Options that appeared to avoid responsibility or weaken trust among customers could be easily identified and filtered out. An old saying tells us, When you're waist deep in alligators, it's hard to remember your original purpose was to clear the swamp. A mission with well-articulated goals helps us avoid many of those alligators and lets us step back and gain better perspective. Missions center our gaze on the right *Why*.

Identity and core values provide a final filter to sift different options. Which course of action is consistent with who we are? Where does it complement, and where contradict, our deepest principles and values? Responsibility to doctors, nurses, and parents gets priority in the Credo, shareholders come last, with the stipulation that they'll receive a "fair return" on their investment. Burke's recall of 31 million bottles rang true to who J&J was, and the event reinforced (structurated) J&J's identity for a generation. Missions remind us of the right *Who*.

James Burke and J&J provide an excellent example of how missions help with short-term, bet-the-company type crises. What does the example say to social innovators and entrepreneurs fighting poverty? Plenty! Individuals and organizations fighting poverty face relentless pressures to drift from their missions; that's why making that mission clear and articulate proves to be so valuable. Your mission must work like the Credo because it helps you avoid the diversions we spoke of earlier.

Clients, partners, or other stakeholders push or pull us to increase the scale and scope of activities. Donors or paying clients feel free to suggest (coerce?) the organization into expanding the operation. These have a flavor of the month feel to them, except that the pressure comes every month. Focusing on the original superordinate goals gets really hard when we've lost count of how many alligators are in the pond. Abandoning these leads to death by drift; without a clear sense of *why* we have no reason to say no to any *what*.

Finally, and perhaps most tragically, our identity moves from something core, central, and enduring to being epiphenomenal and a fundamental order gets reversed.[20] Who we are becomes secondary rather than primary, and what we do drives who we are. We climb the ladder of success only to find it's leaning against the wrong wall. Missions make sure that walls come before ladders; *who* drives *why*, which determines *what*.

CONCLUSION

Matthew Boulton outlined his vision for the steam engine in one prescient letter written in 1769. His vision resonated with Watt, who worked to bring Boulton into the partnership from the receipt of that letter until they joined forces four years later. Boulton's expansive vision defined the business—to "serve all the world" with steam engines, and he articulated the goals and values of eighteenth-century England—the "love of a money-getting ingenious project." The vision ultimately led Boulton and Watt to develop the rotary engine and change "all the world."

Having a vision isn't enough, however, to create lasting and meaningful change. In the case of the steam engine Boulton and Watt tapped into, and helped create, the emerging ecosystem that was British industry in the eighteenth century. Our work to eliminate poverty requires similar acumen. Vision provides the foundation; the edifice of our work requires serious day-to-day effort. But we can't do it alone. Little p poverty represents an ecosystem; we have to partner with others to provide a systemic response. Systems and partnerships are the topic of the next chapter.

CHAPTER NINE

ECOSYSTEMS OF DEVELOPMENT

Systems to Fight a System

Omwana takulila nju emoi—A child does not grow up only in a single
home.

—Banyoro proverb[1]

WATT REFERRED TO his new contraption as his brat, and Boulton's letter of 1769
acknowledged that Watt sought an economic midwife to bring his "brat into
the world."[2] As with all innovations and inventions, Watt's machine behaved
like a temperamental child; it worked when it wanted to, erupted when things
went wrong, and forced its parent to learn and develop new ways of thinking
and acting. Watt and Boulton were the steam engine's rightful parents; without Watt the engine would not have been conceived nor born, and Boulton's
financial and organizational mastery nurtured the machine's growth and development into the engine of industrialization.

While the intellectual and financial lineage of the steam engine appears
a settled matter, Watt's machine embodies the Banyoro proverb above, as it
had many homes, many uncles and neighbors that played pivotal roles in the
machine's childhood. Glasgow provided the foundation; from the university's
labs to the college green where the key conceptual advances occurred. The nascent machine could call London home as well; without the royal patent the
engine never would have survived infancy. A commercially viable engine hails
from Birmingham and Boulton's Soho works, and its apprenticeship filled in
nearby Coalbrookdale and the further coal producing region of Cornwall.

The uncles who helped develop and grow the invention create an impressive list of the finest minds of eighteenth-century England. Some would be
counted in Watt's stock of social capital, and we've met many of them in
Chapter 2. Joseph Black, the leading authority on the principles of latent heat,

played a pivotal technical role; Dr. William Small, physician and friend of Black, provided emotional and economic support through access to his friend, industrialist John Roebuck.[3]

Others lay outside the social capital account and were purely professional interactions. The crazy uncle Iron Mad Wilkinson, Chapter 7's main character, configured the boiler so that the young engine could realize its full potential, as well as the testy William Murdock, with whom Watt designed the sun and planet gear. Murdock, a Scot like Watt, brought an inventive mind and sharp mechanical skills to Boulton & Watt; although he often clashed with Watt, the partnership paid off as Watt enlisted Murdock to help design and build the sun and planet system so critical to the rotary engine.[4]

The circle extends outward, to distant associates such as Joseph Priestley, the minister and fellow Lunar Society member who preached the moral worth of invention, innovation, scientific investigation, and economic progress. We can't forget Watt's contemporary at Glasgow, Adam Smith, whose writings echoed Priestley's teachings but for a more secular audience.[5] The steam engine also owes its existence to the kindness of strangers, from the MPs (members of Parliament) who accepted Watt's original (and later revised) calls for patent protection to the craftsman at Soho who precisely manufactured the delicate value-added guts of the young engine, which consisted of a set of intricate valves and tubes.

Watt fathered the engine and Boulton acted as midwife. Yet in a larger sociological sense the invention was an offspring of the ecosystem of the British Enlightenment. The machine was a creation of the mix of scientific inquiry and economic innovation that characterized the spirit of the times, as we discussed in Chapter 3. Watt's engine, in no small way, owes its heritage to the entire system of government, business, and theology that characterized eighteenth-century England. This chapter focuses on the importance of systems in fighting and defeating little p poverty.

Poverty is a system, and fighting it requires the systemic response; one part of which is to employ the system typified by the five types of capital. Another element of our response entails creating and maintaining effective ecosystems, sets of partnering organizations and individuals that can accomplish more as a collective whole than acting on their own. Creating effective partnerships takes more than just a desire to do so, and the chapter focuses on tangible steps to create effective ones. We begin, however, with a short primer on the nature of systems so we can understand how to create our own ecosystem to fight little p poverty.

SYSTEMS: A PRIMER

Dietrich Dörner directed the institute for theoretical psychology at Germany's Otto-Friedrich University and won many prizes for his work in systems analysis. His classic book, *The Logic of Failure*, describes a simulation Dörner ran to teach people about systems and their complexity.[6] The simulation centers on the fight against poverty among the Moros, a fictitious tribe of desert-dwelling West Africans, and their cattle. The Moros wander from one watering hole to another in the Sahel region with their herds of cattle and also raise a little millet.

As the simulation begins, things aren't going particularly well for the Moros. Tsetse flies ravage their cattle, preventing any significant increase in herd size. With sparse herds the Moros eke out a meager existence on the Sahel and fight to survive. Their situation appears as dreadful as it is sustainable; the Moros have lived like this since time immemorial. How much of a difference could policy, and money, make in improving the situation? Dörner's participants receive all the tools *and* all the money policy-makers or philanthropic donors might use to improve the well-being of the Moros and their herds.

The tsetse fly emerges early as a devastating scourge among the Moros; if the flies can be controlled or eliminated, the herds will be stronger both *in* time (stronger cattle with more milk and meat) and *over* time (enough of the herd will survive to reproduce multiple times). Participants eagerly wage war on the tsetse fly. As the herd begins to grow, participants begin drilling wells into the regional aquifer to improve irrigation, which combined with fertilizers increases the pasturage for the cattle. These interventions have the positive side benefit of boosting the millet harvest. Within a few short years the Moros enjoy surplus cattle and millet, which they sell to generate cash income. Life looks great!

By about year twelve the first clouds appear on the horizon as the expanded herds begin to seriously overgraze the desert; the Sahel ceases to yield increases in pasturage even in the face of more water and fertilizer, which participants increasingly employ over the next few years. The tribe and their herds exceed the nature-imposed limit on agricultural productivity. The wells do, however, drain the underlying aquifer at an increasing rate. Within a couple more years, the cattle begin not only eating the tops of the grass but pulling up the roots as well. The new foraging pattern slows the rate at which grass grows and increases the rate of soil erosion.

By about year seventeen participants eventually face the unsavory choice of a massive slaughter of the herd or watching as the herd starves itself almost to extinction. Either way the Moros suffer their own death by slow starvation. After two decades the situation for the Moros moved from survival to prosperity to a crisis that threatens their continued existence as a people. What drives this wild cycle of boom and bust?

The cattle crisis arises from a failure of Dörner's students to understand the complex system of interactions that constituted life on the Sahel. The environment featured lots of individual components—many visible but others not—woven together through a set of complex and dynamic interactions that over time creates a true system. Dörner advised his students to learn to think in systems. If we really want to eliminate poverty, we must also understand the deep nature and underlying structure of systems for both poverty and efforts to fight it.

Systems thinker, environmental activist, and McArthur fellow Donnella Meadows noted:

> Hunger, poverty, environmental degradation, economic instability, unemployment, chronic disease, drug addiction, and war, for example, persist in spite of the analytical ability and technical brilliance that have been directed toward eradicating them. No one deliberately creates those problems, no one wants them to persist, but they persist nonetheless. *That is because they are intrinsically systems problems—undesirable behaviors characteristic of the system structures that produce them.*[7]

The Sahel, the cattle, the Morosians, and countless other elements exemplify a system, or set of elements all inter-related to each other. Donnella Meadows adds this important notion to the definition of a system: "[A] system is a set of things—people, cells, molecules, or whatever—interconnected in such a way that they produce their own pattern of behavior over time . . . . The system, to a large extent, causes its own behavior."[8] To think in systems requires that we understand four important concepts: systems are all about wholes, not parts; relationships form the basis of a system; systems maintain a dynamic equilibrium; and they act in nonlinear ways.

Articles, books, and institutes exist that focus on each element, and I hope merely to provide an introduction and overview to key concepts; to learn more about each important element, you'll need to dive much deeper. My goal lies in helping you respond to the system of poverty you face, and so what follows is really a 30,000-foot overview.

Wholes

The study of systems is the study of wholes, not of parts. The parts are important in their own right, but the essence of a system is synergy: the whole system is something different from, and greater than, the collection of individual parts. Systems exist, or sometimes organize, to achieve some important purpose, a purpose that each element performing its individual function can't achieve on its own. Human bodies are complex wholes, made up of subsystems; so are markets and communities. The combination of the elements and their interrelations create and define the system's capabilities.

Most of our training focused on analytics or using models and tools to deeply understand individual elements. Analysis, the art of breaking things down into individual components, provides, at best, half of what we need to understand and respond to systems; we really need synthesis skills, the ability to put parts back together and to see the whole. To fight poverty as a system, we need a new way of thinking, one that focuses on wholes, and holistic solutions, instead of a preoccupation with parts.[9]

Synthesis is the skill of the generalist, hence it proves problematic for individuals and their organizations. Marketlike systems, including the ones that fund much of the war on poverty, accept Adam Smith's logic and reward divided labor, or organizations that attack single problems. The need to solve the problems of poverty, just like the Morosian cattle example, depends on our collective—almost certainly not our individual—ability to create synthetic solutions. The implication: winning the war on poverty means creating effective relationships, the next foundational element in systems thinking.

Relationships

Relationships determine the connections between different elements in a system. Dörner's planners falsely assume that the tsetse fly problem affects *only* herd size, or that the relationship is simple and sequential. In reality the tsetse fly exist in a meshed, complex relationship with other elements of the Sahel ecosystem. Attacking the tsetse fly affected herd size *and* the amount of grass *and* the water supply. Simple relationships look like trees with branches; focus on the roots and you impact the branches. Complex relationships look more like a star circumscribed by a pentagon, where each element has a connection with each other element.

In a tree structure, the combined network contains fewer relationships than elements. Roots and branches are two elements, but only one connection; the number of connections between n elements of a decision tree is n-1. In a star, or meshed network, the five points or elements have ten relationships; the formula is that n elements produce $(n^2$-$n)/2$ connections.[10] If you double a meshed system with five elements and ten relationships you get ten elements, but forty-five relationships! Interventions have multiplicative, not additive, effects on the performance of the system.

It's hard to plan for the multiplicative effects of our efforts to fight poverty, but we improve our odds of foreseeing some of those consequences when we enlist more expertise than our own. Once again, our training and the markets we operate in engrain tree-like thinking; we can describe very well the direct impact of our programs. When we recruit different perspectives to our efforts we begin to get at indirect effects that might be anticipated. That recruitment effort works best over time as we create and sustain meaningful partnerships with other organizations. In systems fashion, however, this creates its own challenge: that of balancing the needs and interests of multiple parties.

Homeostasis

All human systems, as opposed to mechanical ones, are open—they have to interact with the larger environment to get the resources they need for survival.[11] Systems maintain homeostasis, or dynamic equilibrium, based on the nature of the relationships between the elements of a system; specifically, whether the relationships amplify deviations from equilibrium or dampen them, or whether a system operates on positive or negative feedback loops.

Deviation amplifying loops arise when the elements of the system *positively* reinforce each other. Virtuous circles and vicious cycles share a similar structure and property, as they both propel a system further and further from some baseline equilibrium.[12] Deviation dampening loops occur when the elements correlate *negatively* with each other; as one element increases the other decreases. These loops work to stabilize systems, provide resilience, and maintain the baseline equilibrium.

Morosian society subsisted for generations because the negative feedback loop dominated, or drove the system's overall performance. The philanthropic interventions of Dörner's participants allow the positive loop to dominate Morosian dynamics, causing both boom and bust. Eventually, however, the natural constraints on the system (geographic, geologic, and biological) reassert their dominance over the human systems (money, wells, and fertilizers). The Morosian case illustrates the challenge of truly sustainable interventions and the role of homeostasis in alleviating systems of poverty.

Social entrepreneurs initiate positive feedback loops into systems rife with self-correcting negative ones; poverty persists without sustained movement away from a fairly entrenched baseline in the lives of our clients. Those we work closely with can help those efforts in two ways. First, their unique perspective helps us see deviation dampening loops, often hidden from our view; they help us avoid death traps and avoidable errors. Second, and perhaps more important, their own programs may dovetail with ours to augment and extend the deviation amplifying effects we seek. Collective action may create many synergies in our work, but systems analysis suggests nothing is guaranteed; the last key principle describes this reality.

Nonlinearity

Complex systems are nonlinear; they evolve in path dependent and idiosyncratic ways.[13] Path dependence means, simply, that where we've been determines where we are, which will, in turn, drive where we go next. To understand the present we must understand the past and the road taken. The case of the Morosian cattle illustrates the point: the water crisis of an exhausted aquifer traces its origin back to early, seemingly innocuous decisions to eradicate the tsetse.

Path dependence has a twin named sensitivity to initial conditions: small differences in initial conditions lead to big differences as the system iterates.[14] Small differences in starting conditions, perhaps average annual rainfall between two areas of the Sahel, may make a huge difference in the carrying capacity of the area for cattle. Two systems that look very similar at the outset result in systems that look very different at the outcome as a result of very small differences.

Path dependence and sensitivity to initial conditions suggest that no two systems are the same, with the corollary that no two interventions will yield exactly the same results. Efforts to transplant successes in the fight against poverty from one situation to the next, even though the problems appear similar, will never produce identical outcomes. Local partners can often help us overcome the challenges of path dependence, and they can help us initiate our efforts in ways that create positive, rather than negative, initial conditions.

Thinking in systemic terms means that we have to ask a different set of questions; it also means that any illusions we have of solving problems on our own are just that, illusions. Eliminating poverty is not a singles game like tennis. Football provides a more appropriate analogy; successful teams have at least two dozen specialized roles. OK, maybe we don't need a network of twenty-five to create an effective system to fight poverty, but we'll need several partners if we want to win. The next section considers some methods for creating effective partnerships, the fundamental building block of any human work system.

CREATING EFFECTIVE PARTNERSHIPS

Diné, Inc., coordinates its efforts fighting poverty on the Navajo Nation from its leader's home in Flagstaff, Arizona. The home proves adequate for all staff meetings, as the organization employs no more than a handful of coordinators and directors at any one time. Given their small size, and the vastness of the Big Rez, Diné has to partner with others if they hope to create real and lasting change.

One recent partnership involved the creation of a local Food Policy Council in Northwestern Arizona. Diabetes has reached epidemic status among the Navajo, with an incidence rate almost four times greater than that of the U.S. population baseline.[15] The health problem has varied and complex causes, one of which being that Navajos abandoned their traditional diet in favor of the fat and sugar–rich diet found in fast food, packaged grocery items, and carbonated beverages. The Food Policy Council came together to attack this critical issue.

The council brings together a diverse group: concerned Navajos who see their lives and way of life threatened by reliance on nontraditional foods; *bilagáana* citizens in the local communities who care about the issues; university staff doing a long-term public health and nutrition project in the area, and local church food banks. The council represents the first time these different actors have joined forces to tackle critical issues and share knowledge.

The Sisters of St. Jude run a food pantry in Tuba City; they benefited from that knowledge exchange. The sisters distribute emergency food aid packets to Navajo families (about 800 to 850 per month) and sell food boxes. The Food Policy Council discussions led them to produce a new, traditional food–laden box to sell. Their sales of boxes went from 20 to 30 a month to more than 60. Tribal officials saw the value of such a multi-stakeholder partnership in tackling nutrition challenges among the Navajo; the first Navajo Nation food summit took place in Gallup, New Mexico, in May of 2012.

Diné, Inc., established the partnership as part of a federal grant, but they never took ownership of the group. That fell to individual council members, who elected their own chair, wrote their own bylaws, and continued to run the council after Diné backed away to pursue other objectives. Partnerships create wins for all involved, when the roles and resources of each member create meaningful leverage.

Roles and Resources

We can think of three important sets of actors in the fight against poverty. Government, in spite of its flaws, has a clear role to play; so does business, even with its supposed short-term and financial focus. Civil society organizations represent the third leg of that stool. Each must play a role, but those roles vary from project to project. The five types of capital suggest some apparent matches. Government should focus on institutional capital, while business contributes organizational and physical capital. Civil society adds its skills in social capital, and everyone has a stake in and role to play regarding human capital.

This thinking leads to a simplistic division of labor that contributes much to our collective failure because it fails to create truly collective action: divvying up the five capital accounts just pools labor but fails to leverage it. If we think of the five types of capital more thoroughly, as I've suggested, we'll see a vastly different picture. Each social sector plays a vital role in creating, maintaining, and evolving each of the five types of capital. While the exact contribution of each party to the various types of capital changes over time, there are some general tendencies.

Government, when it works well (and that's a big proviso in many pockets of poverty), has a general talent for creating and sustaining long-lived things such as institutions, organizations, and bundles of physical capital. The rule of law and its various courts and regulatory bodies, broad education policy and school buildings, or roads, bridges, and their attendant authorities serve as excellent examples of long-lived capital investments. Tax and investment policies also create a climate that fosters the development (or the degradation) of social, human, and organizational capital.

Business moves in pursuit of clearly identified opportunities for gain, often opportunities provided by government. The U.S. Department of Defense invented the Internet in 1951 with Project Lincoln, which worked to provide a national system of linked computers that could monitor Soviet bombers on the move.[16] The Internet revolution would wait until government granted access to the network and profit-oriented entrepreneurs and businesses could exploit its power as a tool for communication and commerce. Today, businesses invest billions in backbone servers, common protocols, and drive training in engineering, materials science, and business. Government may create, but business can scale meaningful innovations.

Civil society organizations represent, perhaps, the oldest and broadest category of social actors. Civil society organizations are private, nonprofit, distributing, self-sustaining organizations.[17] These organizations legitimate the efforts of both government and businesses; however, they also focus their energies on projects that fall outside the purview of the state or the reach of the market. Churches and related organizations such as Catholic Relief Services fall into this category; so do private universities, think tanks, media organizations, and innumerable special interest organizations. These organizations shape the system through their own investments of time, money, and energy, but also by ratifying (or not) other actors and actions.

Because the nature of the ecosystem that you will join and develop will be complex and context specific, it's impossible to identify a set of different organizations you should seek to partner with. The elements, or the "what," of each system will prove incredibly idiosyncratic; however, there are some common features of the processes that create strong partnerships and vibrant ecosystems.

Creating Solid and Sustainable Alliances

Harvard Business School's Rosabeth Moss Kanter spent a good portion of her illustrious academic career looking at how firms create successful alliances, formal organizational arrangements with more complexity than a simple contract but much less than a merger. She uses a simple alliterative model to convey a set of attributes about creating effective alliances: the eight I's of successful We's.[18] These eight I's provide a simple mnemonic tool to identify good partners and forge strong relationships.

Individual excellence. The first criterion for creating a successful alliance is to be excellent, if not world class, at what *you* do. You'll only attract alliance partners as good as you, so if you're not excellent your ecosystem will be weak and ineffective. A chain is really only as strong as its proverbial weakest link; make sure your partners are outstanding, and then you can both work to make each other stronger. As you become excellent and skilled you'll find lots of people who want to partner with you to make them better. Don't partner with just anyone. Individual excellence creates its own positive feedback loop, and you will, over time, be only as good as the company you keep.

How do you become excellent? Two things matter. First, hire excellent people. Mission-driven organizations often hire based on mission consistency; we want people who are, like us, passionate and committed to the work. Competence gets overlooked in the rush for consistency; however, building an excellent organization requires both. Second, focus and attention to detail provide the mastery experiences you need to become world class; self-efficacy applies in-house as well as in the field. When we master individual elements, we become better partners in the creation of synthetic wholes.

Importance. The partnership has to meet the superordinate goals of everyone involved. Otherwise, one or more parties will lack the commitment and attention to detail that make an ecosystem work and thrive. How do you determine your goals? Your mission statement, of course! That's why a clear mission anchors any effective action, including fighting poverty. That's why mission comes before partnerships in this book. If your partners lack a clear mission or vision, how can you be sure the alliance meets major objectives for them? Looking for, or at, their mission is a good first step. Be careful of mission mismatches, for they'll haunt your efforts down the road.

Interdependence. Successful partners *need* each other because neither can accomplish alone what both can do together. Make sure your ecosystem needs you, in a value creating way, and make sure you need that particular system. Diné, Inc., had contacts with each future Food Policy Council member. Each member had unique assets or access to resources. Everyone brings something of real value to the discussion table, and they all work to implement decisions they make.

We know from Chapter 4 about the perils of dependency; strive for interdependence. Interdependence doesn't come naturally to many of us, independence does. The vision of the lone cowboy solving problems appeals to many who call themselves entrepreneurs. Interdependence requires individual excellence plus a dose of humility that can admit the relevance of the excellence of others to our own efforts. It also means, in very practical terms, creating organizational space in which responsibilities can be meaningfully divided between partners to allow all the opportunity to exercise and leverage their unique yet complementary skills.

Investment. Partners invest in each other and the relationship to demonstrate their commitment to each other by putting substantive skin in the game. Investments come in many forms. It may be as simple as lending a partner office space, or communications equipment. Substantial, often risky, investments come when we share data or proprietary operating systems and techniques with our partners. Sharing the client, or donor, list or investing in introducing our partners to key stakeholders in sustaining our own operations represents a substantial commitment to the endeavor. Resource hording kills partnerships!

Some see investment as a mechanism to protect our own interests in alliances; by exchanging mutual hostages each side has greater incentive to adhere to agreements.[19] This dark view contrasts with a more positive view: by investing significant resources and by creating vulnerability, we lay the foundation for effective trust and cooperation that enables our collective work to truly advance.[20] Skin in the game, financial or otherwise, signals our desire to win, not merely our desire to hedge potential losses.

Information. Open communication means that partners share *all* information required for success. This certainly includes the initial sharing of visions, strategies, and operating plans, but perhaps more important is the sharing of everyday information. To quote Ludwig Mies van der Rohe, "God is in the details."[21] Detailed information aggregates into a monitoring system of the alliance and its practical objectives that allows the parties individually and jointly to make needed adjustments to make things work. Communication also strengthens social capital and the working bonds between partners; the big things matter, but the little things may matter more.

Sharing information represents both a technical and human task, each with its own challenges. On the technical side getting data bases to sync or having systems that can incorporate the information sent by the other party can require substantial investment. The human challenge lies in jointly analyzing information rather than merely collecting it; meetings and reviews become an essential element of successful alliances.

Integration. Successful alliance partners integrate their operations and develop common ways of operating to make the effort more efficient. Happy couples find that replacing mine and yours with ours reduces conflict, improves performance, and provides another touch point for the relationship to deepen. The key here is *shared* or common ways of operating; effective alliances take the best system from each party and avoid the appearance, or reality, of a hostile takeover. Integration begins in the field, where the real work gets done; getting field people to work together creates a foundation for others and greatly enhances other processes, such as information exchange.

The real payoff comes when people and systems do more than just work together; they work to create new solutions to common problems.[22] Integration promotes trust, which enables innovative solutions to emerge and, when well done, it also subjects those innovations to critical review from multiple perspectives. Integration creates early costs and discouragement as each party had effective procedures, systems, and organizations. Persist, however, because the payoff from integration—in cost savings and innovation—vastly exceeds the initial outlays.

Institutionalization. When couples really want to get serious, or when they create new shared assets such as children, they move their relationship to the next level and get married. Partnerships in the fight against poverty should do the same. Institutionalizing means giving the relationship itself formal status and defining clear roles. Institutionalization may begin by linking web pages and defining administrative responsibilities. The process ends when the parties either merge their organizations (marry) or create a third, special-purpose organization to focus solely on the joint objectives. Institutionalization preserves relationships and deepens commitment because it makes it harder for either party to exit.

Integrity. Finally, the partners engage each other in honest and honorable ways that recognize the fundamental dignity and mutual contribution of each. Integrity means not keeping secrets and operating with transparency; it

TABLE 9.1. Leveraging the Eight I's That Create Successful We's

The Eight I's . . .	. . . create leverage and value through
Individual Excellence	*Strength.* Strong partners push each other to improve and be their best
Importance	*Vision.* A clear vision of the critical needs of joint activities focuses effort
Interdependence	*Complementarity.* Partners contribute what the other cannot in ways that add value
Investment	*Dedication and trust.* Real expenditures of time and money invite commensurate commitments
Information	*Speed and clarity.* Decision quality enhance when made on all available facts/opinions
Integration	*Co-creation.* Integration means realizing synergies and developing new assets/skills
Institutionalization	*Permanence.* Partners stop looking over their shoulders and make long-term commitments
Integrity	*Joy.* Partners enjoy richer relationships that extend beyond work

Source: Eight I's taken from Rosabeth Moss Kanter, "Collaborative Advantage: The Art of Alliances," *Harvard Business Review* 72, no. 4 (August 1994): 96.

means really sharing information, the type of information that matters. It also means not holding grudges or sandbagging negative feedback, allowing these negative actions to sour the relationship and decrease effectiveness.

Integrity means that we treat our partners as we want to be treated. Integrity serves as the wellspring of mutual trust. Integrity allows us not to focus on excessive monitoring or control, which further enhances innovation. We must act with integrity and trust as we enter new alliances; however, mutual trust and reliance upon each other takes time—often years—to build.[23] It also requires that each party understand the moral compass of the other to avoid misinterpreting actions or motives.

The eight I's contribute to a successful system because they help define the elements (individual excellence), set and monitor the system's goals (importance and information), create a strong set of relationships (interdependence, investment, integration, and institutionalization), and create positive and negative feedback loops (integrity) that help a system effectively alleviate poverty. One can't control for nonlinear effects other than to make sure the initial conditions of the partnership system are as solid as possible. Table 9.1 summarizes the eight I's and suggests how they create the leverage of We. That leverage leads to real value, for your organization and your clients.

CONCLUSION

Poverty is a system, and eliminating it requires that we build partnerships with others, and then we combine those working partnerships with others to form more complex ecosystems that effectively fight poverty, be it in sub-Saharan Africa, on the Big Rez, in the Paraguayan Chaco, or in the homes and hearths of single parents. Forming partnerships becomes a natural activity for the mission-driven organization; once we know who we are we can work with others. I repeat once again for emphasis: little p poverty is a system, and its elimination requires systems of interconnected individuals and organizations.

No child grows up solely in her own home; it does take a village to raise that child. If James Watt hadn't developed the steam engine, someone else would have. Eighteenth-century England represented a system primed for invention and entrepreneurial activity; the technology, institutions, knowledge, and relationships that drove the steam engine are as responsible as Watt for its final birth, growth, and success. The system facilitated the formation of explicit partnerships, such as that between Boulton and Watt, and a number of alliances, both formal (with Iron Mad Wilkinson) and informal (with Joseph Black and William Small). From all accounts, Boulton and Watt personally exemplified the eight I's that created a very, very successful We.

Partnerships prove critical, as does mission; however, neither ensures victory in the fight against poverty. Mission tells us who we are, why we act, and what we do. Effective alliances create systems that link us with others who help drive that mission. These two create action. The final piece in creating an effective program to lift people out of poverty comes when we know *how* we're doing and whether those actions we are taking really make a dent in poverty and help us achieve our goals. That raises the issue of measurement. As with the other ideas in the book, James Watt created a unique measurement system to move his engine from margin to mainstream.

CHAPTER TEN

MEASURING IMPACT

Are We Winning?

What gets measured gets done, what gets measured and fed back
gets done well, what gets rewarded gets repeated.

—John E. Jones

ALL ENTREPRENEURS, and their innovations, face a common challenge: breaking into the market, a market often crowded with similar products or services.
By 1777 the young firm of Boulton & Watt confronted the same challenge;
they had just commercialized an engine vastly better than the market-leading
Newcomen engines but had few customers. Added to this they would have to
sell to some of Britain's toughest and cost conscious businessmen, the mine
owners in Cornwall. Coal mining consumed huge amounts of capital to dig
mines up to eight hundred feet deep, move the black substance to the surface,
and transport it to markets. Coal prices, weather, and technical challenges of
deep mining made for an expensive and volatile business.[1]

To induce trial Boulton and Watt relied on creative pricing. Customers
bought an unassembled engine kit and provided their own installation services. Watt authored an instruction manual, *Directions for Erecting and Working the Newly-Invented Steam Engines,* in 1779. Owners not only installed their
own engines, they also provided their own operators. They paid Boulton &
Watt an annual royalty based on the machine's efficiency, one-third of the
cost savings over a Newcomen engine doing the same work. A "duty" equated
work between the two engines; a duty consisted of the pounds of water lifted
by one bushel of coal. Newcomen's engines could lift 5,000 to 9,000 pounds
per bushel, Watt's engine almost 19,000.

Duty worked well until the rotary engine came online in the early 1780s.
Now engines were turning wheels, not pumping water; wheels then turned by

equine power.[2] Watt devised a new measure to calculate the savings of a rotary engine. He counted the number of times a horse could turn a twelve-foot mill wheel over an hour's time, which turned out to be about 144, or 2.4 times per minute. If a horse could pull a steady load of 180 pounds (slightly over the weight of the median American male aged twenty to twenty-nine in 2006) and you can do the math, the average horse pulls about 33,000 foot-pounds per minute. Watt's name for his new measure: horsepower. By 1785, industrial users paid an annual royalty of £5 per horsepower for engines designed by Boulton & Watt.[3]

Horsepower quickly became the global standard for measuring power-generating performance. The common metric allowed buyers and sellers to compare two different engines, for different uses, according to a common standard. Universal measures allow people to compare apples and oranges in terms of something like calories or fructose content. Horsepower became the standard for steam power as well as gasoline combustion engines. In a fitting tribute, the common measure for electrical power is the watt, a unit of measure named in honor of James.

James Watt's steam engine represented a technical marvel that would change the world, one that proliferated once consumers had a way to measure how marvelous the engine really was. A fundamental assumption of economic theory states that markets work best when buyers and sellers can precisely measure—and price—the value of the goods being traded.[4] Measurement matters for success in the economic realm just as much as physical superiority does in the scientific one. This chapter takes up the challenge of measuring the effectiveness of our efforts to eliminate poverty.

THE CHALLENGES *TO* AND *OF* MEASUREMENT

We met Martin Burt in Chapter 5 during a deep dive on human capital. Both Martin and Fundacion Paraguaya serve as wonderful examples of the power of human capital in eliminating little p poverty. Martin committed to build a new school and hotel at the Mbaracayu site to replicate the San Francisco model and lift more youth out of poverty. By mid-2009 Fundacion Paraguaya had recruited an initial group of students, all girls, to the new school and begun the long process of creating a financially self-sufficient operation along the lines of the San Francisco School.[5]

The new school would leverage the unique ecological elements of the

Mbaracayu Reserve while transplanting the model and culture of entrepreneurial education. In addition to the school in the Mbaracayu, Martin was working on projects in other countries, such as Bolivia, Brazil, Nicaragua, Kenya, and Uganda. As his business model began to be copied around the region—and hopefully the world—Martin began to understand and appreciate a key barrier to replication: the amount of funding necessary. He had been lucky there to inherit a fully functioning enterprise at San Francisco, but replicating the model elsewhere would often mean building schools from the ground up.

Commercial financing proved almost impossible: Martin and the bankers could not even speak the same language. Martin instead looked to venture philanthropists, a new breed of social investor. Unlike traditional philanthropists who donated based on the worthiness or appeal of the cause, venture philanthropists based their initial and ongoing support on the potential social return on investment (SROI) of different opportunities.[6] SROI, and the pressure to measure program results, presented Martin with the challenge *to* measure his results as well as the challenge *of* creating and capturing meaningful assessments of impact.

The Challenge to Measure

Pressure to measure outcomes and provide accountability for social endeavors has grown substantially since the turn of the millennium. Before investigating the nuances of evaluation and assessment, it's worth taking time to think about why the demands for tangible progress and outcome measurement have become more vocal and pointed. At least four reasons come to mind.

The Failure of Public Investments. In 2001 the U.S. Congress passed an act known popularly as No Child Left Behind in response to growing frustration over America's faltering educational system and poor educational outcomes.[7] Education represented one sector of public spending where outputs seemed uncorrelated (or even negatively correlated) to inputs, particularly inputs measured in dollars. Health care, foreign aid (discussed in Chapter 1), and other public sector services exhibited the same problems. Coincidentally, William Easterly's critique of foreign aid, *The Elusive Quest for Growth*, appeared the same year.[8]

The remedy in No Child Left Behind came in setting clear performance standards for both students and schools and placing heavy (some would say inordinate) emphasis on measurement against those standards. The focus on measurement spilled over into health care, with outcome measures and the quality movement, and into other social sectors. The Grameen model and the proliferation of microlenders legitimated the idea that social investments should generate returns in the spirit of for-profit business investments. A focus on measurement and accountability of social services had, I believe, roots in deeper cultural trends in American and global society.

The rise of economic analysis and material values. Gary Becker, the modern founder of the human capital movement, once wrote that any element of human life that combined rational, goal-directed behavior with choice could be subject to economic analysis: it would be conceptually possible to monetize all decisions, if money stood as an adequate proxy for utility.[9] Things like cost-benefit analysis and attempts to create marketlike processes in traditionally noneconomic activities, such as health care or philanthropy, represent the logical outcome of the dominance of economic analysis.

The rise of economic analysis followed on the heels of a quantum increase in the availability of consumer goods and rising incomes since the end of World War II. A long-term decline in religious participation in all Western societies occurred simultaneously and resulted in a society dominated by secular, consumerist values where materialism and economic utility have become the prevalent definition of a good and meaningful life. Max Weber saw materialism and an attendant decline in aesthetic values as the natural and logical end of the spirit of capitalism, an end that left people trapped in an iron cage.[10]

Materialism provides a cognitive backdrop for, and normative justification of, a measurement driven society. The fundamental premise of materialism is that happiness translates into products and services whose values can be measured by the prices we pay and the assets accumulated on the balance sheet. Materialism facilitates a focus on money, but also on other tangible goods and services; this breadth of focus becomes apparent in the next driver.

The Frustration with Income as a Measure of Development. Development economics held as a central tenet that economic growth served as the goal and measure of progress. If economic output rose a country must be better off, and one way of measuring personal incomes is per capita GDP. In 1990 Pakistani economist Mahbub ul Haq devised a new measure that broadened the myopic focus on income and drew from a larger vision of development: "The objective of development is to create an enabling environment for people to enjoy long, healthy and creative lives."[11]

The human development index added a measure of health, life expectancy at birth, and education, expected and actual mean years of schooling, to GDP per capita in the hope of measuring other aspects of poverty and its elimination. Other measures emerged over the next decade, such as the Global Entrepreneurship Monitor (GEM), begun in 1999 by the London Business School and Babson College; or the World Bank's ease of doing business index in 2002.[12] Each of these measures assesses the escape from poverty as more than simply having more income; by measuring these things you could establish the value of your program even though incomes may not rise.

The rise of social entrepreneurship. The idea of using the market and market forces to create economic development is hardly new, but the rise of social entrepreneurship as an identifiable field probably dates to the 1990s.[13] One impetus came through a focus on sustainability and the triple bottom line for businesses; business ought to be about, and ought to measure, more than just economic profit. Things like environmental impacts and carbon footprints have emerged, but so has a concern with the social impact of business and its operations, including how those operations affect those living at the base of the pyramid.

Harvard Business School strategist Michael Porter and his colleague Mark Kramer advocate a new focus by traditional businesses, governmental agencies, NGOs, and social entrepreneurs on shared value: "policies and operating practices that enhance the competitiveness of a company while simultaneously advancing the economic and social conditions in the communities in which it operates."[14] They note that the lofty goal of shared value entails some very detailed work in measurement to define and scope areas for the creation of shared value and ways to catalog the outcomes, or value created.

Measurement, specifically the notion of SROI, fits hand in glove with the mindset of social entrepreneurs. They want to create businesses with sustainable social impact. Sustainability means attention to financial profitability and the long-term ability to rely on internally generated funds rather than donations. Social impact means observing, cataloguing, and measuring how the venture improves the lives of its clients and participants. Foundations and other civil society organizations have taken up the measurement banner as a response to calls for philanthropy to become more businesslike in its operation.[15]

The challenge for people like Martin to measure the outcomes of their activity has deep roots and is unlikely to fade away. While a strong consensus around the need for measurement exists, the process, or the challenge *of* measurement, has to be adjusted to the nuances of each operation or program. We know why we want measurement, but we lack clarity about how to do it most effectively. To this topic we now turn.

The Challenge of Measurement

Friedrich August von Hayek received the 1974 Nobel Prize in economics. His acceptance speech highlights the problem of measurement in the social sciences, and he titled it *The Pretense of Knowledge:*

> Unlike the position that exists in the physical sciences, in economics and other disciplines that deal with essentially complex phenomena, the aspects of the events to be accounted for about which we can get quantitative data are necessarily limited and may not include the important ones. . . . And while in the physical sciences the investigator will be able to measure what, on the basis of a prima facie theory, he thinks important, in the social sciences *often that is treated as important which happens to be accessible to measurement.*[16] (Emphasis added)

Poverty is a social problem, facing the same measurement challenges as the social sciences. Put simply, those fighting poverty may default to outcomes that are easy to measure, rather than ones that indicate a true exit from poverty. We end up working in areas where we can show measurable progress; however, measurable progress does not mean real progress on the critical, underlying issues. To the extent that SROI measures attempt to monetize the returns to social activities they fall prey to Hayek's pretense of knowledge in spades, because monetization happens only with easy to measure outcomes.

A Google search for the topic "social return on investment" returns more than 250,000 websites; narrow the search to SROI methodologies and you cull that list by a factor of almost ten. Many different models of SROI exist, and listing some but not others may create a false sense of priority or legitimacy.[17] Most SROI measures have common features and recommend a similar sequence of activities.

1. Identify relevant stakeholders. Social initiatives behave like a rock dropped into a pond; they target a set of direct clients, but also the effect spreads out like ripples in a pond. Identify all relevant *primary* stakeholders:

people or organizations that have direct and regular contact with your organization such as clients and suppliers. This will be the focal group, but then move out to *secondary* stakeholders, those with whom you deal directly but irregularly. Government regulators or donors may fall into this group.

Finish the list by noting *tertiary* stakeholders, ones you deal with indirectly but who feel the impacts of your programs. Family members of clients and their communities fall into this category. While "stakeholder analysis" looks like an innocuous step in the process, the actual practice of determining who will be affected, and to what degree, takes time and care to include all the relevant parties.[18]

2. Determine costs. What does it cost to deliver the product or service? How are those costs allocated between capital and operating expenses? How do they behave over time (for example, do costs decrease as learning occurs or increase as new clients enter the system)? For many ventures this may be the easiest step, if you have solid accounting systems and enough experience to know how costs behave over time and economic cycles.

3. Determine the financial and nonfinancial benefits of the program. Programs like education could be measured in monetary outcomes, such as increased earning power. Earning power serves as the most common financial measure used to calculate SROI, even when the effect on some social intervention and earning appears quite tenuous. Financial benefits have the advantage that they can be counted to create a *quantitative* measure, much like horsepower.

Nonfinancial benefits can't be counted, and estimating them raises a host of issues. How exactly do you capture the relevant *qualitative* outcomes from, for example, childhood immunizations, improved nutrition, or the noneconomic value of literacy and education? How do we value health? Does it mean something more than measurable lost days at work? Much like stakeholder analysis, this step sounds much easier than it is in practice—few guidelines exist about how to quantify the total benefits of social ventures.

4. Monetization. All models of SROI rely, ultimately, on the tools of discounted cash flow analysis, often referred to as the Net Present Value (NPV) of a venture. A tool from the field of corporate finance, NPV calculates the present value of future cash flows and provides you with an estimate of the lifetime return of a project.[19]

NPV helps businesses make capital expenditure decisions by telling them how long it will take for a return and what that return will look like. The method has no provision for monetary values, so all nonfinancial benefits get excluded, the first problem with monetization. You can imagine the pressure to make everything quantifiable as a benefit to earning power so they can be included in the model.

5. Choose an appropriate time horizon and discount rate. Programs have different impact horizons. Some, such as disaster relief, lend to measurement in days or months. Others, such as education or training programs, need years or decades to assess their impact. Choosing the right time horizon matters because if you choose a short time horizon (say two years), the true impact of programs may not be apparent. However, choosing a longer time horizon introduces the problem of cross-contamination: how much of later earnings, for example, could be attributed to early interventions? Longer time horizons also dictate a higher risk premium to compensate for the inherent uncertainty in forecasting cash flows far into the future.

6. Calculate and report SROI. This step, given the difficulty of the previous ones, proves relatively simple. You match monetary benefits and costs in each period for a set number of periods, say, five years or twenty years, and plug the numbers into any spreadsheet program and hit the calculate key. This is the value, in today's dollars, of all those future benefits and costs.

Beyond the technical challenges of monetization over a murky future, SROI suffers from other, more fundamental problems. Should social investment become a competitive market?[20] Decision-makers typically use NPV to decide which projects to fund—with the rule being to fund the projects with the highest NPV. While this works great for business investment, social activities arguably operate on a different logic. If infant nutrition programs have higher NPVs than adult literacy programs, should investor/donors with scarce resources fund only the former? What happens to valuable programs, such as adult literacy, that don't make the cut?

SROI may also stifle innovation in the social sector because NPV analysis always favors short-term projects with quicker payback horizons. Innovative programs tend to have long lead times to bring projects to measurable fruition. Many innovative projects fail during the first few iterations, only becoming successful after administrators get down learning and experience curves. If NGOs or others fighting poverty are subject to SROI measurement criteria for their survival, they work with a clear disincentive for experimentation and innovation. While beneficial in the short run, social impact measurement may prove destructive in the long run.

At the deepest level, SROI reduces work on social issues to economic criteria. While this aligns with the cultural trends toward materialism and consumerism, economic analysis may displace other motivations, such as a concern for social justice or for aesthetic beauty. Do people have a *right* to education and literacy, clean water, and adequate food? Or are these good only to the extent they improve earnings? SROI threatens social entrepreneurship and traditional philanthropy with their own versions of the iron cage by blurring the line between societal, moral, and economic values.

Social innovators face real pressures to measure their impacts; donors or other investors expect evaluation for the reasons laid out above, and probably many others as well. SROI, with its focus on monetizing the value of social projects, represents a dangerous trap. Is there a better way? In what follows I'll lay out some guidelines and principles for creating measures that work. They will be only general principles, however, because the specifics of your situation will determine how your measures look, feel, and work.

CREATING MEANINGFUL IMPACT MEASURES

The drawbacks of using SROI mentioned above suggest some broad outlines of what effective measures will do. Good measures will incorporate *intrinsic* benefits (what it means to someone's humanity to be literate) as well as *instrumental* value (how literacy affects health, income, or family relationships) for the areas you work in. They do this by explicitly recognizing qualitative gains from programs. They attend to concerns of fundamental rights, human dignity, and lofty principles as much as they focus on increased welfare, asset accumulation, and the mundane practices of moving ahead.

Good measures allow for, and encourage, innovation within your organization; they track current performance but leave space for projects with longer lead times or higher levels of risk to grow. A balanced scorecard approach suggests that innovation and current performance aren't trade-offs: they represent two distinct facets of long-term organizational success.[21] Similarly, good measures will look inside the organization for outcomes on staff members and associates as well as externally for impacts on clients. Development matters as much to the helpers as to those helped.

These represent overarching characteristics of good measurement tools. Just as in the last chapter, the demands and particulars of your organization, its people, places, and programs will drive the specific measures you adopt to assess impact, as will the culture and institutional norms and values held by the populations you serve. Your measures must be consistent with legitimate action within those constraints. Here are, however, some practical guidelines for you to consider.

Measure the right M: Mission consistency, not monetary benefit. Trying to monetize the benefits of your work runs two risks. First, you'll have to omit several measures that don't monetize—specifically any qualitative impacts. Second, and perhaps more important, you risk pulling your organization away from its core mission. After all, what gets measured gets done, and it's usually what's rewarded as well. To invoke an analogy used earlier, if your mission is to clear the swamp don't measure how many alligators you're killing. It's a short hop from there to becoming an alligator extermination service rather than a swamp drainer. Measure the water level, and it better be receding!

Returning to the mission, you need to make sure that measures assess the impact of your core activities; what business you are in should drive how you measure success. Take CE Solutions and their early work in stoves. If their business were stove design and construction they might measure increases in BTUs per model for each type of stove; if it's stove distribution and sales, then the number of stoves sold. If, however, their mission entails something like community development, then they'd want to measure something like penetration: how many homes within a community use new stoves? How many meals get cooked on these stoves?

As CE Solutions gets closer and closer to its real mission, the measures that matter may not be convenient or easy to obtain; that's the problem Hayek alerted us to. In the rush to produce some type of cost-effective measurement it becomes a simple thing to focus on those easily measured as opposed to those that earnestly matter. Don't trade efficiency for effectiveness: take the time to measure what leads to real, lasting progress.

Measures should include values and identity. FedEx values people, so customer and employee satisfaction serves as an impact measure. They also value things like innovation (measured as new products or services) and integrity (accounting restatements or compliance?). Similarly, Catholic Relief Services needs to include some way to evaluate the extent to which their work honors the sacredness and dignity of all stakeholders; this probably entails something more complex and nuanced than a simple survey that asks people to rate the extent to which they feel dignified. Clearly we've left monetization far behind, but our measures reinforce what matters most to us and who we are.

Consistency Counts. Chapter 3 discussed the time horizon involved in creating lasting and meaningful change; it's measured in decades, not days. Watt's story of the steam engine reinforces the idea that real development takes time. The best way for measures to reflect this reality is to use the same ones over time. However tempting it may be, don't change the measures you use from year to year, because you need to measure changes over longer time horizons than a single year.

I do research in the area of corporate philanthropy and social responsibility. I've accessed two different data bases to do this work. One data base measured aggregate corporate philanthropic contributions over time. While the dollars remained constant, the compilers changed the categories to which firms donated over time, often from year to year. The other data set used the same assessment protocols *and* categories of behavior for more than twenty years; they added new categories but never changed an existing one. Guess which data yields greater insight?

Avoid changing what you measure and how you measure it. Create stable measures! Beware of special circumstances or events that encourage you to create *this* separate measure for that year, or to change how you measure your core impact to incorporate *that* one-off event. You'll lose the validity of measuring progress the same way in each time period. People take years to emerge from poverty into prosperity, and if you set up a robust set of measures you'll capture their progress year by year in a consistent and reliable manner.

Creating reliable measures makes a world of difference, but make sure you create valid measures.[22] If your mission involves providing skill-based training for employability, then completion of the training, maybe along with grades, provides one reliable measure of performance. A valid measure—one that gets at the real value created—may focus on the number of graduates with jobs, or the number of offers per candidate. The numbers may fluctuate from year to year more than grades, but job placement represents a more valid, market-based measure of success than merely grades or graduates.

Triangulate where possible to get better readings. Orienteers, navigators, seismologists, and pilots all employ the principle of triangulation to accomplish their work safely and effectively. Seismologists in Salt Lake City, for example, may receive data about an earthquake with an epicenter three hundred miles from the city. Good information, but the quake could have occurred anywhere within a three-hundred-mile radius. If they know the distance of the epicenter from Denver they narrow the epicenter to two possible points (where Denver's and Salt Lake's circles cross). If they know the distance from Phoenix, then the quake can be precisely located as the single intersection between the three circles. Multiple data points and sources enable more accurate assessments and actions.

Several methods of triangulation can be employed to improve your assessments. An easy step would be to supplement checklist assessments by your field staff with a survey of clients. Third-party evaluators provide another way to assess programs without the contamination of staff known to your clients. The gold standard best practice involves comparing a cohort using your intervention against a control group of similar people who don't take part in your program. This additional step allows you to calibrate how much your intervention impacted clients versus nonclients, not merely how much it affected some clients versus others.

Triangulation, particularly creating and monitoring control groups, becomes expensive very quickly. Doing double-blind control studies isolates impact in drug studies, but few of us fighting poverty have millions to spend on rigorous research protocols like the large pharmaceutical producers. Recognizing that constraint, force yourself and your organization to triangulate in some way; you'll be surprised at the improvement in the richness and detail of the assessments you get. Some expense of time and money makes sense, because the ultimate value of the assessment depends on the quality of the underlying data: garbage in, garbage out. After you have good data, understand what it says, which brings us to the next implementation principle.

Measure more than impact; try for causality as well. If you follow the principles laid out above, you should end up with a fairly strong set of measures about your participants, programs, and outcomes. You'll have data about ultimate outcomes like self-reliance, improvements in income, or other indicators of the movement out of poverty. You'll have a set of program-level measures, such as which types of interventions different people participated in, or their performance on related tasks; you will probably have data on individuals as well, including demographics and some understanding of their history or personality characteristics.

With that data you can build *causal* models, groups of measures that explain and predict each other. Causal models show how the different things you do interact with the people you serve to bring about certain outcomes. One simple version of a model would look at how individual level measures—say, about someone's previous level of education or hometown—influenced their participation in your programs. Participation in those programs, things such as the number of training sessions attended or facility gained with different skills, can be juxtaposed to tangible outcomes to determine how much impact your program makes.

The key to establishing causal relationships depends on analysis, and Excel or a number of simple statistical software packages can provide you with the tools. More important, however, causal relationships mean that you have to have some theory of action—what causes what, and why.[23] You already have some theory that guides your actions; that's why your interventions have the designs and features they do. Meaningful measures, and some thoughtful analysis of those data, allow you to test the validity of your theory. You'll see whether your theory of action proves correct, and you'll elaborate that theory as you see other relationships emerge.

These principles and guidelines should help you create strong data and create robust, reliable, and valid assessments of the impact of your programs. The overall architecture of the process keeps the measurement process consistent and aligned with the larger strategy and efforts of your organization. Understanding how and where you create impact requires one final step.

Use the assessments to make changes. Collecting data takes time and energy, and so does the analysis that determines how your programs contribute to poverty elimination. Your measurement work will tell you some things you want to hear, and some you don't. Use both types of results to improve performance. If CE Solutions finds, for example, that certain individual characteristics and traits predict success in the field, they may be able to shorten their training regimen by focusing their selection efforts toward potential clients with certain traits.

Far too many organizations, be they businesses, governments, universities, or civil society–based, expend tremendous resources to gather data, and even more to crunch the numbers or read the qualitative reports, but then fail to act on what they find. The value of assessment lies in continual improvement, not just cajoling donors or other stakeholders. Measurement often discourages change, however, because when we implement something new our performance usually declines. It takes courage and insight to fight the natural tendency to "make the numbers look good" and learn from our programs, but it's the only way for our measurement programs to make a difference.

Dedicate time to analyzing the results and discussing implications for changes in what you do or how you do it. We all schedule time for employee performance reviews; the same logic and scheduling protocols should exist for program reviews. Use your findings as a platform for a deep and substantial analysis; incorporate both the positive and negative aspects your measures reveal. Good assessment work consumes valuable time and scarce cash; don't turn that investment into an expense by failing to learn from and act upon what those assessments reveal.

CONCLUSION

James Watt's clever pricing scheme to get their engines in use would not have succeeded over the long term except for the development of horsepower. Comparing performance between two engines would be straightforward, but most mine owners had only one type of engine. When the steam engine created rotary power, having a robust and legitimate measure of performance facilitated its acceptance in the marketplace.

Luckily for you and me, we don't have to create our own global standard of measurement for what we do. We face the same fundamental pressure and challenge they did, however. If we want our programs to survive and thrive, we have to prove they add value. That means, put simply, that you must accept the challenge *to* measure. You must solve the challenge *of* measuring as well. This chapter has provided some guidance as to how to create and manage your own assessment process; you must customize it to your mission and your market.

The measurement of qualitative outcomes such as the virtues of justice, fairness, and dignity defy easy solution and will—and should—keep you up at night, because these larger virtues pose a question: what does it mean to exit poverty? Is it simply reaching an income level that puts one above the poverty line, or a collection of assets that bestows the title of self-reliant?

The book opened with the claim that it's not about the money. Part I argued that it takes much more than money—the five types of capital—to move people from poverty to prosperity. Part II focused on organizational capital—specifically, how you can build an organization capable of winning the war on little p poverty. Money can't be the only *means* of eliminating poverty. Chapter 11 closes the book with an argument that we should not equate the possession of more money with the *end* of poverty. Prosperity means something more, that people flourish in all aspects of their lives: economic, social, moral, and spiritual. Aristotle had a term for such flourishing; he called it Eudemonia.

CHAPTER ELEVEN

EUDEMONIA

Human Flourishing and the End of Poverty

What is the meaning of life? To be happy and useful.
—Tenzin Gyatso, 14th Dalai Lama[1]

SOMETIME IN 1812 Ned Ludd sent this to a woolen mill master in Huddersfield, an industrializing town southwest of Leeds:

Sir,

Information has just been given in, that you are a holder of those detestable Shearing Frames, and I was desired by my men to write to you, and give you fair warning to pull them down, and for that purpose I desire that you will understand I am now writing to you, you will take notice that if they are not taken down by the end of next week, I shall detach one of my lieutenants with at least 300 men to destroy them, and further more take notice that if you give us the trouble of coming thus far, we will increase your misfortunes by burning your buildings down to ashes, and if you have the impudence to fire at any of my men, they have orders to murder you and burn all your Housing.[2]

Ned Ludd never lived; the name cloaked a radical, antitechnology movement known as the Luddites, a group who viewed the emerging Industrial Revolution as a plague to be resisted by whatever means necessary, including violence, mayhem, and threats of murder. Watt's engine, particularly the rotary motion version that could power factory machinery, contributed to a radical restructuring of English society. Some of those effects were decidedly good, others questionable.

The macroeconomic effects of the Industrial Revolution occurred simultaneously with the appearance of Watt's engine. Between 1700 and 1780 English

GDP grew about 0.65 percent per year. From 1780 to 1801 those figures would double to 1.4 percent, and would rise to 1.9 percent annually in the three decades from 1801 to 1831, almost 300 percent greater than a century before. Scientific patent applications followed a similar trajectory. The 1760s saw 205 patent awards, compared with 92 in the previous decade. Patent grants would more than double again in twenty years to 477 in the 1780s, and again by 1800, with 924. Technology and industry transformed English society. The rest of the world would follow during the nineteenth century.[3]

The population of England grew dramatically in the second half of the eighteenth and first half of the nineteenth centuries. In 1701 England had just over 5 million citizens; it would take six decades to exceed 6 million, in 1761. Within two decades the country had added another million, and by 1796 the population reached 8 million. That population lived increasingly in cities. Take Leeds, for example, since it's close to the focus of the Luddite aggressions. In 1700 Leeds was a burgeoning community of between 5,000 and 7,000 people; within a half-century the city had grown to 16,000. By 1800 the population tripled again, to 53,000.[4]

Wages and standard of living tell a more complex story. Some evidence suggests that real wages increased between 1700 and 1750 but then declined dramatically between about 1770 and 1800. Numbers create a fuzzy picture, however, because the composition of the labor force and family earning patterns mean that wages probably do not reflect the overall standard of living. Wages went up for skilled laborers such as blacksmiths, or the emerging professions of boilermakers and iron puddlers. Earnings remained stagnant, or declined, for unskilled labor; it seems that some things never change. The percentage of poor vagrants rose ninefold, from 0.9 percent in 1759 to 8.2 percent by 1801. Some people won, others lost.[5]

Two secular trends in the nature of labor and wages seem clear. First, the rise in wage work as the primary method of earning. As families moved from towns to cities and the factory became the dominant mode of employment, wages became the sole source of people's livelihoods. Karl Marx viewed wage labor as akin to slavery in his attacks on capitalism.[6] Second, the shift to factory production altered the nature of work. Textile work shifted from domestic to factory production, and skilled hand labor could now be commoditized through steam-powered machinery. One historian describes this change as "nothing less than catastrophic, a violation of the sacred nature of the home."[7]

It was to these changes that Ned Ludd and his movement took such violent opposition. They saw in the Industrial Revolution the destruction of their very way of life, not merely their livelihoods. Industrialization would bring to the economic realm the type of formalism and a shift away from tradition and custom as a way of organizing life, replacing that with rational/legal institutions and economically motivated organizations. The Luddites, and other protesters, saw themselves as worse, not better, off.

The development of the steam engine, and the Industrial Revolution it fostered, produced both positive and negative effects for British society. I do not intend to pass judgment on the moral worth of the Industrial Revolution with this brief accounting of some of its larger social impacts, but rather the story illustrates the poignant reality that *any* development produces both good and not so good outcomes. Whether the Industrial Revolution was saintly or satanic, then, depends on the perspective we use to define whether people became better off.

What constitutes "better off?" What does it mean to get out of poverty? Should it mean more than just having more income? This chapter considers the end goal of the fight on poverty. The five types of capital discussed in the previous chapters represent the *means* of *getting* people out of poverty, and we'll consider here what role they play in realizing the *end* of people *being* out of poverty. The end of poverty comes when people attain Eudemonia, a term from Aristotelian philosophy—or when they flourish, according to psychologist Martin Seligman.[8]

EUDEMONIA AS THE END OF POVERTY

Amartya Sen won the Nobel Prize in economics in 1998 for his work in welfare economics. Sen's choice was unpopular among many in the profession, and their disdain was captured by *Wall Street Journal* editorial writer Robert Pollock, who called Sen's work the "muddleheaded views of establishment leftists" and suggested that "it would be nice to see the committee recognize that from time to time by refusing to give an award, rather than default to someone of such debatable merit."[9] Sen's crime against doctrinaire economics? The view that development entailed more than income; that development meant an expansion in human capabilities and freedom, and that qualitative gains mattered just as much as quantitative ones.

Capability deprivation, Sen's term for poverty, arises from a lack of income. It manifests itself as the lack of ability to purchase basic necessities or advanced consumer goods, but also in terms of things like access to medical care or adequate educational opportunities. The social status, not merely the economic standing, of the poor also excludes them from active involvement in the political, civic, and religious life of their communities. The poor lack the freedom to exchange for things they desire but also lack fundamental dignity, rights, and legal standing in many places.[10]

Sen's call, what Pollock decried as muddleheaded leftism, was for a "many-sided approach" that involves sustained action by government actors. Governments work to create freedom first by ensuring a basic set of rights and liberties for people, then moving on to encourage capabilities such as education or health care to reach the poor. Redistribution schemes and a restricting of incentives that guide business and market activity should help create a better opportunity set for those with low incomes. The end of poverty for Sen encompasses a focus on human rights, but also healthy doses of individual liberty to choose the outcomes in life people value.

Whether Sen's view of development as freedom represents a muddleheaded distortion or a more correct focus on market forces misses the central point. Mainstream economics and Sen's response both deal with poverty as a Big P phenomenon amenable to solution at the highest levels of both abstraction and action. Little p poverty, at the level of individuals and communities, requires ends appropriate to those actors. Certainly greater aggregate income helps, and well-established political rights prove critical; however, the focus needs to be at the individual level, on individual human flourishing.

Eudemonia, Flourishing, and Little p Poverty

Eudemonia is a Greek word that means "having a good guardian spirit": that is, the state of having an objectively desirable life, universally agreed by classical Greek philosophers and citizens as the supreme human good. This objective character distinguishes it from the modern concept of happiness: a subjectively satisfactory life. The quest for happiness, for the Greeks, entailed pleasure, but also concepts such as justice, fairness, and opportunity.[11] Eudemonia comes to individuals; it represents the exit from little p, but maybe not Big P, poverty; the concept has become relevant again in modern psychology through the work of Martin Seligman.[12]

Seligman began his career as a professional psychologist in 1967 amid what he termed a focus on negative psychology. Psychotherapy in the 1960s entailed identifying and remedying the various causes of psychological distress, be they neuroses, psychoses, or other mental maladies. Psychologists worked from the deep belief that eliminating the causes, and consequences, of psychic dysfunction represented the end goal of their work. Psychic health was the absence of dysfunction; if you weren't sick you must be healthy.

Martin saw the flaw in this argument: the absence of illness does not equal health, particularly if psychic health requires active effort and investment on the part of individuals. Positive psychology builds on the core insight that being healthy means more than just not being sick. Creating a life worth living requires attention to a different type of health. What is the good life for Seligman? "Happiness, flow, meaning, love, gratitude, accomplishment, growth, better relationships—constitutes human flourishing. Learning that you can have more of these things is life changing. Glimpsing the vision of a flourishing human future is life changing."[13]

The PERMA acronym captures the five elements of Seligman's model of eudemonia. The first element, P, stands for *positive emotion*. Positive emotion can be defined as any pleasurable emotion or sensation; it captures very well the notion of utility that economists think of. Positive emotion could be the satisfaction of a good meal, the visual and tactile pleasure found in a bouquet of flowers, the joy and curiosity we feel when learning new things, or the hope we hold for the future. Positive emotion represents a necessary condition for happiness; it's hard to be happy without feeling good.

Engagement, or the E, can best be described by Seligman's term of flow: when we become so involved in a task or activity that we seem to lose our own sense of being and become completely absorbed in what we are doing. Time flies, not only when we are having fun but also when we are deeply engaged in some active pursuit. Engagement requires that we operate at the edge of our abilities, and the things we are doing require our full attention and best effort; engagement entails stretch, and we have to reach and work to flourish. Positive emotion may be transitory, but engagement contributes to more lasting growth and development.

The R in the model stands for *relationships*. Humans are gregarious creatures, social by nature. The creation and maintenance of positive, healthy, and developmentally sound relationships fills a core human need. Positive relationships build on a foundation of fundamental respect for another or others, a concern for their well-being as much as our own, and a willingness to give of ourselves to help others be happy and succeed. Strong relationships reflect back these same principles onto us; our respect for ourselves improves, as does our vision of lasting satisfaction.

Meaning, M, is the next element in the PERMA acronym. Meaning gets at a deep human need to see ourselves as a part of something bigger than the microdrama of our own lives. We have a need to find transcendent meaning, to be a part of something larger than ourselves. To be truly happy we must have an answer to the question Why am I here? What purpose does my life serve? A sense of purpose and meaning helps us through the sad and difficult times of our lives, times when positive emotions flee, engagement eludes us, and maybe even our relationships suffer. Meaning bestows a deep and persistent sense of happiness that creates long-term flourishing.

The final element of the PERMA model is *achievement*, or A. Achievement means at its core getting things done. Achievement, however, gets at more than just getting up or doing our daily work. It comes when we accomplish challenging goals, master new skills or difficult subjects, win contests, or move our lives forward in fundamental ways. Achievement provides a measure of our skill and prowess, and as we achieve difficult new tasks or master skills, it also provides us with a measure of our growth and development. Achievement allows us to look backward at a legacy of accomplishment, remembering the pleasure we felt at the time but also engendering its own unique retrospective joy.

PERMA, human flourishing, or Eudemonia all stand at the end of the journey from poverty to prosperity. They capture a richer set of outcomes than money income as they describe some of the things money can buy, but many other sources of happiness money can't buy. Flourishing, at least as Seligman describes it, is an individual-, or maybe a family-, or community-based measure. The outcome of eliminating poverty in the lives of individuals is reflected in things that directly touch them: personal pleasure, engaging activities, real relationships, a sense of meaning, and tangible accomplishments. Self-reliance and the five types of capital don't just help people out of little p poverty; they contribute to flourishing as well.

SELF-RELIANCE, THE FIVE CAPITALS, AND EUDEMONIA

A focus on self-reliance and the five types of capital, as the means of eliminating poverty provide ample guidance and motivation for the fight against poverty. It makes sense to lift our eyes and look at the ends of our efforts as well, if only to avoid creating groups of Luddites among those we help. Development work creates winners and losers, goods and not so goods; if we keep our eye on eudemonia we can, hopefully, avoid eliminating economic poverty but deepening its emotional or spiritual dimension. Let's look at how self-reliance contributes to flourishing and then consider some obvious overlaps between the five capitals and eudemonia.

Self-Reliance. Self-reliance helps us weather the storms of life without drowning and it helps us welcome opportunities when the sun shines. At a deeper level self-reliance allows us to express our full humanity; it represents a fundamental alignment between the lives we daily live and our true selves.[14] Self-reliance develops and manifests autonomy, a fundamental need of humanity and a marker of eudemonia. I don't want to diminish this broad, systemic interaction by isolating one-to-one relationships between the elements of self-reliance and flourishing; however, some links seem obvious.

We feel greater levels of positive emotion when we've played a central role in creating the conditions where those emotions manifest themselves. To the extent that *responsibility* spurs us to action, that sense of obligation to be engaged deepens and sweetens the subjective satisfaction we derive from those actions, as we know we played an active part. Positive, energizing relationships arise when two independent individuals come together to form an interdependent whole.

Self-efficacy provides a foundation for achievement and engagement. We rarely attain that which we don't believe we can; without that fundamental belief we give up when the path to goal achievement seems out of reach. Self-efficacy leads us try new things, to not rest on a sense of past accomplishment and thus to make continuous improvement a defining aspect of eudemonia. Engagement comes only when we truly stretch ourselves and become immersed in tasks and activities; self-efficacy allows us to be comfortable operating at the limits of our capacity. Immersion requires not only focus, but confidence as well. Both arise from our belief that we can do hard things.

The essentials of day-to-day living don't leave much time for finding transcendent meaning, and those in poverty find their days consumed with the essentials of meeting their basic needs. The cultural institutions that provide people with a sense of meaning, from the organized denominations of Christianity to which most Ghanaians, Paraguayans, and our single mothers belong, to the rich oral traditions of the Navajo, all present a larger panorama of humanity and our lives as an essential part of their teachings. The *long-term orientation* of the self-reliant resonates with this larger perspective, as finding transcendent meaning entails a process over time as well as events in time.

Institutional capital. Cognitive and normative institutions create meaning. The steam engine reflected one set of cognitive/normative institutions, the allure of "money getting" projects.[15] Ned Ludd and his followers held dear another set, a set that valued family and honored traditional ways of working. At the level of institutions, the goods and bads of development become most apparent. Moving forward means, of necessity, moving away from existing cultural patterns, norms, and world views. It means adopting new mental maps and moral compasses.

As we work to build institutional capital, particularly by influencing the mental and moral maps our clients use, we must be cognizant which institutions we displace, and what we displace them with. What displaces more traditional ways of life is often a focus on wealth, material possessions, and the devaluation of intrinsic relationships and the ascendance of instrumental ones: getting ahead becomes the sole (soul's) measure of value. The trick here involves helping people adopt elements of the spirit of capitalism consonant with the meaning systems they live in, but leaving ample room for traditions and values that avoid the descent into materialism as a moral good. We need to make sure the dyes we use enhance, rather than destroy, meaning.

Social capital. Social capital centers on relationships, so this becomes a very natural fit with the PERMA model. For Seligman a flourishing relationship, whether thick or thin, will be rich in bonding capital. Instrumental relationships that help us get ahead fill only part of our deep human needs; they help fill the stomach but do little for the soul. Positive relationships build on respect and trust; they engage the whole person and create emotional, intellectual, and spiritual connections as well as economic ones.

Chapter 4 focused on the double-edged nature of most social capital, and those lessons apply here as well. We must avoid building and encouraging relationships that do little beyond provide economic resources, and attend to a broader vision of positive relationships, ones that fill the soul and meet our instinctual needs for attachment and belonging with others. The importance of bonding capital helps us maintain an appropriate focus on critical relationships; we need to help people strengthen the relationships that matter most to them as well as cultivate ones that move them forward economically.

Human capital. Human capital speaks to the Achievement component of eudemonia. Achievement requires all the virtues of the heart, as most things worth achieving take persistent, diligent, and courageous work. Accomplishing difficult and challenging goals requires hard, diligent, and sustained effort. In today's world the head and hands also contribute to achievement because without relevant cognitive skill and physical dexterity people find their ability to reach new heights limited.

The work we do to strengthen human capital helps our clients achieve economic outcomes; eliminating poverty constitutes an achievement of massive proportion. Human capital must have a holistic focus on work that enhances people's intellectual and practical skills as well as helping them incorporate important elements of the Protestant work ethic. Increased human capital may spill over to other domains such as family or leisure activities and encourage or assist goal achievement in these areas as well.

Organizational capital. We often become absorbed, engaged, and lost in organized activities. Many of life's most challenging tasks, from engagement in business activities to raising children, happen within the context of organization because organization happens only when we've reached the limit of our personal capabilities. Whether activities take on a formal character, such as an official league, or reflect the informality of a pick-up game, the structure, constraints, and stretching that come through work and play with others create opportunities for immersion that prove difficult to achieve on our own.

Our work to strengthen organizational capital among the poor gives them more opportunities to engage. People become engaged when they have a clear sense of what they do, and how their role contributes to the larger task at hand. Structure encourages engagement, as it provides clarity and focus. Ownership contributes as well, and the positive emotion it generates through possessing the spoils of organized activity makes it easier for us to commit fully and engross ourselves in activities.

Physical capital. Strangely, the concreteness of physical capital plays a substantial role in creating positive emotions or satisfaction. Some satisfactions come without physical capital, such as watching a beautiful sunset, and some are by-products of other types of capital and flourishing, such as the joy of relationships. In many cases, however, solid and liquid capitals produce satisfaction and pleasure. The assets we have create economic value for us, but they also spawn satisfaction. Having money allows us to have more fun, and

TABLE 11.1. Eudemonia, Self-Reliance, Capital Accounts, and Values

Eudemonia . . .	arises from/promotes self-reliance, . . .	the capital accounts, . . .	and values
Positive Emotion	Responsibility	Physical Capital	Kindness Gratitude Admire beauty
Engagement	Self-efficacy	Organizational Capital	Loyalty/duty Self-control Curiosity
Relationships	Responsibility	Social Capital	Love others Accept love Fairness
Meaning	Long-term orientation	Institutional Capital	Perspective Leadership Integrity
Achievement	Self-efficacy	Human Capital	Bravery Persistence Hope

Source: PERMA elements originate in Martin E. P. Seligman, *Flourish : A Visionary New Understanding of Happiness and Well-Being* (New York: Free Press, 2011).

the physical things we have, such as cars, hearths, or homes, generate genuine pleasure.

To the extent that our work deals with physical capital we should consider how that capital contributes to positive emotions, but also where the landmines of negative emotion lay hidden. Technologies such as computers or other communications devices exhibit this quality; think of the negative impacts on people who lead overconnected lives: stress, detachment from relationships, and an emerging narcissism. Ned Ludd and his followers found little positive emotion in the technology of their day; let's work to help people realize the satisfaction that the proper use of physical capital can bring.

The organizations you build and strengthen, based on the principles outlined in Part II, also play a role in realizing eudemonia. The values that ground your organization and its work will drive the particular elements of the PERMA model that your associates, clients, and partners experience. I argued earlier that values may be your most critical *input*; the complement realizes that values contribute directly to your ultimate *outcomes* as well. Table 11.1 summarizes the ties that bind self-reliance, the five types of capital, and the core values of your organization to enhanced flourishing and eudemonia.

CONCLUSION

Our efforts to eliminate poverty must build from a platform that includes the whole person. People have needs greater than food, water, and shelter, and we must remember that the way we help people economically prosper can assist or detract their whole person from finding joy and happiness in life. Just as the means for fighting poverty required a more holistic view than just money, so too must we focus on a larger sense of what it means to truly eliminate poverty. Poverty ends when people have both food and flourishing.

You first met Freddie in Chapter 2. The last time I saw Freddie he spoke excitedly about his life and work. As chairman of the Teteh Quarshie Market Association, he's diligently engaged with the city of Accra to obtain a long-term lease for the shops in the market. With a long-term lease the shop owners could make greater investments to upgrade the quality of the market and compete more effectively for business. Freddie hopes to see a small restaurant open up, as well as better amenities for the expatriate shoppers that frequent the shops. The market association provides Freddie with deep meaning and an opportunity to achieve some worthwhile, and tremendously difficult, goals.

Freddie continues to produce beautiful carvings and stretch his skills. His business now supports the next generation, as he's paying for a nephew to attend high school and saving money for his younger children's education, including university studies. Family, friends, and the other shop owners represent a rich network of positive relationships in his life. Finally, to talk with Freddie is to feel his satisfaction with life. He welcomed me with a warm hug and huge smile, a smile indicative of a full, flourishing life.

It's not about the money! As I've argued in these pages, money—and physical capital more generally—contributes to the elimination of poverty and the achievement of eudemonia. So do other types of capital. Little p poverty gives way to individual and family flourishing when self-reliance leads individuals to acquire, employ, leverage, and preserve all five types of capital. The design and activities of the organizations you create, guide, and inspire, rather than merely the dollars you spend, become the decisive foot soldiers in an ultimately winnable fight against little p poverty. I opened with the question "Is poverty permanent?" At the little p level, I answer with a resounding NO. The war can be won; through the principles of self-reliance permanent poverty *will* yield to enduring eudemonia.

REFERENCE MATTER

NOTES

Introduction

1. UN General Assembly, 2000. *The United Nations Millennium Development Declaration* (55/2), New York City, p. 4. See http://www.un.org/millennium/declaration/ares552e.pdf, accessed 13 August 2012.

2. C. K. Prahalad popularized the notion of the "bottom of the pyramid." C. K. Prahalad. 2005. *The Fortune at the Bottom of the Pyramid*. Upper Saddle River, NJ: Wharton School Publishing. The management literature on the topic continues to grow; for example, see S. L. Hart. 2007. *Capitalism at the Crossroads*. 2nd ed. Upper Saddle River, NJ: Wharton School Publishing; and T. London and S. L. Hart. 2011. "Creating a fortune with the base of the pyramid." In *Next Generation Business Strategies for the Base of the Pyramid*, ed. London and Hart, 249. Upper Saddle River, NJ: FT Press.

Chapter 1

1. For a review of development economics, see D. Ray. 1998. *Development Economics*. Princeton: Princeton University Press. Management scholars took up the baton with the publication of C. K. Prahalad. 2005. *The Fortune at the Bottom of the Pyramid*. Upper Saddle River, NJ: Wharton School Publishing (see Introduction, n. 2)

2. J. Haughton and S. R. Kandker. 2009. "What is poverty and why measure it?" In *Handbook on Poverty + Inequality*, 1–9. Washington, DC: World Bank.

3. H. W. J. Rittel and M. M. Webber. 1973. "Dilemmas in a general theory of planning." *Policy Sciences* 4: 155–69.

4. Data from http://gbk.eads.usaidallnet.gov/data/detailed.html, excel file "historical dollar-data," Economic assistance 1946–2010, accessed 16 August 2012.

5. J. Sachs. 2005. *The End of Poverty: Economic Possibilities for Our Time*. New York: Penguin Books.

6. Ibid., 236.

7. W. Easterly. 2001. *The Elusive Quest for Growth: Economists' Adventures and Misadventures in the Tropics*. Cambridge, MA: MIT Press. And W. Easterly. 2006. *The White Man's Burden: Why the West's Efforts to Aid the Rest Have Done So Much Ill and So Little Good*. New York: Penguin Books.

8. Easterly, *The Elusive Quest for Growth*, 74–75.

9. Easterly, *The White Man's Burden*, ch. 11.

10. M. Yunus. 2006. Nobel Lecture. Oslo, Norway (10 December). Text can be found at http://www.nobelprize.org/nobel_prizes/peace/laureates/2006/yunus-lecture-en.html, accessed 17 August 2012.

11. P. Chavan and R. Ramakumar. 2002. "Microcredit and rural poverty: An analysis of empirical evidence." *Economic and Political Weekly* 37 (10): 955–65. A more recent review can be found in J. C. Brau and G. M. Woller. 2004. "Microfinance: A comprehensive review of the existing literature." *Journal of Entrepreneurial Finance and Business Ventures* 9 (1): 1–26.

12. P. Mosley and D. Hulme. 1998. "Microenterprise finance: Is there a conflict between growth and poverty alleviation?" *World Development* 26 (5): 783–90; see p. 786.

13. J. C. Brau, S. Hiatt, and W. Woodworth. 2009 "Evaluating the impacts of microfinance institutions using Guatemalan data." *Managerial Finance* 35 (12): 953–74.

14. L. Daniels and D. Mead. 1998. "The contribution of small enterprises to household and national income in Kenya." *Economic Development and Cultural Change* 47 (1): 45–71.

15. See Chavan and Ramakumar, "Microcredit and rural poverty," 959, for a discussion of the limiting effects on business growth of microloans.

16. J. Jacobs. 2000. *The Nature of Economies*. New York: Vintage Books. In this vein my distinction between growth and development mirrors that of Joseph Schumpeter in describing the difference between industrial and entrepreneurial activity. See J. A. Schumpeter. 1936. *The Theory of Economic Development*. Cambridge, MA: Harvard University Press.

17. See http://www.britannica.com/EBchecked/topic/287086/Industrial-Revolution, accessed June 2010.

18. See R. Stark. 2005. *The Victory of Reason: How Christianity Led to Freedom, Capitalism, and Western Success*. New York: Random House; D. L. Landes. 1999. *The Wealth and Poverty of Nations: Why Some Are So Rich and Some So Poor*. New York: W. W. Norton and Company; and D. C. North and R. P. Thomas. 1973. *The Rise of the Western World: A New Economic History*. Cambridge: Cambridge University Press.

19. Material for this section is drawn from B. Madsen. 2002. *Watt's Perfect Engine: Steam and the Age of Invention*. New York: Columbia University Press; J. Gribben. 2002. *Science: A History*. New York: Penguin Books; and G. Weightman. 2007. *Industrial Revolutionaries: The Making of the Modern World, 1776–1914*. New York: Grove Press.

20. "Capital." In *Oxford English Dictionary*. 2009. Oxford: Clarendon Press.

21. W. R. Scott. 2008. *Institutions and Organizations*. 3rd ed. Thousand Oaks, CA: Sage, 48.

22. See R. Friedland and R. R. Alford. 1991. "Bringing society back in: Symbols, practices, and institutional contradictions." In *The New Institutionalism in Organizational Analysis*, ed. W. W. Powell and P. J. Dimaggio, 232–66. Chicago: University of Chicago Press.

23. A. Portes. 1998. "Social capital: Its origins and applications in modern sociology." *Annual Review of Sociology* 24: 1–24.

24. M. Walzer. 1994. *Thick and Thin: Moral Argument at Home and Abroad*. Notre Dame, IN: University of Notre Dame Press.

25. G. S. Becker. 1962. "Investment in human capital: A theoretical analysis." *Journal of Political Economy* 70 (5, part 2: "Investment in human beings"): 9–49. Quotation from p. 9.

26. A. Savvides and T. Stengos. 2009. *Human Capital and Economic Growth*. Stanford: Stanford University Press.

27. M. Weber. 1947. *The Theory of Social and Economic Organization*. New York: Macmillan.

Chapter 2

1. H. W. Dickinson. 1936. *James Watt: Craftsman and Engineer*. Cambridge: Cambridge University Press. Material also taken from A. Carnegie. 1905. *James Watt*. London: Oliphant Anderson.

2. Conversion of £1,750 to dollars done 28 August 2012 at
http://www.umich.edu/~ece/student_projects/money/denom.html. Conversion from 2003 dollars to 2010 dollars uses conversion factors found at http://oregonstate.edu/cla/polisci/faculty-research/sahr/sahr.htm.

3. Car Lira, *Biography of James Watt: A Summary*. See http://www.egr.msu.edu/~lira/supp/steam/wattbio.html and http://www.clockmakers.org/.

4. Dickinson, *James Watt*, 21.

5. Ibid., 23.

6. R. W. Emerson. 1989. *Ralph Waldo Emerson and Self Reliance: Adventures in American Literature: Pegasus Edition*, ed. Bernard Brodsky. Orlando, FL: Harcourt, 221.

7. B. M. Friedman. 2005. *The Moral Consequences of Economic Growth*. New York: Vintage Books, ch. 2: "Perspectives from the Enlightenment and its roots."

8. N. D. Smoak. 2007. "Beliefs." In *Encyclopedia of Social Psychology: Volume 1*, ed. R. F. Baumeister and K. D. Vohs, 110–11. Thousand Oaks, CA: Sage Publications.

9. See C. Williams. 2007. *Management*. 4th ed. Mason, OH: Southwestern Publishing, ch. 13. A more academic treatment can be found in J. G. Nicholls. 1984. "Achievement motivation: Conceptions of ability, subjective experience, task choice, and performance." *Psychological Review* 91 (3): 328–46.

10. Plato's "Crito" represents an early and excellent discourse on the role of duty in public life. See Plato. 1994. "Crito." In *The Collected Dialogues of Plato*, ed. E. Hamilton and H. Cairns, 27–39. Princeton: Princeton University Press. Aristotle takes up individual duties in the "Nicomachean Ethics" and the "Politics." See Aristotle. 1941. "Nicomachean ethics." In *The Basic Works of Aristotle*, ed. R. Mckeon, 935–1126. New York: Random House. Also Aristotle's "Politics," on pp. 1127–324 of the same volume.

11. A. Comte. 1896. *The Positive Philosophy: Volume 2*, trans. H. Martineau. London: George Bell and Sons, 98. Quotation taken from Friedman, *The Moral Consequences Of Economic Growth*, 30.

12. My own research in Ghana highlights the importance of parental influences on children's sense of responsibility and the associated behaviors. See P. C. Godfrey, W. G. Dyer, and J. G. Mangum. March 2009. "Managing smart: The capital accounts

of successful entrepreneurs in a developing economy." Paper presented at the Western Academy of Management, Heber City, UT.

13. The early work of Kluckhohn and Strodtbeck around value orientation theory remains an authoritative voice on the subject. M. D. Hills. 2002. *Kluckhohn and Strodtbeck's Values Orientation Theory*. For a synopsis of the theory, see http://scholarworks.gvsu.edu/orpc/vol4/iss4/3, accessed 27 August 2012. The original work is F. R. Kluckhohn and F. L. Strodtbeck. 1961. *Variations in Value Orientations*. Evanston, IL: Row, Peterson.

14. A. Bandura. 1994. "Self-efficacy." In *Encyclopedia of Human Behavior: Volume 4*, ed. V. S. Ramachaudran, 71–81. New York: Academic Press.

15. Bandura's own summary after twenty years can be found in A. Bandura. 1997. *Self-efficacy: The Exercise of Control*. New York: W. H. Freeman. Self-efficacy tends to be an applied construct, and most literature reviews tend to be discipline, or application, specific. Two reviews of interest for economic self-reliance are N. G. Boyd and G. S. Vozikis. 1994. "The influence of self-efficacy on the development of entrepreneurial intentions and actions." *Entrepreneurship: Theory and Practice* 18 (4): 63–90; and G. Sadri and I. T. Robertson. 1993. "Self-efficacy and work-related behaviour: A review and meta-analysis." *Applied Psychology* 42 (2): 139–52.

16. G. Joët, E. L. Usher, and P. Bressoux. 2011. "Sources of self-efficacy: An investigation of elementary school students in France." *Journal of Educational Psychology* 103 (article 3): 649–63.

17. G. Hofstede. 1980. *Culture's Consequences*. Thousand Oaks, CA: Sage Publications; 2nd ed., 2001, Sage. Hofstede, along with his son, Gert Jan, and Michael Minkov, published a third volume in the series: G. Hofstede, G. J. Hofstede, and M. Minkov. 2010. *Cultures and Organizations: Software of the Mind*. New York: McGraw-Hill.

18. J. A. Schumpeter. 1942. *Capitalism, Socialism, and Democracy*. New York: Harper and Brothers, 84.

19. "Husband." In *Oxford English Dictionary*. 2009. Oxford: Clarendon Press.

20. I learned this principle from Steve Gibson, founder of the Academy for Creating Entrepreneurs in the Philippines.

21. International Fund for Agricultural Development. 2009. "Ghana—informal financial services for rural women in the Northern Region." New York: United Nations; and E. Aryeetey and C. Udry. 1995. "The characteristics of informal financial markets in Africa." In *Yale Economics Department Working Papers*, 42. New Haven: Yale University.

22. Aristotle began this conversation by noting the importance of Eudemonia, or human flourishing. For a description of this concept, see J. H. Randall. 1960. *Aristotle*. New York: Columbia University Press. For more recent additions to this thinking, Pope John Paul II, a theologian, outlined an expansive view of human progress in John Paul II. 1991. *Centessimus Annus*. Washington, DC: Office for Publication and Promotion Services, United States Catholic Conference. More recently, psychologist Martin Seligman has advanced the concept of human flourishing in his field. For an example, see M. E. P. Seligman. 2011. *Flourish: A Visionary New Understanding of Happiness and Well-being*. New York: Free Press.

23. See Bandura, *Self-efficacy*; and Joët, Usher, and Bressoux, "Sources of self-efficacy."

24. This question comes from S. Johnson. 1993. *Yes or No?: The Guide to Better Decisions*. New York: HarperCollins Publishers.

Chapter 3

1. See E. W. Hulme. 1896. "The history of the patent system under the prerogative and at common law." *Law Quarterly Review* 46: 141–54, 143.

2. W. Blackstone. *Commentaries on the Laws of England: 1765–1769, Book II (The Rights of Things)*, ch. 21, p. 346. See http://avalon.law.yale.edu/18th_century/blackstone_bk2ch21.asp, accessed 21 August 2012.

3. See http://www.ladas.com/Patents/USPatentHistory.html for a brief description. See also C. Dent. 2009. "Generally inconvenient: The 1624 Statute of Monopolies as political compromise." *Melbourne University Law Review* 33 (2): 415–53; and Hulme, "The history of the patent system."

4. David Landes puts great stock in the role of patent law in creating incentives for economic development. See D. S. Landes. 1999. *The Wealth and Poverty of Nations: Why Are Some So Rich and Others So Poor?* New York: W. W. Norton.

5. R. J. Sullivan. 1989. "England's 'age of invention': The acceleration of patents and patentable invention during the industrial revolution." *Explorations in Economic History* 26 (4): 424–52.

6. B. M. Friedman. 2005. *The Moral Consequences of Economic Growth*. New York: Vintage Books, 37.

7. A. Smith. 1776/1965. *An Inquiry into the Nature and Causes of the Wealth of Nations*. New York: Modern Library. Smith's famous passage, found in book IV, ch. 2, para. 9, reads: "By directing that industry in such a manner as its produce may be of greatest value, he intends only his own gain, and he is in this, as in many other cases, led by an invisible hand to promote an end which was no part of his intention."

8. B. Madsen. 2002. *Watt's Perfect Engine: Steam and the Age of Invention*. New York: Columbia University Press; and G. Weightman. 2007. *Industrial Revolutionaries: The Making of the Modern World, 1776–1914*. New York: Grove Press, ch. 1, n. 19. Both note the importance of the patent and its value to the invention. See also, for a description of the patent's importance, E. Robinson and A. E. Musson. 1969. *James Watt and the Steam Revolution: A Documentary History*. London: Adams and Dart; New York: Kelley.

9. See D. C. North. 1990. *Institutions, Institutional Change and Economic Performance*. New York: Cambridge University Press, 1990; and D. C. North. 1991. "Institutions." *Journal of Economic Perspectives* 5 (1): 97–112.

10. North's work stands in stark contrast to the abstract, theoretical work initiated and justified by Milton Friedman. See M. Friedman. 1953. *Essays in Positive Economics*. Chicago: University of Chicago Press.

11. W. R. Scott. 2008. *Institutions and Organizations*. 3rd ed. Thousand Oaks, CA: Sage, 48. See also W. R. Scott, M. Ruef, P. J. Mendel, and C. A. Caronna. 2000. *Institutional Change and Healthcare Organizations*. Chicago: University of Chicago Press; M. Granovetter. 1985. "Economic action and social structure: The problem of

embeddedness." *American Journal of Sociology* 91 (3): 481–510; K. Thelen. 1999. "Historical institutionalism in comparative politics." *Annual Review of Political Science* 2: 369–404.

12. Institutional historian Thomas Ertman argues that the rules and game co-evolve; we see the regulatory structures and cognitive-normative elements interacting with each other to create relatively unique macrosocial institutions such as government. See T. Ertman. *Birth of the Leviathan: Building States and Regimes in Medieval and Early Modern Europe.* New York: Cambridge University Press, 1997.

13. A great description of the rational choice view, and how it compares with other views, can be found in J. L. Campbell. 2004. *Institutional Change and Globalization.* Princeton: Princeton University Press.

14. D. C. North and R. P. Thomas. 1973. *The Rise of the Western World: A New Economic History.* Cambridge: Cambridge University Press.

15. P. Bolton and M. Dewatripont. 2005. *Contract Theory.* Boston: MIT Press. This very advanced textbook outlines the fundamental assumption that all trade occurs through contracts subject to adjudication.

16. I. R. Macneil. 1985. "Relational contract: What we do and do not know." *Wisconsin Law Review*: 483–525; and I. R. Macneil. 2000. "Relational contract theory: Challenges and questions." *Northwestern University Law Review* 94 (3, Spring): 877–907.

17. M. Weber. 1947. *The Theory of Social and Economic Organization.* New York: Macmillan.

18. Statistics taken from Navajo Nation, Division of Economic Development. *2009–2010 Comprehensive Economic Development Strategy. Window Rock, AZ: Navajo Nation Division of Economic Development,* 24.

19. Data from http://navajonationdode.org/Office_of_Educational_Research_and_Statistics_1.aspx, accessed 23 August 2012.

20. See E. P. Yazzie and M. Speas. 2007. *Diné Bizaad Bináhoo'aah (Rediscovering the Navajo language): An introduction to the Navajo Language.* Flagstaff, AZ: Salina Bookshelf, ch. 7. The claim of 140 clans comes from http://navajo-arts.com/clans-navajo.html, accessed March 2012.

21. The above citation also quotes Phil Bluehouse in their description of the concept.

22. J. R. Farella. 1984. *The Main Stalk: A Synthesis of Navajo Philosophy.* Tucson: University of Arizona Press.

23. See D. C. North. 1990. *Institutions, Institutional Change and Economic Performance.* New York: Cambridge University Press; C. Seelos and J. Mair. 2007. "Profitable business models and market creation in the context of deep poverty: A strategic view." *Academy of Management Perspectives* 21 (4): 49–63.

24. See L. Pritchett and F. DeWeijer. 2011. "Fragile states: Stuck in a capability trap?" *World Bank Development Report,* background paper; see http://www.hks.harvard.edu/fs/lpritch/NEW%20docs,%20ppts,%20etc/Fragile%20States%20-%20stuck%20in%20a%20capability%20trap.pdf. See also J. W. Meyer and B. Rowan. 1991. "Institutionalized organizations: Formal structure as myth and ceremony." In *The New Institutionalism in Organizational Analysis,* ed. W. W. Powell and P. J.

DiMaggio, 41–62. Chicago: University of Chicago Press.

25. M. Weber. 1958. *The Protestant Ethic and the Spirit of Capitalism,* trans. Parsons. New York: Charles Scribner's Sons.

26. T. Hillerman. 1990. *People of Darkness.* In *The Jim Chee Mysteries.* New York: Harper and Row, 59.

27. A. Giddens. 1996. *In Defense of Sociology.* Cambridge: Polity Press. See also W. H. Sewell. 1992. "A theory of structure: Duality, agency, and transformation." *American Journal of Sociology* 98 (1): 1–29.

28. Material in this section taken from K. Bobroff. 2004–6. "Diné bi beehaz' áanii: Codifying indigenous consuetudinary law in the 21st century." *Tribal Law Journal* 5, http://tlj.unm.edu/volumes/index.php.

29. W. Channell. 2008. "Law as relationship: Toward a more effective and ethical legal reform." *Economic Self-Reliance Review* 10 (2): 20–28.

30. J. P. Kotter. 1996. *Leading Change.* Boston: Harvard Business School Press.

31. This argument is explained very well in P. Pierson. 2004. *Politics in Time.* Princeton: Princeton University Press.

32. N. Machiavelli. 1513. *The Prince.* New York: SoHo Books, ch. 6.

Chapter 4

1. Information about the statue, its description, and inscription at http://www.westminster-abbey.org/our-history/people/james-watt, accessed 3 September 2012.

2. A. Carnegie. 1905. *James Watt.* New York: Doubleday, Page and Company, 5.

3. J. Uglow. 2002. *The Lunar Men: Five Friends Whose Curiosity Changed the World.* New York: Farrar, Straus and Giroux, 28.

4. B. Marsden. 2002. *Watt's Perfect Engine: Steam and the Age of Invention.* New York: Columbia University Press, 14, and H. W. Dickinson. 1936. *James Watt: Craftsman and Engineer.* London: Cambridge University Press, 20.

5. Marsden, *Watt's Perfect Engine,* 24.

6. Dickinson, *James Watt,* 30.

7. Uglow, *The Lunar Men,* 101.

8. See Marsden, *Watt's Perfect Engine,* 70–71, for a complete description of these events.

9. Letter from Small to Watt, 5 February 1769, in E. Robinson and A. E. Musson. 1969. *James Watt and the Steam Revolution.* New York: Augustus M. Kelley, 54–56.

10. Robinson and Musson, *James Watt and the Steam Revolution,* 15.

11. P. S. Adler and S. W. Kwon. 2002. "Social capital: Prospects for a new concept." *Academy of Management Review* 27 (1): 17–40. The first definition comes from M. A. Bellivea, C. A. O'Reilly III, and J. B. Wade. 1996. "Social capital at the top: Effects of social similarity and status on CEO compensation." *Academy of Management Journal* 39: 1568–93. The second comes from K. Pennar. 1997. "The ties that lead to prosperity: The economic value of social bonds is only beginning to be measured." *Business Week,* December 15, 153–55.

12. R. D. Putnam. 2000. *Bowling Alone: The Collapse and Revival of American Community.* New York: Simon and Schuster; see, esp., ch. 1. Quotations taken from p. 22.

13. See M. Granovetter. 1985. "Economic action and social structure: The problem of embeddedness." *American Journal of Sociology* 91 (3): 481–510. Philosopher Michael Walzer makes a distinction between thick and thin sources of morality; I like his notion enough to include it in several places. See M. Walzer. 1994. *Thick and Thin: Moral Argument at Home and Abroad.* Notre Dame, IN: University of Notre Dame Press.

14. See Putnam, *Bowling Alone.*

15. For the economic value of reciprocity, see E. Fehr and S. Gachter. 2000. "Fairness and retaliation: The economics of reciprocity." *Journal of Economic Perspectives* 14 (3): 159–81.

16. L. Bernstein. 2001. "Private commercial law in the cotton industry: Creating cooperation through rules, norms, and institutions." *Michigan Law Review* 99: 1724–90.

17. The data in this paragraph taken from S. McLanahan and I. Garfinkel. 2012. "Fragile families: Debates, facts, and solutions." In *Marriage at the Crossroads,* 142–69. Cambridge: Cambridge University Press. The quotation at the beginning of the paragraph appears on p. 147.

18. All data drawn from U.S. Census Bureau, 2009. "Custodial mothers and fathers and their child support," http://www.census.gov/prod/2011pubs/p60-240.pdf.

19. McLanahan and Garfinkel, "Fragile families."

20. J. W. Bauer, K. D. Rettig, and S. Seohee. 2008. *The Cost of Raising Children,* ed. University Of Minnesota Extension. Minneapolis: University of Minnesota. See http://www.extension.umn.edu/distribution/familydevelopment/components/00178full.pdf, accessed 3 September 2012.

21. Some of this research has been written up; for example, see R. J. McClendon and J. Humberstone. 2008. "Education—a powerful asset for single mothers." *Economic Self-Reliance Review* 10 (1): 34–39.

22. Adler and Kwan, "Social capital," 23.

23. M. Woolcock and D. Narayan. 2000. "Social Capital: Implications for development theory, research, and policy." *World Bank Research Observer* 15 (2).

24. A. Spicer, G. A. Mcdermott, and B. Kogut. 2000. "Entrepreneurship and privatization in central Europe: The tenuous balance between destruction and creativity." *Academy of Management Review* 25 (3): 630–49.

25. M. Weber. 1947. *The Theory of Social and Economic Organization.* New York: Macmillan.

26. M. Acquaah. 2007. "Managerial social capital, strategic orientation, and performance." *Strategic Management Journal* 28 (12): 1235–55.

27. E. Durkheim. 1933/1984. *The Division of Labor In Society.* New York: Free Press.

28. A. Portes and J. Sensenbrenner. 1993. "Embeddedness and immigration: Notes on the social determinants of economic action." *American Journal of Sociology* 98 (6): 1320–50.

29. The crab mentality has been described in the Urban Dictionary, and there is even a Wikipedia entry. See http://www.urbandictionary.com/define.php?term=crab%20mentality; and http://en.wikipedia.org/wiki/Crab_mentality; accessed 3 September 2012.

30. W. W. Powell and L. Smith-Doerr. 1994. "Networks and economic life." In *The Handbook of Economic Sociology*, ed. N.M. Smelser and R. Sedberg, 368–402. Princeton: Princeton University Press, see 393. Quoted in Adler and Kwan, "Social capital," 30.

31. R. K. Payne. 1996. *A Framework for Understanding Poverty*. Highlands, TX: Aha! Process pp. 14, 23

32. I am indebted to my good friend and colleague Wade Channel for this nice turn of phrase.

33. See P. C. Godfrey, W. G. Dyer, and J. G. Mangum. March 2009. "Managing smart: The capital accounts of successful entrepreneurs in a developing economy." Paper presented at the *Western Academy of Management*, Heber City, UT.

34. The big chief problem has also been discussed in *Culture Matters*, 2003. Ed. L. E. Harrison and S. P. Huntington. New York: Basic Books.

35. B. Uzzi. 1997. "Social structure and competition in inter-firm networks: The paradox of embeddedness." *Administrative Science Quarterly* 42: 35–67, for example, has been cited more than five thousand times. Parts of our conversation have been re-printed in Uzzi. 2008. "Keys to understanding your social capital." *Economic Self-Reliance Review* 10 (2): 4–11.

Chapter 5

1. S. Yusuf. 2009. *Development Economics through the Decades: A Critical Look at 30 Years of the World Development Report*. Washington, DC: World Bank.

2. J. Uglow. 2002. *The Lunar Men: Five Friends Whose Curiosity Changed the World*. New York: Farrar, Straus and Giroux, 101. The quotation directly below appears on the same page as well.

3. Ibid., 288.

4. W. Rosen. 2010. *The Most Powerful Idea in the World*. New York: Random House, 175. Pp. 178–87 detail the development of the sun and planet gears.

5. B. Marsden. 2002. *Watt's Perfect Engine: Steam and the Age of Invention*. New York: Columbia University Press, 117–20.

6. G. Weightman. 2007. *The Industrial Revolutionaries: The Making of the Modern World, 1776–1914*. New York: Grove Press, 57.

7. R. Turner, S. L. Goulden, and B. Sheridan, eds. 1981. *Great Engineers and Pioneers in Technology*. New York: St. Martin's Press, 293.

8. Ibid., 292.

9. The wording of the Nobel Committee, http://www.nobelprize.org/nobel_prizes/economics/laureates/1992/, accessed May 2012. The seminal work in human capital is G. S. Becker. 1962. "Investment in human capital: A theoretical analysis." *Journal of Political Economy* 70 (5, part 2: Investment in human beings): 9–49. His book-length treatment is G. S. Becker. 1964. *Human Capital: A Theoretical and Empirical Analysis with Special Reference to Education*. Chicago: University of Chicago Press.

10. Quotations taken from an interview with Becker at http://www.linezine.com/7.1/interviews/gbbmthc.htm, accessed May 2012.

11. A. Smith. 1776/1965. *An Inquiry into the Nature and Causes of the Wealth of Nations*. New York: Modern Library, 32.

12. A. Savvides and T. Stengos. 2009. *Human Capital and Economic Growth*. Stanford: Stanford University Press, 32–33.

13. R. K. Payne. 1996. *A Framework for Understanding Poverty*. Highlands, TX: Aha! process, 37–40.

14. Information from this section compiled by research assistants, as well as my own travels to Paraguay. Material can be found in the teaching case Godfrey, P. C. Fundacion Paraguaya (A): The San Francisco School, Globalens case ID #1429216.

15. Data on these countries available at http://data.worldbank.org/country, accessed 7 September 2012.

16. Quotation from personal interview with Martin Burt in P. C. Godfrey. 2011. Martin Burt: A conversation with a social entrepreneur, GlobaLens, Case ID #1429214. Available at http://www.globalens.com/search.aspx?q=godfrey

17. See D. A. Kolb and R. Fry. 1975. "Toward an applied theory of experiential learning." In *Theories of Group Process*, ed. C. Cooper. London: John Wiley.

18. C. Harmon and I. Walker. 1995. "Estimates of the economic return to schooling for the United Kingdom." *American Economic Review* 85 (5): 1278–86; O. Ashenfelter and A. Krueger. 1994. "Estimates of the economic return to schooling from a new sample of twins." *American Economic Review* 84 (5): 1157–73; P. Miller, C. Mulvey, and N. Martin. 1995. "What do twins studies reveal about the economic returns to education? A comparison of Australian and U.S. findings." *American Economic Review* 85 (3): 586–99.

19. Victor Niederhoffer on long-term stock returns, at http://www.dailyspeculations.com/scholarly/LongTermStockReturns.html, accessed 28 March 2012.

20. Taken from Godfrey, *Martin Burt*.

21. L. E. Harrison. 2003. "Introduction, why culture matters." In *Culture Matters*, ed. Harrison and S. P. Huntington, xvii–il. New York: Basic Books.

22. B. M. Friedman. 2005. *The Moral Consequences of Economic Growth*. New York: Alfred A Knopf, 44.

23. M. Weber. 1958. *The Protestant Ethic and the Spirit of Capitalism*. New York: Charles Scribner's Sons, 80.

24. Taken from Godfrey, *Martin Burt*.

25. R. Ditella, S. Galiana, and E. Schargrodsky. 2004. "Property rights and beliefs: Evidence from the allocation of land titles to squatters." *Ronald Coase Institute Working Paper Series* http://www.coase.org/research.htm, accessed 24 June 2013. See p. 3 for the description of the setting. Their view of the value of property rights stands in contrast to the writings of Desoto, who argues that property rights give the poor collateralizable assets. See H. Desoto. 2000. *The Mystery of Capital*. New York: Basic Books.

26. Paul Tough. "What if the secret to success is failure?" New York *Times,* 14 September 2011. Martin Seligman discusses the principles in M. E. P. Seligman. 2011. *Flourish: A Visionary New Understanding of Happiness and Well-being*. New York: Free Press.

27. Taken from Godfrey, *Martin Burt*.

Chapter 6

1. Edmund Burke, quoted in H. W. Dickinson. 1937. *Matthew Boulton*. Cambridge: Cambridge University Press, 24.

2. From Sketchley's Birmingham Directory of 1767, 56. Cited in Dickinson, *Matthew Boulton*; and J. Uglow. 2002. *The Lunar Men*. New York: Farrar, Straus and Giroux, 17.

3. Dickinson, *Matthew Boulton*, 29.

4. Uglow, *The Lunar Men*, 25.

5. Ibid., 63.

6. Ibid., 64.

7. Ibid., 68.

8. Ibid., 215.

9. Ibid., 287; and B. Marsden. 2002. *Watt's Perfect Engine: Steam and the Age of Invention*. New York: Columbia University Press, 103–4.

10. See, for example, R. Daft. 1992. *Organization Theory and Design*, 4th ed. St. Paul: West Publishing Company, 7.

11. M. Weber. 1947. *The Theory of Social and Economic Organization*. New York: Macmillan.

12. J. H. Turner. 2004. *Human Institutions: A Theory of Societal Evolution*. Lanham, MD: Rowman and Littlefield; see 207 for details.

13. Human limitations as a foundation for organization was a fundamental insight of organizational theorist Chester Barnard. C. I. Barnard. 1938. *The Functions of the Executive*. Cambridge, MA: Harvard University Press.

14. A. Smith. 1776/1965. *An Inquiry into the Nature and Causes of the Wealth of Nations*. New York: Modern Library; see bk. I, chs. 1 and 2.

15. Uglow, *The Lunar Men,* 212.

16. J. G. March and H. Simon. 1958. *Organizations*. New York: Wiley.

17. Barnard, *The Functions of the Executive*, 5.

18. M. C. Jensen and W. H. Meckling. 1976. "Theory of the firm: Managerial behavior, agency costs, and ownership structure." *Journal of Financial Economics* 3 (4): 305–60.

19. A. A. Alchain and H. Demsetz. 1972. "Production, information costs, and economic organization." *American Economic Review* 62: 777–95.

20. The "agency theory" model has its detractors, as well. See R. L. Martin. 2012. *Fixing the Game*. Boston: Harvard Business Review Press, for a recent critique of the Jensen and Meckling model.

21. Information in this section taken from P. C. Godfrey. 2012. *Community Enterprise Solutions: Replicating the Microconsignment Model*, GlobaLens, Case ID # 1-429-331. Available at http://www.globalens.com/search.aspx?q=godfrey.

22. G. Van Kirk. 2010. "The Microconsignment model: Bridging the "last mile" of access to products and services for the rural poor." *Innovations/ Tech4Society. Boston: MIT Press Journals*, http://www.mitpressjournals.org/userimages/ContentEditor/1265821130874/INNOV-TECH4SOCIETY_127-153_van-kirk_12-30-09.pdf: 144.

23. Information on Micro-Consignment can be found at Microconsignment.com, "What is the MCM?" accessed February 2012.

24. For example, see L. Pritchett and F. DeWeijer. 2011. "Fragile states: Stuck in a capability trap." World Bank, *World Development Report* 2011 background paper; see http://www.hks.harvard.edu/fs/lpritch/NEW%20docs,%20ppts,%20etc/Fragile%20 States%20-%20stuck%20in%20a%20capability%20trap.pdf.

25. See http://www.doingbusiness.org/ and http://www.doingbusiness.org/rankings for rankings of the world's 183 countries based on the ease of doing business.

26. Material in this section has been adapted from P. C. Godfrey. 2011. "Toward a theory of the informal economy." *Academy of Management Annals* 5 (1): 231–77.

27. See note 25, above, for a listing of all countries, accessed 10 September 2012.

28. Data available from the U.S. Small Business Administration, accessed 11 April 2012. This data came from http://www.gpmlaw.com/practices/family-owned-business. aspx.

29. Uglow, *The Lunar Men*, 215.

30. D. North, J. J. Walls, and B. R. Weingast. 2009. *Violence and Social Orders*. Cambridge: Cambridge University Press; chs. 1 and 5 elaborate on the power of formal organizational templates in stabilizing advanced societies.

31. T. Beck, A. Demirguc-Kunt, and R. Levine. 2005. "SME's, growth, and poverty." *National Bureau of Economic Research Working Papers*. Cambridge, MA: Working paper 11224, http://www.nber.org/papers/w11224, accessed 24 June 2013.

32. P. Mosley and D. Hulme. 1998. "Microenterprise finance: Is there a conflict between growth and poverty alleviation?" *World Development* 26 (5): 783–90.

33. H. Desoto. 2000. *The Mystery of Capital*. New York: Basic Books. This work provides an excellent description of these hurdles in the developing world.

34. R. Laporta and A. Shleifer. 2008. "The unofficial economy and economic development." *Working Paper Series*, 1–75. Washington, DC: National Bureau of Economic Research.

35. See Godfrey, *Community Enterprise Solutions*, for figures and data.

Chapter 7

1. Material on the Weald and its contribution to early iron making at http://my-geologypage.ucdavis.edu/cowen/~gel115/115CH10.html, accessed June 2012.

2. An excellent, yet accessible, history of cannon development was written by Denver University engineering professor Dr. James Calvert. This material can be found at http://mysite.du.edu/~jcalvert/tech/cannon.htm, accessed June 2012.

3. W. Rosen. 2010. *The Most Powerful Idea in the World*. New York: Random House, 144.

4. R. Turner, S. L. Goulden, and B. Sheridan, eds. 1981. *Great Engineers and Pioneers in Technology*. New York: St. Martin's Press, 258.

5. Rosen, *The Most Powerful Idea in the World*, 165; see also Turner, Goulden, and Sheridan, *Great Engineers and Pioneers in Technology*, 280.

6. Turner, Goulden, and Sheridan, *Great Engineers and Pioneers in Technology*, 281.

7. Ibid.

8. My reference text makes this quite clear. See, for example, W. Nicholson. 1995. *Microeconomic Theory: Basic Principles and Extensions*. Fort Worth, TX: Dryden Press.

9. The history of QWERTY, as well as some of the controversy surrounding it, is described by S. Liebowitz and S. E. Margolis. 1996. "Typing errors." *Policy* (Winter): 22–28.

10. V. Chandra and S. Kolavalli. 2006. "Technology, adaptation, and exports—how some developing countries got it right." In *Technology, Adaptation, and Exports—How Some Developing Countries Got It Right,* ed. Chandra, 1–48. Washington, DC: World Bank.

11. E. K. Stice and J. D. Stice. 2006. *Financial Accounting: Reporting and Analysis,* 7th ed. Mason, OH: Thomson/Southwestern: 32–33, 537, 545.

12. P. Chavan and R. Ramakumar. 2002. "Microcredit and rural poverty: An analysis of empirical evidence." *Economic and Political Weekly* 37 (10): 955–65; see p. 959 for the results around technological investment.

13. C. K. Prahalad. 2005. *The Fortune at the Bottom of the Pyramid.* Upper Saddle River, NJ: Wharton School Publishing.

14. See A. Karnani. 2007. "The mirage of marketing to the bottom of the pyramid." *California Management Review* 49 (4): 90–111.

15. P. C. Godfrey. *Fundacion Paraguaya (A): The San Francisco School,* GlobaLens Case ID #142921. Available at http://www.globalens.com/search.aspx?q=godfrey.

16. Information on the school from http://www.mbertoni.org.py/vi/mbaracayu/cem/historia/, accessed 12 September 2012.

17. See S. B. Karpman. 1968. "Fairy tales and script drama analysis." *Transactional Analysis Bulletin* 7 (26, April), at http://www.karpmandramatriangle.com/pdf/Drama-Triangle.pdf, accessed 12 September 2012. For a modern take, see L. L'abate. 2009. "The drama triangle: An attempt to resurrect a neglected pathogenic model in family therapy theory and practice." *American Journal of Family Therapy* 37 (1): 1–11.

18. J. Collins. 2001. *Good to Great.* New York: Harper Business, ch. 7.

19. Information for this section from https://www.engineeringforchange.org/news/2012/02/04/ten_solar_cookers_that_work_at_night.html, accessed June 2012.

20. See http://www.climatehealers.org/olddump/home.html, accessed 12 September 2012.

21. This story was related to me by Warner Woodworth, noted social entrepreneur and my colleague at BYU.

22. See J. R. Farella. 1984. *The Main Stalk: A Synthesis of Navajo Philosophy.* Tucson: University of Arizona Press.

Chapter 8

1. See http://www.jquarter.org.u k/webdisk/morejwatt.htm, accessed June 2012.

2. E. Robinson and A. E. Musson. 1969. *James Watt and the Steam Revolution.* New York: Augustus M. Kelley, 62–63.

3. A. Smith. 1767/1982. *The Theory of Moral Sentiments.* Indianapolis, IN: Liberty Fund.

4. A. Smith. 1776/1965. *The Wealth of Nations.* New York: Modern Library. The famous passage is found on p. 351: *"[He] intends only his own security; and by directing that industry in such a manner as its produce may be of the greatest value, he intends only his own gain, and he is in this, as in many other cases, led by an* invisible hand *to promote*

an end which was no part of his intention. Nor is it always the worse for the society that it was no part of it. By pursuing his own interest he frequently promotes that of the society more effectually than when he really intends to promote it."

5. R. M. Cyert and J. G. March. 1963. *A Behavioral Theory of the Firm.* New York: John Wiley and Sons.

6. See www.davebarry.com for details. The quotation excerpted here is taken from http://www.searchquotes.com/search/Mission_Statement/, accessed 7 May 2012.

7. "Dilbert's creator strikes a believable pose in hoax." *Los Angeles Times*, 16 November 1997. See http://articles.latimes.com/1997/nov/16/news/mn-54489, accessed 7 May 2012.

8. D. W. Johnson and R. J. Lewicki. 1969. "The initiation of superordinate goals." *Journal of Applied Behavioral Science* 5: 9–24.

9. I've taught these principles in my classes for years. The original framework of the three questions came from my mentor Charles Hill. See, for example, C. W. L. Hill and G. R. Jones. 2012. *Strategic Management* Theory. Mason, OH: Cengage Learning, 14.

10. See http://about.van.fedex.com/mission-strategy-values, accessed 12 September 2012.

11. See http://crs.org/about/mission-statement/, accessed 12 September 2012.

12. P. Drucker. 2005. "Managing oneself." *Harvard Business Review* 83 (1): 100–109.

13. See M. Friedman. 1970. "The social responsibility of business is to increase profit." *New York Times Magazine,* September 13, 33, for the premier articulation of this principle in modern times.

14. See http://about.van.fedex.com/mission-strategy-values, accessed 12 September 2012.

15. See http://crs.org/about/guiding-principles.cfm, accessed 12 September 2012.

16. Darrell Rigby, "Top 10 management tools," http://www.bain.com/publications/articles/management-tools-2011-mission-and-vision-statements.aspx, accessed 8 May 2012.

17. Don Babwin. "Tylenol tampering case remains unsolved, in 25 years." *USA Today*, 29 September 2007, at http://www.usatoday.com/news/health/2007-09-29-tylenol-poisonings_N.htm, accessed 8 May 2012.

18. Statistics taken from http://www.mallenbaker.net/csr/crisis02.php; and information from the University of Florida's Interactive Media Lab, http://iml.jou.ufl.edu/projects/spring01/hogue/tylenol.html. Both accessed 8 May 2012.

19. See http://www.jnj.com/connect/about-jnj/jnj-credo/, accessed 13 September 2012.

20. S. Albert and D. A. Whetten. 1985. "Organizational identity." In *Research in Organizational Behavior*, ed. L. L. Cummings and B. M. Staw. Greenwich, CT: JAI.

Chapter 9

1. I originally had wanted to use "It takes a village to raise a child." I tried to document the source at http://www.h-net.org/~africa/threads/village.html, and found that "It takes a village to raise a child" has no attribution as an African proverb. The one quoted above does seem traceable to the Bunyoro region in Western Uganda.

2. E. Robinson and A. E. Musson. 1969. *James Watt and the Steam Revolution*. New York: Augustus M. Kelley, 62–63.

3. J. Uglow. 2002. *The Lunar Men: Five Friends Whose Curiosity Changed the World*. New York: Farrar, Straus and Giroux.

4. W. Rosen. 2010. *The Most Powerful Idea in the World*. New York: Random House, 179–80.

5. B. M. Friedman. 2005. *The Moral Consequences of Economic Growth*. New York: Alfred A Knopf; see ch. 2 for this discussion.

6. D. Dörner. 1996. *The Logic of Failure: Recognizing and Avoiding Error in Complex Situations*. Cambridge, MA: Perseus Publishing. The discussion of the Moros occurs primarily in chs. 1 and 2.

7. D. Meadows. 2008. *Thinking in Systems: A Primer*. White River Junction, VT: Chelsea Green Publishing Company, 4

8. Ibid., 11.

9. The foundational work in differentiating analysis from synthesis is B. S. Bloom, M. D. Engelhart, E. J. Furst, W. H. Hill, and D. R. Krathwohl. 1956. *Taxonomy of Educational Objectives: The Classification of Educational Goals. Handbook 1: Cognitive Domain*. New York: Longmans, Green.

10. Chester Barnard, a systems theory proponent in the field of management, recognized the challenge of multiplicity more than seventy-five years ago. See C. I. Barnard. 1938. *The Functions of the Executive*. Cambridge, MA: Harvard University Press.

11. L. Von Bertalanfy. 1968. *General System Theory: Foundations, Development, Applications*. New York: George Braziller. See pp. 124–32, but esp. p. 125.

12. K. E. Weick. 1979. *The Social Psychology of Organizing*. 2nd ed. New York: McGraw-Hill, cf. ch. 3, 72–88.

13. Path dependence features heavily in the works of economists, sociologists, and complexity scientists. A significant academic literature exists in all three fields. The version of path dependence presented here comes from complexity science; see J. Gleick. 1987. *Chaos: Making a New Science*. New York: Penguin Books.

14. Meteorologist Edward Lorenz discovered this effect, also known as the butterfly effect, when he failed to enter numbers to the sixth digit to the right of 0 in his forecasting models. These minuscule initial differences (on the order of 1 millionth) caused his forecasts to diverge early and become unrecognizable as time elapsed. See ibid., ch. 1.

15. J. C. Will, K. F. Strauss, J. M. Mendlein, C. Baltew, L. L. White, and D. C. Peter. 1997. "Diabetes mellitus among Navajo Indians: Findings from the Navajo health and nutrition survey." *Journal of Nutrition* 127 (10): 2106S–2113S.

16. "Mitch Waldrop, DARPA and the internet revolution," pdf at http://www.darpa.mil/About/History/History.aspx, accessed June 2012.

17. L. M. Salamon, H. K. Anheier, R. List, S. Toepler, S. W. Sokolowski, et al. 1999. *Global Civil Society: Dimensions of the Nonprofit Sector*. Baltimore, MD: Johns Hopkins Center for Civil Society Studies, 3.

18. R. M. Kanter. 1994. "Collaborative advantage: The art of alliances." *Harvard Business Review* 72 (July/August): 96–108.

19. See, for example, O. E. Williamson. 1985. *The Economic Institutions of Capitalism*. New York: Free Press.

20. R. C. Mayer, J. H. Davis, and F. D. Schoorman. 1995. "An integrative model of organizational trust." *Academy of Management Review* 20 (3): 709–34.

21. Speaking about restraint in design, see *New York Herald Tribune* (28 June 1959) quotation found at http://architecture.about.com/od/20thcenturytrends/a/Mies-Van-Der-Rohe-Quotes.htm, accessed 17 September 2012.

22. J. B. Barney and M. H. Hansen. 1994. "Trustworthiness as a source of competitive advantage." *Strategic Management Journal* 15 (special issue): 175–90.

23. For an elaboration of these principles, see T. M. Jones. 1995. "Instrumental stakeholder theory: A synthesis of ethics and economics." *Academy of Management Review* 20: 404–37.

Chapter 10

1. W. Rosen. 2010. *The Most Powerful Idea in the World.* New York: Random House, 169–70.

2. J. Uglow. 2002. *The Lunar Men: Five Friends Whose Curiosity Changed the World.* New York: Farrar, Straus and Giroux, 376.

3. B. Marsden. 2002. *Watt's Perfect Engine: Steam and the Age of Invention.* New York: Columbia University Press, 131.

4. J. McMillan. 2002. *Reinventing the Bazaar: A Natural History of Markets.* New York: W. W. Norton.

5. Material taken from P. C. Godfrey. 2011. *Fundacion Paraguaya (B): Measuring Social Impact.* GlobaLens teaching Case ID #1429217. Available at http://www.globalens.com/search.aspx?q=godfrey.

6. For an early description and study of SROI, see A. Lingane and S. Olsen. 2004. "Guidelines for social return on investment." *California Management Review* 46 (3): 116–35.

7. Information on the act and its history can be found at http://www.ed.gov/esea, accessed June 2012.

8. W. R. Easterly. 2001. *The Elusive Quest for Growth: Economists' Adventures and Misadventures in the Tropics.* Cambridge, MA: MIT Press.

9. G. Becker. 1976. *The Economic Approach to Human Behavior.* Chicago: University of Chicago Press.

10. Robert Putnam documented the decline of religious participation in the United States in R. D. Putnam. 2000. *Bowling Alone: The Collapse and Revival of American Community.* New York: Simon and Schuster. Pope John Paul II outlined the prevalence of secularism in John Paul II. 1991. *Centessimus Annus.* Washington, DC: Office for Publication and Promotion Services, United States Catholic Conference. Weber's concern over the iron cage of capitalism can be found in M. Weber. 1958. *The Protestant Ethic and the Spirit of Capitalism.* New York: Charles Scribner's Sons.

11. Information on the history of the human development index, and the quotation in the text, can be found at http://hdr.undp.org/en/humandev/, accessed 14 June 2012.

12. For the Global Entrepreneurship Monitor, see http://www.gemconsortium.org/, accessed 14 June 2012. The ease of doing business rankings can be found at http://www.doingbusiness.org/rankings, accessed 19 September 2012.

13. A history of the academic study of social entrepreneurship can be found at J. C. Short, T. W. Moss, and G. T. Lumpkin. 2009. "Research in social entrepreneurship: Past contributions and future opportunities." *Strategic Entrepreneurship Journal* 3: 161–94.

14. M. E. Porter and M. R. Kramer. "Creating shared value." *Harvard Business Review* 89 (February 2011): 62–77. Quotation taken from p. 67.

15. The Acumen fund provides one such example of measuring SROI as a criterion for involvement. For a discussion of their methodology, see http://www.acumenfund.org/uploads/assets/documents/BACO%20Concept%20Paper%20final_B1cNOVEM.pdf, accessed 19 September 2012.

16. F. A. Hayek. 1989. "The pretense of knowledge." *American Economic Review* 76 (6): 3–7. Quotation found on p. 3.

17. A Google search of SROI methodologies yields over 33,000 hits. A quick view of the first page reveals that a number of different organizations advance their own version of SROI. See also Godfrey, *Fundacion Paraguaya (B)*.

18. For tips on identifying stakeholders effectively, see R. E. Freeman, J. S. Harrison, and A. Wicks. 2008. *Managing for Stakeholders: Survival, Reputation, and Success*. New Haven: Yale University Press.

19. For those unfamiliar with NPV analysis, please see a standard finance textbook. Mine is R. A. Brealey, S. C. Myers, and A. J. Marcus. 1995. *Fundamentals of Corporate Finance*. New York: McGraw-Hill.

20. These arguments also appear in Godfrey. 2011. *Fundacion Paraguaya (C): Challenging SROI*. GlobaLens teaching case #1429218. Available at http://www.globalens.com/search.aspx?q=godfrey.

21. A. Chatterji and D. Levine. 2006. "Breaking down the wall of codes: Evaluating non-financial performance measurement." *California Management Review* 48 (2): 29–51.

22. C. M. Christensen and M. E. Raynor. 2003. "Why hard-nosed executives should care about management theory." *Harvard Business Review* 81 (9): 66–74.

23, Ibid.

Chapter 11

1. Dalai Lama, from www.widsomquotes.com/happiness, accessed June 20 2012.

2. Letter found in K. Morgan. 1999. *The Birth of Industrial Britain: Social Change, 1750–1850*. New York: Longman, 136.

3. N. Crafts. 1981. "The industrial revolution." In *The Economic History of Britain since 1700*, ed. R. Floud and D. McCloskey, 47. Cambridge: Cambridge University Press. Patent data from T. May. 1987. *An Economic and Social History of Britain, 1760–1970*. New York: Longman, 23.

4. R. Schofield. 1981. "British population change, 1700–1871." In *The Economic History of Britain since 1700*, ed. Floud and McCloskey, 64. Cambridge: Cambridge University Press. Data on urbanization found on p. 88.

5. R. Brown. 1991. *Society and Economy in Modern Britain, 1700–1850*. New York: Routledge. Ch. 15, "Wages," discusses the challenges to measuring changes in real wages as well as the secular trend in British working life.

6. K. Marx. 1848/1977. *The Communist Manifesto.* In *Karl Marx: Selected Writings,* ed. D. Mclellan. London: Oxford University Press.

7. Brown, *Society and Economy in Modern Britain,* 319.

8. Aristotle's discussion is found in Aristotle. 1941. *Nicomachean Ethics.* In *The Basic Works of Aristotle,* ed. R. Mckeon, 935–1126. New York: Random House. The concept of Eudemonia is also discussed in J. H. Randall. 1960. *Aristotle.* New York: Columbia University Press.

9. R. L. Pollock. "The Wrong Economist Won." *Wall Street Journal,* 15 October 1988, A22.

10. A. Sen. 1999. *Development as Freedom.* New York: Random House. Ch. 4 focuses on capability deprivation, and chs. 5–11 detail his broad approach to development as freedom.

11. S. Blackburn, ed. 1996. *The Oxford Dictionary of Philosophy.* Oxford: Oxford University Press, 127.

12. M. E. P. Seligman. 2011. *Flourish: A Visionary New Understanding of Happiness and Well-being.* New York: Free Press.

13. Ibid., 2.

14. J. Kabat-Zinn. 2009. *Full Catastrophe Living.* New York: Delta Trade Paperbacks, 61.

15. From Matthew Boulton's letter in Chapter 8, found in E. Robinson and A. E. Musson. 1969. *James Watt and the Steam Revolution.* New York: Augustus M. Kelley, 62–63.

INDEX